Caught in the Crossfire

Caught in the Crossfire

A YEAR ON ABORTION'S FRONT LINE

SUE HERTZ

PRENTICE HALL PRESS

New York · London · Toronto · Sydney · Tokyo · Singapore

PRENTICE HALL PRESS
15 Columbus Circle
New York, NY 10023

Copyright © 1991 by Sue Hertz

PRENTICE HALL PRESS and colophons are registered trademarks
of Simon & Schuster, Inc.

Library of Congress Cataloging-in-Publication Data

Hertz, Sue.
Caught in the crossfire: a year on abortion's
front line/Sue Hertz.
p.   cm.
Includes bibliographical references and index.
ISBN 0-13-381914-0
1. Abortion—United States.   2. Pro-choice movement—United
States.   3. Abortion—Government policy—United States.   I. Title.
HQ767.5.U5H47   1991
363.4'6'0973—dc20   91-2676
CIP

Manufactured in the United States of America

10   9   8   7   6   5   4   3   2   1

First Edition

To my parents, for the love and stability
every child should have.

Acknowledgments

I had often read that authors never wrote a book alone, but it wasn't until I started this project that I realized how dependent I would be on others for support and guidance.

I am forever indebted to Carolyn Coman for her open ear, encouragement, and sense of story; to Jane Harrigan for her insightful editorial suggestions and her empathy; and to Jan Waldron for her enthusiasm and diligence on the later drafts. For help on the manuscript, I also thank Nancy Bolick, David Horsey, Becky Rule, Bruce Ballenger, Anne Raver, Marjorie Howard, my students at the University of New Hampshire, and, of course, my editor, Toni Sciarra.

Thanks to Susan Levine and Jeff Davis for their friendship and sofa bed, and to my parents for the endless supply of newspaper clippings. In addition, I thank the following for listening to me ad nauseum: Barbara Tindall, Chris Welch, Lisa Miller, Phil Hertz, Bill Steelman, Pete and Wrecker McKenzie, Lucy and Skip Hancock, Chuck Finnegan, Donna Qualley, Suzanne and Fred Myers, Tory Poulin, Kathleen Megan, Peter Pach, Dan and Marcia Edson, Evelyn Iritani, Paula Dalrymple, Andy Merton, Don Murray, Colin McEnroe, Sandy Beckwith, Joan O'Connell, Gin Evans, Marcia and David Goldscholl, Dan Hogan, Beth Fischer, Margaret Shirley, and the late Thomas Williams. Although she disagreed passionately with the premise of this book, Susan Harrington supplied me with humor and ratatouille for which I am grateful. To Tish, I am obliged for the morale boost, and to Lance Hidy for his time behind the camera.

Thanks also to Michael DePorte and the UNH English Department for relieving me of some of my teaching responsibilities to allow me more research and writing time.

I am also grateful to Leslie Loveless and Susan Newsom from the Planned Parenthood League of Massachusetts; Glenda Barkin of Repro Associates; Ulla Wallin of the Crittendon Hastings House; Ann Baker of the 80 percent Majority Campaign; the Brookline Police Department and Town Counsel; and Hema Ramachandran of the UNH library.

Many thanks belong to my agent, David Black, without whom this book would not be.

My deepest appreciation of all, though, goes to the women and men of Preterm Health Services for their patience, honesty, and willingness to share their world.

Contents

Introduction

Ever since the United States Supreme Court legalized abortion in 1973, hundreds of thousands of newspaper and magazine articles and books have covered the politics of abortion—fetal rights versus mothers' rights, state rights versus federal rights, government versus individual rights. Legal scholars have pondered whether abortion should be decided by legislation or litigation. Moralists, philosophers, and physicians have argued at what point life begins. Yet in the eighteen years since the *Roe* v. *Wade* decision, which declared that banning abortion violates a woman's constitutional right to privacy, never had the issue incited such passion as it did in 1989.

The reason: *Webster* v. *Reproductive Health Services*, a Supreme Court case which challenged a 1986 Missouri law that forbid public hospitals or other tax-supported facilities and public employees (including doctors, nurses, and other health-care providers) to perform abortions not necessary to save the mother's life, and required elaborate and expensive medical viability testing on fetuses thought to be twenty weeks or more. Buoyed by a conservative Supreme Court and newly elected President George Bush, who advocated "adoption, not abortion," those who called themselves prolife hoped that the justices would use the case to dismantle *Roe* v. *Wade* and send the issue back to the states, a move that could drastically curtail abortion availability. Those who called themselves prochoice went on the defensive, praying that *Roe* would stay intact, fearing any restrictions the justices might inflict.

What followed the high court's announcement in January 1989 to hear the case three months later was a war of words, demonstrations, and more media coverage than the nation could digest. Throughout that winter and spring and the months that followed the Supreme Court's *Webster* decision in early July, both sides of the battle took their fight to the streets, both wrangling to blast their rhetoric on the evening news.

Ironically, scant attention was paid to those most affected by the Supreme Court's action and the future of abortion access: the people struggling to provide abortions and the people struggling with the decision to have an abortion. This is the story of the people behind the rhetoric, the people caught in the crossfire of the abortion war during one of the most turbulent years in abortion's history.

Many names have been changed to protect individuals' privacy. The abortion clinic on which this story focuses, Preterm Health Services in Brookline, Massachusetts, did not and will not benefit financially from this book. After months of thoughtful debate, Preterm's staff agreed to open its doors to me only in the hope that the public would better understand abortion's complexity and the need to keep the procedure safe and legal.

Caught in the Crossfire

CHAPTER ONE

The Clinic

T HIS is it, Carolyn Wardell told herself as she steered her blue Hyundai through the early morning mist into the back parking lot of Preterm Health Services. This is the day they'll get us. Her stomach fluttered, just a little. It seemed to her that she should feel scared or nervous at the thought of hundreds of abortion foes blocking her doors and bobbing poster-size photographs of dismembered fetuses under her office window. Instead, she felt excited. Facing the invasion couldn't be any worse than waiting for it to happen.

Three times in the past five months, Preterm had prepared for an attack by Operation Rescue, and each time the militant antiabortion group had struck elsewhere. Well, almost each time. On a Saturday in January, the day after Carolyn had taken over as director of her clinic in Brookline, Massachusetts, a woman had secured herself by the neck with a Kryptonite bicycle lock to the clinic's back door. Some of the staff had suggested leaving her there, but Carolyn wanted her gone. As Brookline fire fighters struggled to drill open the sturdy lock without puncturing the woman's neck, a brigade of other antiabortion soldiers drove across the state to Worcester, where they jammed the elevators and blocked the doorways of an office building that housed a Planned Parenthood clinic. More than 100 were arrested. Back at Preterm, the fire fighters resorted to prying off the door handle with the Jaws of Life.

Now, two months later, Carolyn's gut told her that those soldiers, who never revealed what clinic they planned to seize next, would be at Preterm's doorstep in less than two hours. They couldn't ignore the clinic that performed 10,000 abortions a year, the largest provider in

1

New England, forever. Besides, this rescue had been billed as the big one: a regional rescue that could lure hundreds, perhaps a thousand, antiabortionists from around New England. This could be the first rescue to boast enough people to successfully block Preterm's wide front entrance and back door.

Even the police seemed primed. The sun wouldn't rise for another half hour and already two cruisers sat, engines idling, one in front of Preterm and one in back. As Carolyn slid out of her car into the predawn blackness, another car door slammed, cracking the eerie quiet. She turned to see Lin Sherman, one of Preterm's telephone counselors, walking toward her through the nearly empty parking lot.

"It's nice to have the cops out back," Carolyn said. "It feels like they're protecting us."

"They sure are," Lin replied. "They wanted to know what *I* was doing here."

Carolyn unlocked the back door and stepped into the hallway, one of the few areas that was lit in the five-story medical office building which loomed above the back parking, a giant concrete square. As Lin turned left toward the phone room, Carolyn continued straight down the hallway to the front door to welcome more of her staff and the television crew that hoped to film a rescue from inside an abortion clinic. The media, like the local abortion providers and the police, had learned of the rescue through prochoice women who had infiltrated the antiabortion group. Either at meetings or in a newsletter, Operation Rescue leaders announced the date of the next blockade, and the "moles," as the prochoice spies were called, were quick to forward the message.

Carolyn tried to suppress a smile when she noticed the cameraman filming her from his spot on the front steps. If she'd known, she would have changed from her sneakers into one of the pairs of heels she kept in the bottom drawer of her file cabinet. She hadn't even had a chance to slip out of her coat or comb her hair.

"Good morning," she said to the TV crew as she opened the door with a self-conscious giggle. Media attention was still new to Carolyn. In the two months that she had been Preterm's director, Carolyn had sent most reporters and photographers to the clinic's spokeswoman, Fran Basche. A former journalist, Fran seemed to know instinctively how to answer the questions without stumbling over her thoughts or saying something that she, or the clinic, would later regret. Carolyn was more prone to speak her mind, a trait which some would hail as honest and others, Carolyn herself included, would call blunt.

Carolyn Wardell was a small woman, a few inches over five feet tall, with soft, curly brown hair and pale, almost translucent skin. Her face was delicate and her voice was so gentle that she often considered using a microphone to be heard at all-staff meetings. But her gaze was direct and her handshake firm. When she walked she marched, always with a sense of purpose, or at least she looked like she had a sense of purpose as she strode through the clinic, arms swinging. Five years before, Carolyn had been Preterm's administrative secretary, regarded as quiet and efficient, a good detail person. Her superiors had quickly recognized her talent for organizing and troubleshooting and the promotions began. A counselor by training, Carolyn leapt from secretary to office manager to director of counseling to director of the abortion clinic to assistant director of all of Preterm's services, which included gynecology, sterilization, and breast cancer screening. When the clinic's director left in January 1989, Carolyn was the likely replacement. Carolyn was a clear thinker with a cool temperament, the previous clinic director told Preterm's board of directors when recommending Carolyn for the job; she wouldn't buckle in a crisis.

Carolyn, too, believed that she wouldn't buckle in a crisis, not even during an Operation Rescue attack. If the troops struck, she would organize her staff into action, something she felt she did well. Carolyn had never bought into the frenzy that in the early days had propelled Preterm's staff to sleep at the clinic the night before a threatened rescue. Fearing that Rescue would strike before dawn the next day, some staffers wanted to make sure that people were inside to answer calls from frantic patients. Although ideally Rescue would have liked to blockade before the clinic opened and staff and patients arrived, in the five months that the antiabortion group had been waging war against abortion providers in the Boston area, never had the troops arrived at a clinic before 7 A.M. Carolyn felt that she had plenty of time to help prepare Preterm for a possible assault if she were inside the building before six o'clock. Besides, sometimes a handful of abortion foes snuck inside the clinics even after the staff had already arrived, chaining themselves to urinals, banisters, examination tables, anything that didn't move. Last month, six of them had locked themselves together by the neck and lay like sardines on the floor of a procedure room at one local clinic. In front of another, they had lain down on Beacon Street, refusing to move as cars piled up for blocks and traffic froze.

Even though Carolyn disagreed down to her marrow with the protesters' belief that abortion is evil, she didn't condemn the protests— only their methods. She wished that they would stay on the sidewalk with their signs and songs, but she understood the need to demonstrate against something that they felt was wrong. God knows, she had spent much of her twenties shouting about the injustices of the Vietnam War.

Yet her understanding didn't erase her annoyance. The abortion foes had always struck on a Saturday, and it was hard enough being a thirty-nine-year-old single mother working full-time, without spending precious weekend days at Preterm. Her only hesitation in accepting her promotion to director was that she feared her new job would require too many Saturdays at the clinic preparing for demonstrations, too many Saturdays away from her four-year-old daughter.

Last night when she had dropped Lorena off at a friend's, Lorena was sobbing for her mother not to leave. She was still hysterical when Carolyn called a few hours later. "Oh, God," Carolyn had thought, "I'm traumatizing my daughter." Carolyn had gone to sleep sad and frustrated that Lorena was being hurt by a situation her mother couldn't control. Carolyn couldn't stop Operation Rescue from attacking any more than she could stop women from getting pregnant. She couldn't shrug off her responsibility to try to keep Preterm functioning. Her Saturday staff of forty depended on her to protect their right to provide abortions, and their patients' right to receive them.

And on this Saturday, she felt more keenly than ever her responsibility to tell the public what abortion providers had to endure to fulfill their lawful services to women. That's why she had agreed to let the "Chronicle" TV crew in. She wanted the crew to help her show what it was like to gear up for an attack: to rearrange patient schedules, staff schedules, child-care schedules, and then wait, and wait, for the protesters to arrive. If Preterm wasn't hit, perhaps the audience would understand the extraordinary drain of the wasted effort. If it were attacked, well, that was a lesson in itself.

There wasn't much to do now but wait. Sitting at one of the secretaries' desks, Carolyn smiled as Fran Basche flew into the administrative office. Fran always moved quickly, but today she charged into her office as if she were being chased. Reentering the administrative area, she greeted Carolyn and the TV producer, a woman named Maggie. Fran was perfect for TV. Not only did she look good with her wavy, dark hair cropped at her shoulders, her wide smile, and classic features but also she could stun any interviewer into silence with a blizzard of words. Fran could talk faster than most people could think, and what amazed Carolyn was that she made sense.

A few months shy of thirty, Fran had joined Preterm a year and a half before, tossing her job of writing press releases about computers to promote a cause to which she was committed. She liked to say that she simply woke up one morning and it hit her: She spent most of her days talking about computers. "Computers!" she would repeat, aghast.

Since the first threatened rescue last October, whenever a public discussion was arranged Fran had dealt with TV reporters, newspaper reporters, and the antiabortionists. The task had required all of Fran's tact and self-restraint. Just the day before, she had had to clench her teeth as she sat in a television studio with two of Operation Rescue's leaders as all three waited to appear together on a talk show. One of the leaders, Bob Delery, mentioned that a veteran rescuer wouldn't be at Saturday's demonstration because his wife had recently miscarried. The couple had ten daughters; now they were trying for a son. "Sounds to me like that woman should be rescued," Fran had thought. But she had kept quiet. She couldn't, however, contain herself on the air when Delery slammed the clinics for not describing fetal development to patients.

"I think in nine months they know they'll have a baby," Fran shot back. The antiabortionists were forever arguing that women were ignorant of what abortion meant, that patients didn't understand that they were killing a potential child. Why then, Fran thought, was Preterm a vale of tears?

Usually cool in public, Fran was prone to private rages against the antis, as she dubbed them. "I think they're all sexually repressed," she would rant. "And they hate women." To refocus her energy, she prepared for rescues with the aggression of Mike Tyson and the finesse of Martha Stewart. She arranged for the patients to wait out the attack in a safe spot, usually the Episcopal church a block away. She recruited volunteers to help escort patients and answer phones. And she bought food, lots of food, although she'd cut back since the first threatened attacks. Last fall, Fran had fortified the staff with bagels and doughnuts and boxes of cereal, even bananas for the cereal. She was thrilled when a nurse brought in homemade noodle pudding. Somehow the cornucopia made the event seem more festive, less intense. But with each false alarm, the incentive to soften the tension faded. For this rescue, Preterm's table boasted a mere two dozen blueberry muffins, a tray of Danish, a cinnamon coffee cake, and cartons of cream for the good coffee Fran had bought—not the industrial-strength brew the clinic usually served; coffee even the cops on private detail politely declined to drink.

Fran leaned against the doorway which led into Preterm's administrative area and watched the TV people meander up and down the hall, checking their lights and audio equipment. Soon they would concentrate on her, tagging behind her, monitoring her every move to document the tension level inside the clinic. Before Operation Rescue, Fran's work with the media had been limited to a few interviews with newspaper reporters on special features, such as the one about married women having abortions. While no story on abortion lacked in controversy, her pre-Operation Rescue quotes seemed almost innocuous compared to what she had to say about the injustice of Operation Rescue blockades, about the violation of a woman's legal right to an abortion. These days her words were potent, and she worried that they might be too potent if Operation Rescue actually hit Preterm.

While Fran appeared confident on the outside, inside she was anxious. Last August, when the providers had heard whispers that local abortion foes were creating their own chapter of Operation Rescue, the nation's most radical antiabortion outfit, Fran had worried how this new threat would affect her job, her life. Would she have Saturdays free, ever again, to spend with her boyfriend? Would she stay calm at a rescue? She'd always handled crisis well in the past, but would a siege by antiabortion fanatics push her over the edge? Would the tension reduce her to tears in front of reporters? Now, after five months of false alarms, she was still left to wonder how she'd react to hundreds of protesters outside her clinic's doors.

In her quiet moments, however, Fran, like Carolyn, admitted that a part of her was titillated by the challenge. Preparing for an attack was a lot more invigorating than the duties that had consumed her first year at Preterm: explaining the diaphragm to high-school seniors, or calling doctors' offices suggesting that they refer patients to Preterm for breast screening, tubal ligations, or abortions. When the first Operation Rescue newsletter had landed on her desk, Fran had said a silent prayer, thankful that this hadn't happened the year before when she was just learning the different effects of high- and low-estrogen birth-control pills.

"It's starting to feel a little bit like a war to me," Fran told the "Chronicle" cameraman as he filmed her for the news special that would air the following week. She was controlled, relaxed, unflinching as the camera followed her as she picked up the receiver of a ringing phone. "Hi, this is Fran," she said, looking straight ahead, not at the camera. "Nothing happening yet." It was 6:45 A.M. The camera trailed her outside as she taped a "NO TRESPASSING" sign on the front door. "Assuming, of course," she said, "that they can read." She returned inside, wondering if she should have said that.

As the minutes rolled by, the Saturday staff filtered in, first a couple of nurses, then some counselors and medical assistants. The doctors wouldn't be in for another half hour. Ordinarily, patients began arriving at seven o'clock, but because of the rescue, Carolyn had pushed the first appointment up to nine. She had figured that if Operation Rescue had arrived early as was its practice, the invaders might already be stuffed into police vans by the time patients showed up.

As Fran talked to the TV people, Carolyn patrolled the hallway, peering out the front door, then the back. Nothing greeted her but a raw gray day in early March. It was 6:50 A.M.

•   •   •

Preterm Health Services operated out of the first and fourth floors of a medical building at 1842 Beacon Street in the Boston suburb of Brookline, which was known to the right-to-life community as "abortion row" for the three abortion clinics it harbored on a two-mile strip. Planned Parenthood was the closest to the Boston border. The first of the three Beacon Street clinics, it was housed in a turn-of-the-century brownstone on the left. A mile up the wide thoroughfare, which was divided by trolley tracks and lined with sycamores and oaks and elegant apartment buildings, was Repro Associates. The only for-profit clinic of the three, Repro functioned behind an unmarked door. Easily overlooked, it was tucked between the post office and a gourmet delicatessen in the middle of Coolidge Corner, Brookline's shopping center. Stores sprawled for blocks up Beacon and down cross streets, offering everything from Oriental rugs to silk pants to cream cheese and lox. When Operation Rescue hit Repro, hundreds watched, from elderly women parading to the post office to computer whizzes heading into Radio Shack to silver-haired CEOs driving by en route to the golf course. No one escaped the scene.

Beyond Coolidge Corner, beyond more apartment buildings, more trees, beyond Washington Square and its cluster of delis and dry cleaners, stood Preterm. The building's modern facade was nondescript; a combination of concrete and windows hulking uncomfortably between brownstones and brick. Nowhere on the outside did it say Preterm. Patients usually knew they had arrived when they saw the raised numbers of the street address, 1842, and the picketers.

From the moment Preterm opened in August 1973, just seven months after the Supreme Court had legalized abortion in *Roe* v. *Wade*, picketers were as much a part of the clinic's routine as pregnancy tests.

They had figured out the clinic's schedule immediately: Abortion patients were scheduled on Tuesday, Thursday, Friday, and Saturday morning, and the rest of Preterm's hours were devoted to its other services: gynecology, breast cancer screening, and sterilization. Although many of the picketers didn't believe in contraception, they didn't stand in front of the clinic and pray for the young women heading inside for Pill prescriptions during the hours Preterm provided general gynecological service; they protested only on abortion days. Shuffling in circles, waving signs, silently praying, two, three, sometimes six or seven abortion foes clustered in front of the building during the week, and as many as ten to fifteen on Saturdays, the abortion clinic's busiest day. While some protesters confronted patients entering the building, pressing pamphlets on them and pleading "please don't kill your baby," they were, for the most part, benign, regarded by the staff with more pity than trepidation.

Before Operation Rescue had lured new faces and numbers to the clinics, the staff had known most of the picketers by name, or sometimes by costume. There was the man who dressed as Santa Claus every Christmas and held a sign that said "Please don't kill my kids." There was old Bill Clarke, who warned patients of God's wrath, and Constance Smith, the former nun with the waist-length brown hair. And there was Bill Cotter, the computer programmer who stood stone-faced and rigid, telling patients that they could be hurt inside those doors, that not only would their babies die, but that they could, too.

All the clinics' staffs knew Bill Cotter, for he had haunted clinics from Worcester to Boston for years. But Preterm seemed to be his favorite. He was always in front of Preterm. He began his vigil, or "sidewalk counseling" as he called it, at 6 A.M. When his reinforcements arrived between seven and nine o'clock, he left for his day job of testing computer boards at Honeywell. In December 1988, four months after he celebrated his thirty-seventh birthday, he quit his job to focus all his attention on Operation Rescue and stopping abortion. Since then, he frequently paced the sidewalks until late morning, jogging between the front and back entrance, holding out pamphlets to patients, and telling the women that he had help for them. So low-key was his presentation that few patients or their partners stopped to talk to Bill Cotter, as they sometimes did with other, more aggressive, picketers. Ignored, Cotter would return to his post in front of Preterm's steps, sometimes holding up a poster featuring an illustration of an eleven-week fetus for anyone mounting the steps to see.

Standing over six-feet tall, Bill Cotter was pale, with a square face and deep-set brown eyes. He rarely smiled, but when he did, his mouth lifted, as if in effort, to one side. The Preterm staff snickered about the strong but quiet presence of "Billy," as they referred to him, the man of few words and even fewer changes of clothes. When word leaked out that Cotter was not just a soldier of Boston's Operation Rescue, but its general, some staffers were stunned. While Billy C. had showed some vigor in his crusade—he occasionally invaded clinics, locking himself to utility carts, doors, other people—he hardly seemed to exude the charisma to inspire hundreds of abortion foes to sit on cold sidewalks for hours and risk arrest. "He's such a lump," Fran said. "He has such a blank look, like a robot. It's scary to think of people listening to him."

Whether Bill Cotter was responsible for galvanizing the forces was hard to tell, but there was no disputing that since the fall of 1988, the local abortion foes had become more aggressive, just as abortion foes across the country had become aggressive. The momentum had begun to gather when Vice President George Bush, who advocated "adoption, not abortion," became the undisputed forerunner of the 1988 election. With the hope that Bush and a conservative U.S. Supreme Court would overturn *Roe* v. *Wade*, the once muffled voice of the antiabortion troops became louder and louder. Enemies of abortion who had watched on national TV a group called Operation Rescue blockade clinics in Atlanta during the Democratic National Convention saw a new tactic and began to form their own Operation Rescue satellites. Although the satellites shared the same name as the original group, which was based in Binghamton, New York, they didn't share resources. Bill Cotter insisted that Operation Rescue: Boston functioned autonomously, with only spiritual—and tactical—guidance from Binghamton.

Preterm's staff wasn't concerned with what had ignited the local antis, only with how to deal with the invigorated picketers. Never had they been so feisty. Instead of returning to prayer after patients disregarded their spiel, the demonstrators shadowed the women and their escorts, shouting that their babies had brain waves and feelings and thumbs that they sucked. The protesters' literature became more graphic, replacing illustrations of rosy-cheeked infants with photos of bloodied fetal parts and decapitated fetal heads. One woman protester trailed Preterm staffers as they walked to one of the local lunch spots, yelling, "How did you get into this death business anyway?"

Usually, the staff disregarded the taunts, sailing by the picketers, noses pointed toward the clinic. Pretending that two or three protesters were invisible was easy; ignoring 500 protesters blocking the door to your office building was impossible.

• • •

Preterm's telephone lines weren't supposed to open for another forty-five minutes, but Lin was already at her desk in the phone room. If the antiabortion warriors surrounded Preterm, the lines would open early and patients would call, anxious and scared. Lin hadn't thought twice about hopping into her Ford Escort at 4:30 that morning to drive the fifty-five miles from her home in Worcester to Brookline. After two years as a Preterm phone counselor, she knew that her voice could soothe the most desperate patient.

Lin was a large woman—"obese" was how she described herself—who was most comfortable in slacks and T-shirts and sneakers. The phone-room counselors, most of whom were either in college or fresh out of college, were "her kids." No matter how frantically busy she was, she would stop whatever she was doing to answer their questions. For the moment, though, she didn't have to worry about their questions since the other phone counselors wouldn't arrive for at least another half hour. The phone room was empty, save for herself and Ralph.

Ralph was the teddy bear Lin's twenty-four-year-old son had given her for protection. Last October, when Operation Rescue had threatened its first Massachusetts attack, her son had spent the night at Preterm with Lin and four other staffers who feared the rescuers would beat them to the clinic that Saturday morning. "You be there for your patients," he had told Lin. "And I'll be there for you." After all the false alarms, though, no one slept on the waiting-room couches anymore, and Lin's son no longer accompanied his mother. He had offered Ralph as his substitute.

Even without waking up on a clinic sofa to a battalion of men in blue standing guard outside in the dark, Lin was jumpy this morning. It was the lack of control that disturbed her, the lack of predictability. She'd feel better once Operation Rescue struck somewhere, preferably not Preterm. "I worry about my patients out there," she said. If only she knew what to expect, or at least how many protesters there'd be.

Outside on the front steps, Carolyn and a handful of staffers searched the passing traffic for Operation Rescue scouts—people as-

signed to scope out the preparedness of the clinics. Every time a car slowed down, Carolyn held her breath. A maroon sedan crept by, pulled a U-turn, parked briefly across the street, then sped away. "We're gonna be hit," mumbled a staffer. Carolyn returned inside to the phones, which rang with calls from the other clinics. It was 7:10 A.M. Nothing had happened anywhere.

•   •   •

The sky was still dark and the mist still heavy as Sergeant Bill McDermott and his partner, George Driscoll, struggled to follow the caravan of cars that had just left Our Lady Help of Christians Church in Newton. The two Brookline detectives had arrived at the church in their unmarked cruiser at 5 A.M., early enough to count the cars streaming into the parking lot and watch the antiabortionists file into the church. Catholics were directed upstairs for mass. Protestants were led downstairs for a prayer service. Sipping coffee, the two cops had tried to estimate how many people would sit in front of an abortion clinic entrance later in the morning. Four hundred, McDermott thought, maybe more.

When Bill Cotter had created Operation Rescue:Boston, McDermott and Driscoll were assigned to gather intelligence on the local group and its affiliates around the country. At first glance, they seemed an unlikely team. A Vietnam vet with a penchant for stogies and horse racing, McDermott was a dark Irishman with the height and thick build of the football lineman he was in college. Driscoll, who at thirty-three was nearly ten years McDermott's junior, was slight and fair, a recent law school graduate who favored khakis and polo shirts. McDermott mumbled. Driscoll articulated. Their superiors thought that combining McDermott's experience as a detective and his solid rapport with the Boston Police Department (with which Brookline would have to work), and Driscoll's legal background might squelch the recent outbreak of civil disobedience. McDermott had the contacts and savvy to gather the necessary intelligence on the antiabortionists, while Driscoll would make sure that the Brookline police were handling the arrests properly in case Cotter and company filed claims of police brutality, as members of Operation Rescue were doing across the country.

It didn't take Driscoll and McDermott long to become familiar with Operation Rescue's shroud of secrecy, its policy that no one but the top two or three leaders knew the details on how and where the group would attack. The detectives talked to police across the country who had dragged protesters from abortion clinic doors, shattered Kryptonite locks that held five, six, seven people together, and smashed 200-pound concrete slabs to which demonstrators were chained. They talked to Ann Baker, a former nun who had made a career out of tracing and analyzing antiabortion activity, and they talked to local clinic staffs, hoping to plot strategies to keep the clinics open and accessible for patients.

At first, Operation Rescue was a challenge, like any new case would be a challenge. It was fun trying to figure out where the group would hit, how the police should gear up. The detectives weren't afraid for their safety; Bill Cotter and friends were hardly the Black Panthers. It was more a matter of trying to think like the abortion foes, which required insight into their characters. In his nineteen years with the Brookline Police Department, McDermott had made a career out of studying his subjects, learning if they favored lo mein or lasagna, video games or pool. If he understood minor motivations, often it was easier to understand major motivations. But Cotter was an enigma. "Hi, Bill," McDermott would open. "Hi, Bill," Cotter would reply. Despite McDermott's questions, the conversation rarely went further, not even when the sergeant asked Cotter if he had a girlfriend. McDermott couldn't even get a permanent address out of Cotter. Sometimes he lived in Arlington, sometimes Boston, sometimes with his parents in western Massachusetts.

This morning, as the rescuers piled into their vans and station wagons to head to their destination, McDermott couldn't find Cotter in the church parking lot. He and Driscoll had hoped to follow Cotter's car. That way, they wouldn't be taken in by any decoy vehicles headed to nowhere—Rescue's tactic to confuse police. Instead, McDermott had spotted Darroline Firlit, Cotter's executive assistant. A plump woman with a broad, flat face framed by a fringe of bangs and long brown hair, Darroline was known to the cops as a trench fighter. She would do anything to save babies, including snatching fetal tissue from an abortion clinic. She had told reporters that she planned to keep it in her home until she could make proper funeral arrangements. With nearly twenty arrests for blockading clinics around the country on her record, Darroline would be headed to the heart of the action.

McDermott's gut told him that Brookline was the heart of the action for this rescue. Cotter and company read the papers. They knew that many Brookline residents were livid about the $17,000 the town paid in police overtime every Saturday that Operation Rescue threatened a blockade. If Rescue actually hit, which it had done once in November at Planned Parenthood and once in December at Repro, the price tag was even higher. Brookline was forced to shoulder the bill for the food the arrested protesters ate and the hours police devoted to fingerprinting, booking, and guarding the prisoners. If Rescue attacked Brookline this morning, the total cost to the town since last October could reach $100,000. In Rescue logic, McDermott surmised, that meant victory. Even though the chairman of Brookline's Board of Selectmen had vowed that the town would pay whatever it cost to keep the clinics open, Rescue probably figured it could eventually push the town over the brink.

Now, as McDermott and Driscoll followed the caravan south onto the Massachusetts Turnpike, McDermott wondered if he'd been wrong. This was the route to Providence, Rhode Island. Then again, the rescuers could curl back toward Boston and Brookline. Cotter had amassed enough people to hit more than one clinic. Perhaps there was another group of rescuers that the two detectives had missed.

The river of cars veered off at the Allston-Brighton exit, then turned left onto Harvard Street, which led straight into Coolidge Corner.

"Brookline," McDermott said.

Driscoll radioed ahead to the police station, where seventy cops waited to know which clinic they would defend. None were happy to be there. Working a rescue meant either not going to sleep after the midnight shift, or rising before dawn to spend the morning standing around in the cold and lugging limp prisoners, as heavy and inert as bags of wet sand.

For some officers, rescues were more than physically torturous; they presented a conflict of the heart or the spirit. Antiabortion sympathizers on the police force were excused from the private details at the clinics during the week, but on Rescue Saturdays, every cop was expected to work. If some cops' sympathies rested with the rescuers, their professional obligation lay with protecting public safety. Their job was to keep the sidewalks clear and enforce the law, which meant helping women enter the clinic safely and keeping protesters at bay.

Both Driscoll and McDermott were raised Catholic. During their years as patrolmen, neither had refused a private detail at a clinic; abortion wasn't a major issue to either of them. If pressed, they would say that women had the right to decide whether or not to bear a child. When abortion returned to the public limelight, McDermott began listening carefully to discussions on the issue's complexities, but only when women spoke. At forty-one, he clearly remembered watching the birth of his four children, and what having a baby meant to his wife. "When men start having babies, I'll listen to men," he said.

The rescuers parked in the Centre Street lot, which offered twice as many spaces as the entourage needed and was less than a football field away from Repro Associates. The troops could make a direct hit on Repro, or hop on the trolley and head anywhere. McDermott and Driscoll parked across the street and waved to Darroline, who waved back. She wore her battle clothes, McDermott noted—faded blue jeans, a tattered wool coat, heavy boots, nothing that would suffer when police dragged her across frozen pavement from the clinic entrance to the prisoners' bus. Bustling from rescuer to rescuer, Darroline directed her flock. "You go here," she barked. "You go here." McDermott thought she sounded more like a platoon leader than his platoon leaders in Vietnam.

Darroline took her place at the front of the train of people she had assembled, her lips drawn in a tight line. There were at least 100 people behind her, McDermott estimated, each one looking more ragged than the next. The crusaders for the unborn had taken their fashion cue from Darroline, outfitting themselves in worn ski parkas and patched pants, wool hats and thick mittens. Although the sky had brightened, the sun had yet to poke through the heavy cloud cover and the temperature hovered at freezing. Some of the rescuers shivered. It was only 7:30 A.M.; they would be a lot colder by the time their day was over, McDermott knew.

The brigade started marching, with McDermott and Driscoll pursuing by foot in the rear. Dressed in their own heavy outerwear— McDermott in a sweatshirt and nylon shell and Driscoll in a leather jacket—the two detectives almost blended in with the crowd. The giveaway was the walkie-talkie each detective carried. At the first rescue last October, they had tried to hide the radios underneath their coats as they followed the troops into a Boston subway station, but talking into their lapels muffled their message and was about as subtle as waving the device under Bill Cotter's nose. It didn't matter anyway. Police presence at rescues wasn't a secret; it was expected.

Out of the parking lot the army headed, across Beacon Street, and over the trolley tracks. McDermott looked around for more protesters. If all of those who met at the church earlier this morning intended to blockade a clinic, several hundred were missing. Were they on a trolley? In a second wave of cars? Would they hit Repro or another clinic? Most important, McDermott wondered, where the hell was Cotter?

He didn't have time to ponder Billy C.'s absence. The rescuers turned left, and one by one, knelt down before Repro Associates.

•   •   •

Sonia Lewis wondered what would await her at Preterm as she and her husband Edgar drove down Beacon Street. Would the steps be strewn with bodies and the sidewalk clogged with singing protesters? It was a raw day, even for March, a day made for lolling in bed, or reading spy novels. Who in their right mind would voluntarily stand outside for hours with the goal of spending the rest of the day in the Brookline police station?

Obviously quite a few, she noticed as they drove past Repro. Bobbing signs, singing antichoicers, chanting prochoicers, barricades, police—Repro had it all. Preterm had been saved again, she thought.

A little disappointed, a little relieved, she said good-bye to Edgar and slipped out of the car and into Preterm, unobstructed by the usual picketers begging her to quit her job. The only sidewalk activity was a young woman jogging by, her ponytail swinging. Sonia headed straight to her desk, the reception desk, the first stop for any Preterm patient.

Sonia couldn't work up much of a sweat about a Saturday rescue. In sixteen years at Preterm, she had seen and handled just about everything the antis could muster. Once, raising herself to her full five feet two inches, she had confronted a group of eight protesters who had snuck in Preterm's downstairs waiting room, the family room as Sonia called it, and passed out pamphlets explaining the dangers of abortion. "If you believe in Jesus Christ, this is murder," they had shouted.

"You're trespassing," Sonia told them, her head barely reaching one man's chest. "You'll have to leave."

They didn't, until the police arrived twenty minutes later.

When abortion foes had threatened to picket Sonia's home, she had stood on Preterm's front steps, dangling a piece of paper bearing the picketers' names and addresses, which she had found through tracing their license plates. "We all know where each other lives," Sonia had told them, smiling. Later, when one picketer had suggested that she remember the Holocaust, she threw a balled-up napkin at his nose. "You're nothing more than a bigot with a crew cut," she had said, and walked inside. "Isn't she beautiful," he muttered after her.

Sonia hadn't been flattered, even though she took great pride in her appearance, rising at 4:45 A.M. to begin the makeup and hair routine so that she would be at work before seven o'clock. At fifty-seven, she wore her hair high and black and her nails long and sculpted. "She must have seven closets," Carolyn said frequently. "She never wears the same outfit twice." She did, but they always looked different, depending on her accessories, which were as abundant as her outfits. If she wore a gray dress, she wore gray earrings and gray shoes. If she wore a canary-and-black jumpsuit, she wore canary-and-black shoes and bracelets. Her ability to handle heels, two inches high on average, but often as tall as four inches, was a source of pride. "We used to jitterbug in these," she said pointing to her stilettos.

When the U.S. Supreme Court legalized abortion in 1973, Sonia was forty years old and had spent the previous nineteen years driving her three children to Cub Scouts and Girl Scouts, to hockey practice and Hebrew School. She was the mother who brought orange slices to her kids' track meets and chaperoned the postprom parties. She had toyed with the idea of getting a job outside the home, but hadn't taken any firm steps until she heard on TV that Preterm needed older, experienced counselors. That was it. She knew what she wanted to do. She had heard too many stories of botched abortions, of teenagers traveling to New York to wait in grimy waiting rooms for doctors with dirty hands. She had to be a part of helping women exercise their new reproductive rights.

Her qualifications? It may sound corny, she had told her interviewer, but all of her kids' friends talked to her, sought her advice when they were in trouble. And although her last professional job had been screening movies with priests to determine if the films were too racy for Catholic Boston, she was hired. Jane Levin, Preterm's founder, saw in Sonia a wisdom, a natural ability to home in on the key issue. Sonia began as a counselor in the medical area upstairs, then later moved to the reception room downstairs, to be, as Carolyn called her, "the patient advocate." No one calmed frantic patients, or the frantic parents of patients, like Sonia could.

Sonia sipped her coffee and admitted some nine o'clock patients. "Good morning," Sonia said, flashing a bright grin to a young woman who clung to the hand of her boyfriend. "Why don't you sit here." Sonia patted the chair beside her desk. "And you can sit here," she told the boyfriend, pointing to another chair. Her face partially covered by a cloud of dark hair, the patient, whose name was Greta, nodded stiffly. This was her first abortion, she told Sonia, and she was nervous. Donald, her boyfriend, a beefy fellow in a dungaree jacket, sat stoically across from Greta, his legs spread apart, his hands on his knees. Sonia passed Greta a medical chart, explaining the section that patients had to fill out. She didn't mention the possibility of a rescue disrupting the clinic's service; her instincts told her that the day would be quiet. If Rescue was going to hit Preterm, it would have arrived by now.

Down the hall, in the administrative waiting room, Carolyn and Fran sat at the two secretaries' desks. "We gear up and we're let down," Carolyn said, nibbling a piece of coffee cake. "In two weeks, they'll announce another rescue and we'll go through this all again." For the past forty-five minutes the phones had rung with Operation Rescue updates from staffers at the other clinics. The clinic staffs had always been friendly toward each other, but since the advent of Operation Rescue, the women (only a handful of men worked at the clinics, most of whom were either doctors, business managers, or handymen) at Gynecare and the Crittendon Hastings House in Boston and the three Brookline clinics had bonded into a united force. If one had information, the others soon knew it. On Saturdays of threatened rescues, the phone lines between the providers buzzed.

Shortly before eight o'clock, Preterm learned that Repro had been hit. Within half an hour, Leslie from Planned Parenthood called to say that the abortion foes had descended on her clinic in a second sweep. Bill Cotter, who was among the protesters littering Planned Parenthood's front stoop, had been arrested immediately. Most of the clinic's patients were in, she said, but could those who weren't come to Preterm? Planned Parenthood's entrance was still blockaded.

Greta had been scheduled for an abortion this morning at Repro, but when she and Donald spotted the mob in front of the Coolidge Corner clinic, they drove to the nearest phone booth to find another clinic in the telephone directory. On most days, Preterm's schedule was full and walk-ins were asked to return later in the week. Because of the threatened rescue, however, the phone counselors had booked fewer appointments for this Saturday, leaving some openings. Carolyn OK'd Greta, for she didn't envision that her staff would face any hurdles, or bodies, upon entering the building this morning. If the other two clinics have been blockaded, it was unlikely that Operation Rescue had the staff to hit Preterm, too.

"We are never," Carolyn said, "changing our bookings again."

Carolyn returned to her office to change from her high heels back into her sneakers. Since the "Chronicle" crew had left to film the rescue at Repro, she'd choose comfort over fashion. Another wasted morning.

"I'm really disappointed," Fran told Susan Newsom of Planned

Parenthood as they chatted on the phone, adding with a chuckle, "I wore makeup and everything today." She paused. "I . . ." another pause. "Omigod." She dropped the receiver.

"Lock the doors!" the policeman guarding the back door bellowed. "They're coming!"

From every direction, Operation Rescue soldiers raced toward Preterm's entrances. Women with babies. Teenagers in army jackets. Men in workboots. Fran sprinted to the back door, forgetting that Repro's secretary had been injured in December when the demonstrators pushed her behind the door she had tried to block. "Help me," she screamed. Preterm's bookkeeper, Sarah, ran to her aid as Carolyn tried to find the lock button on the fuse box.

"Why isn't that door locked?" the policeman barked.

"It's automatic," Carolyn yelled back. "It opens at eight o'clock." She found the switch and the door lock clicked shut.

Linking arms, the demonstrators jammed the doorways, the steps, and the sidewalks, shoulder to shoulder, five, six, seven deep. Their backs to the clinic, their faces to the street, those at the front entrance sang "Jesus Loves the Little Children," substituting "babies" for "children." At the back door, a leader shouted, "Fifty percent of women having abortions already have children. Isn't that sad?"

"Amen," a priest replied.

"Amen," the protesters echoed.

Sonia would remember for a long time the thud of bodies hitting the glass of the front doors. Swaying and singing, fifty or sixty protesters dammed the outside foyer, blocking out daylight. Sonia could see only the backs of their heads and coats, sometimes a profile when a protester turned slightly. All that separated her from them was a pane of glass, and although Sonia knew that the door was locked, it felt as if they would turn around at any minute and fling themselves into the clinic.

But she couldn't share her fears with the patients. She had to remain composed. Calm. Only three couples had arrived before the protesters had descended, a Hispanic couple, neither of whom spoke much English, a couple in their thirties, and Greta and Donald. In the family room, Sonia found Greta huddled close to her boyfriend, her hand clutching his knee. Both stared blankly at the television set, which blared Saturday morning cartoons.

"Can they get in?" Greta asked Sonia.

"No, you're safe," Sonia said gently, adding that this day, meaning the day of an abortion, was never easy, and she understood that a blockade intensified the trauma. Greta smiled weakly. The youngest child of a close Italian family, Greta worried that the demonstration would lure television cameras, which might photograph her. Her Catholic parents would be appalled if they knew that their twenty-one-year-old daughter had an abortion. They hadn't yet recovered from learning that she lived with her boyfriend, a lobsterman. Greta placed her head on Donald's shoulder.

With as much of a reassuring smile as she could muster, Sonia left the couple and returned to the hallway where she took turns standing on a chair with other staffers. Teetering on her tiptoes, hoping that the chair beneath her was stable, Sonia peered over the heads of the protesters clogging the outside foyer. On the sidewalk below were lots of people, she noted, a good crowd, 100 or more. From her perch, it looked as if every other person in the crowd held a sign. Signs bearing photos of cherubic babies. Signs bearing photos of fetal remains. Signs saying "KEEP YOUR LAWS OFF MY UTERUS." The prochoice contingent must have arrived.

When Operation Rescue had first threatened to blockade Boston area clinics last fall, the local prochoice groups, such as Mass Choice and the Boston chapter of the National Organization for Women, had created an extensive phone tree. On the Saturdays of possible rescues, representatives of these groups monitored the antiabortionists' activities, and when Operation Rescue struck, the prochoicers ran to the phones. Each person they dialed called several other people on the phone tree, and those people called other people. Within an hour, the prochoicers were chanting en masse in front of the targeted clinic. On October 29, 1988—less than six months ago—more than two thousand abortion rights advocates had lined Beacon Street to intimidate Operation Rescue, which had promised a blockade that day. The prochoicers cried victory when they learned that the abortion foes had driven to a clinic in Providence, Rhode Island.

Now, as the chanting outside grew louder, Sonia knew that the prochoice forces were swelling. "Not the church, not the state, women must decide their fate," they yelled. "One, two, three, four, open up the clinic door." At times, it sounded more like a high-school pep rally than a war over crisis pregnancy.

Outside, the noise was deafening—not as bad as at rescues in New York City where the prochoicers blew whistles to drown out the abortion foes' hymn singing—but still annoying to the police. Lugging bodies from the steps to the awaiting police bus was almost easier than standing around; at least when they were busy, the cops could concentrate on something other than the competing chants.

Bill McDermott had stayed at Repro to oversee the final cleanup of the protesters there, sending his partner, who had helped direct the arrests at Planned Parenthood, to Preterm. The detectives' job was to determine who the leaders were of each of the attacks. From what McDermott and George Driscoll could figure, Darroline had been in charge of the Repro siege, and Bill Cotter had led his band of fifty or so to Planned Parenthood in a second wave. Probably 100 or more rescuers had bounced back and forth between the two clinics on the trolley before finally heading to Preterm for the third and final blockade. Constance Smith, the former nun, the third member of what George Driscoll called the "Holy Trinity" of Operation Rescue leadership, seemed to have organized the Preterm blitz. Before being arrested, Constance told a television reporter that she thought Rescue had saved some babies.

"This was their Super Bowl," Jeffrey Allen, the chairman of Brookline's Board of Selectmen, told reporters in front of Preterm, grinning smugly as he watched three policemen lift the dead weight of a limp protester. Repro and Planned Parenthood were open for business and the police were quickly sweeping away the protesters from Preterm's front foyer. By 10 A.M., less than an hour after Operation Rescue had arrived, prochoicers outnumbered the abortion foes two to one, and more women and men carrying the blue-and-white "STAND UP FOR CHOICE" signs continued to jump off the trolley. Bodies still clogged the entryway, preventing any patient or staffer from entering, but Allen said he was confident that Preterm soon would be open.

No one locked inside, though, felt confident that the clinic would ever open on this Saturday, and neither were the patients who called, confused and frantic. "How could you let them do this to you?" one patient cried.

"Where are you?" Lin said calmly, her voice almost a singsong. "Don't panic. Wait at the corner of Dean and Beacon and someone will escort you to the church. No, this doesn't mean that your appointment is canceled."

Telephone counselors had warned each patient who had scheduled for this Saturday that there might be a blockade, and that if the women saw a large group of people in front of Preterm, they should drive to the nearest phone booth and call the clinic for instructions on where they should go to wait out the siege. On this Saturday, Lin was the phone room's anchor, assisted by any of the other staffers, such as Fran, who had arrived early enough to be held captive. The patients who called were told to wait at the corner of Dean and Beacon streets, a few blocks away from the clinic, and a clinic staffer would pick them up and drive them to the designated safe place: All Saints Episcopal Church.

Carolyn paced the hallway, the administrative offices, then the hallway again, furious that she was held hostage inside. It was like being in a submarine: No one could get in, and no one could get out. The poor man who had had an appointment with the dentist on the second floor earlier this morning couldn't leave the building. He just stood by the front door, staring at the backs of the protesters plastered against the glass.

In her most vivid dream of what a rescue would be, Carolyn had never imagined that she would lose control. Most of her staff was outside, arriving at their workplace after the abortion foes had descended. Her only means of communicating with her counselors, medical assistants, nurses, and doctors was by telephoning the church, where one of the nurses, Deb Andrews, and several counselors were stationed with the patients. When Carolyn looked out of her office window on the side of the building, she could see medical assistants clutching each other and crying, looking cold and befuddled. All she could do was hold a sign in the window that said "GO TO CHURCH."

The patients were scared, Deb told Carolyn. Deb, who had been a nurse at Preterm for nearly seven-and-a-half years, had volunteered to be in charge of the church because she wanted to be busy, and she was calm in a crisis. Patients couldn't tell who was prochoice and who was antichoice, she said. By the time they were escorted to the church, some were in tears, most were angry, all wondered if they would get their abortions. Counselors were calming those most upset, and someone was getting coffee.

To hold back the protesters at abortion demonstrations, the Brookline police had recently invested thousands of dollars in barricades. These looked like thick, metal bicycle racks. As Repro and Planned Parenthood were evacuated of protesters, the police loaded up the barricades that had surrounded those clinics and drove them to Preterm. But as the crowd ballooned with the arrival of abortion rights advocates, settling the barricades into two straight lines to create a pathway into the clinic was a struggle. In past demonstrations, the prochoice contingent had stood separate from their opposition, either off to the side or across the street on the median strip. Today, however, the prochoicers and antichoicers blended into one mob, the prochoicers inching toward the clinic entrance as the abortion protesters, most of whom were either kneeling or lying on the ground, were hauled to the prisoner bus. At Planned Parenthood, two prochoicers had been arrested for not cooperating with police orders to move away from the heart of the demonstration. If the two sides of the abortion war weren't separated, a riot would erupt, George Driscoll worried.

At Preterm, the possibility loomed dangerously near. Prolifers shoved prochoicers and prochoicers shoved prolifers as the police lowered the barricades into place. Once the barricades formed a long tunnel from the bottom of Preterm's steps out into Beacon Street, the protesters, prochoice and antichoice alike, began pushing to get to the edge of the metal dividers, as if their presence at the front would determine the demonstration's victor.

"Not a pretty crowd," Driscoll thought as he watched some prochoicers taunt the antichoicers. On the whole, the prochoice contingent had cooperated willingly with the police, but as in any political or social movement, the abortion rights crusade harbored a few extremists. They didn't see the need for boundaries, George thought. The only rules were their rules. "They are no friends of the police," he thought. It was hard enough dealing with Operation Rescue without having to deal with the other side now, too.

George's attention veered to a two-year-old child strapped into a stroller parked in the middle of the demonstration. Weaving through people, he told the woman, who had come to pray in support of Operation Rescue, that if she didn't get the child away from the crowd, he would call the Department of Social Services. She moved the child. Another mother told a reporter for *The Boston Globe* that her three children were safe at this demonstration, that "God would protect them." George Driscoll wasn't so sure, and put in a call to the police station to have someone drive Cotter, who was being fingerprinted and booked, to Preterm to order his people to remove their children from the fracas. By the time Cotter arrived, most of the blockaders had been arrested, and the parents who had brought their children accepted their leader's order without question.

By 10:40 A.M., less than two hours after they had arrived, more than 100 rescuers had been dragged from Preterm's front foyer and steps into two police buses and carted to the station, where they would be fingerprinted, booked, and imprisoned if they refused to pay the fifteen-dollar bail, which they were encouraged by their leadership to do. On Monday, they would be arraigned in Brookline Municipal Court and released. Their trials would be later in the spring.

Once the police bus rolled out, calls and orders flew between the police, Carolyn, and Deb at the church. The police would soon open Preterm's front door, which meant that the patients and staff could finally enter. Inside the clinic, behind the front door, stood Sonia, Carolyn, Fran, and the handful of other staffers who had been held hostage, waiting for the police to open the door so they could get a clear view of the demonstration, or what was left of it.

Shortly before eleven o'clock, two policemen swung open the front doors. Three hundred abortion rights activists erupted in cheers and clapping. They were everywhere—congregated on either side of the barricades, spilling out onto Beacon Street, streaming down the side-walk. Only a few Operation Rescue supporters remained near the building, most of whom were elderly women leaning against the barri-cades, praying fervently, rosary beads dangling from their clasped hands. Forty or fifty other abortion foes stood in clusters away from the prochoice demonstrators, pointedly avoiding contact with their opposition.

Across Beacon Street, a train of patients and staff, their arms linked in solidarity, wound its way toward the clinic. "Murderers!" someone from the antichoice crowd shouted. "You're killing your own children!"

"They're swimming in blood up there," wailed a woman in a red cape and waist-length gray hair, as she touched a huge crucifix that hung from her chin to her abdomen. Her face had been powdered deathly white.

Cheering on the train of patients and staff, a prochoice supporter pushed away a "Pro-Choice equals Pro-Death" sign. The man holding the sign punched her in the face. The women en route to Preterm clung together, arm in arm, looking straight ahead. Some cried.

As the train neared the clinic, the crowd parted, tossing scarves and hats to shield the women's faces from newspaper photographers and television cameras. Once inside, the first patient in line slugged her boyfriend in the arm. "You would have to look straight at the camera," she snapped.

Their faces uncovered, many of the women burst into tears. "I am absolutely furious with those people," said one patient. "They were being threatening. They were trying to psychologically abuse us. They don't know what we're going through. They don't understand it's my choice, it's my body, it's my life."

And they never will, Carolyn knew. She and Fran stood by the doors, watching the thirty-six patients stream in as the crowd outside shouted "Choice! Choice!" Earlier in the morning, Carolyn had felt invulnerable, believing that Preterm could not be stopped by anything Operation Rescue dreamed up. Eager to experience a rescue, Carolyn hadn't considered that there would be more attacks after today. Now even though the police had declared the rescue "a bust"—that the demonstrators hadn't prevented one woman from receiving an abortion—Carolyn was worried. Cotter had shut down business for two hours with less than an army of people. This wasn't the end of the war. This was just the beginning.

CHAPTER TWO # The Opposition

O UTSIDE St. Agatha's Church circled a band of prochoice demonstrators wrapped in wool coats and scarves, their mittened hands
holding signs bearing coat hangers slashed with a red line. No moon-
light lit their vigil and a bitter wind blew. Bill Baird, one of the nation's
most outspoken reproductive rights activists, responsible for bringing
to the Supreme Court the case that ultimately made contraceptives
available to single as well as married people, was among the chanting
men and women. His head bent down against the cold, Baird trudged
along, clutching a six-foot wooden cross, his symbol of women's fate if
abortion became illegal once again.

The chance that the stream of people pouring into the church would
attack Baird's abortion referral service in downtown Boston on Saturday morning for the March 4 regional rescue was unlikely; Operation
Rescue was only interested in physically blockading women from having abortions, not in women wondering where to get one. But Baird
didn't often miss an opportunity to protest when his opposition attracted press attention, and a pre-rescue rally such as this could lure
cameras from every television station in Boston. A dark, stocky man,
Baird told a reporter for *The Boston Herald* that this was "the first time
people are meeting inside a church to conspire to deny women their
constitutional right to abortion."

That wasn't exactly true. Pre-rescue rallies were a critical ingredient
in Operation Rescue's strategy and were held before every major blockade. By firing up the assemblage with song, prayer, and preaching,
Rescue's leaders hoped to inspire newcomers and veterans alike to

25

participate in the next rescue. Last October, hundreds of rescuers had met in a Baptist church the nights before they headed to Gynecare in Boston and to Women's Surgical Services in Providence, Rhode Island. "Baby Choice," a twenty-six-week-old fetus which traveled around the country in a casket to various Operation Rescue functions, laid in state at one of the autumn rallies, the subject of much scrutiny and many tears on the part of the hundreds of abortion foes who filed past her. Rescue's leaders insisted that Baby Choice was an aborted fetus that had been found in a dumpster outside of an abortion clinic on the West Coast. Abortion rights advocates claimed that Baby Choice was a stillborn donated to the abortion foes by a doctor sympathetic to their cause.

Wherever she came from, Baby Choice was nowhere in sight at this rally at St. Agatha's in East Milton, a suburb just a few highway exits south of Boston. No one, though, seemed to notice. The mood inside the Catholic church of heavy wood and dramatic stained-glass windows was festive. Individually and in clusters, the women and men, some carrying infants and toddlers squirming in their fuzzy sleepers, sauntered down the church's two aisles, nodding to acquaintances or stopping to quickly hug a friend before settling into a wooden pew. At the altar stood Bill Cotter, rocking back and forth, heel toe, heel toe, his hands clasped in front of him as he watched the pews fill with people. This was the largest turnout yet: between 500 and 600 potential rescuers would soon listen to Cotter's pleas to help stop the slaughter of innocent human lives. A TV camera crew paraded up and down the aisle, filming the faces in the crowd.

"It's good to be around so many people who think like I do, people who want to save the babies," a thin young woman with pale skin and curly brown hair whispered to the man beside her. The man nodded. He, like the woman, was in his late twenties, a small fellow with hands bearing the callouses and redness that come from working outdoors. His wife had been so furious that he had been arrested on October 29 for blockading the clinic in Rhode Island that she had made him promise not to participate in any more rescues. Rallies, she said reluctantly, were OK. "It's a miracle she let me come tonight," he said. "Praise God."

"Praise God," the woman next to him echoed.

It was nearly 7:30 P.M., a half hour past the designated starting time, when the guitar player began strumming the chords of the opening song. On cue, the congregation rose. "I've been redeemed . . ." the abortion foes sang. "I've been redeemed . . ." One person began to clap,

then another, and another. Soon, the clapping thundered over the voices. Those who didn't clap swayed with their arms stretched high toward heaven, eyes closed, mouths open in song. After the final chord, the congregation joined hands and bowed their heads. "Holy Spirit," the priest at the lectern began, "come upon us with power and might that we may hear and see Jesus."

"Yes, God, yes," hollered a voice in the crowd.

"Yes, sweet Jesus," boomed another.

So mesmerized in worship was one woman that she began speaking in tongues, in a language that sprang from her subconscious and erupted out of her mouth in sharp, clacking sounds. "Lord, Father, hear my cry," repeated another woman over and over. The priest asked that the congregation seek spiritual guidance and forgiveness for the years of inactivity, of letting child sacrifice continue unimpeded since 1973.

"Father, forgive us for being chickens, forgive us for being wimps," the priest prayed. "Lord Jesus, give us strength. We ask for power, peace, and love. Thank you, Lord, for not letting us stay home on Saturday or tempting us to go shopping. We must remember that we are killing if we remain silent."

Behind the priest, Bill Cotter waited for his turn to speak. Cotter's face had a white sheen almost the same color as the oxford shirt he wore underneath his gray suit—his only suit, Sergeant Bill McDermott had often joked. To the people before him, owning one suit wasn't an embarrassment but a source of pride, a symbol of sacrifice. Had Bill Cotter chosen to continue working as a software engineer in one of the big computer companies scattered around the Boston area, he would have earned enough money to buy ten suits. Instead, he had traded a healthy income for whatever Operation Rescue, which existed on donations, could afford to give him. To his followers, Bill Cotter had forsaken comfort for a greater cause. Their cause.

The first worship over, Bill Cotter walked briskly to the lectern. It wasn't time to delve into the tactical details of Saturday's blockade, of where to meet and what to do once the troops arrived at the designated clinic. That would come later, near the rally's end. Since much of Rescue's success depended on surprising the clinics and police, Cotter leaked only a little bit of information at a time. In the Operation Rescue:Boston newsletter mailed to more than 1,500 people, he listed the time and place of the pre-rescue rally. At the rally, he mentioned the meeting spot on Saturday morning. At the meeting spot, he would pass out maps to the targeted clinic.

But now his mission was to make each person in the audience feel so deeply the immorality of killing society's most vulnerable members, the unborn, that all listening would be willing to participate in Saturday's rescue. Recruitment was key. The more people blockading, the longer the arrests would take, the longer the clinic would stay closed. Without numbers, rescues would fizzle.

"We are not doing anything illegal," Cotter told the people, his hands gripping the lectern's sides. "We are saving children and there isn't a Massachusetts law that says saving children is illegal."

Blockading clinics was justified under what Cotter called the "necessity defense." You wouldn't be penalized for trespassing into a burning building to save a child locked inside. Therefore, you shouldn't be punished for saving children whose mothers were walking them toward certain death. To Cotter and the rest of the abortion foes, life began the moment the egg and sperm met. Therefore, that life enjoyed the same right to exist as any living, breathing human. By preventing women from entering the clinic, and perhaps ultimately closing the clinic, the abortion foes were doing what was right. Even if man's law didn't recognize the justness of their action, God would, because under God's law, killing the unborn was a sin. "We are obeying a higher law," Cotter told his audience.

The crowd listened respectfully to his monotone as Cotter quoted the Massachusetts abortion law, reciting that abortion was defined as "the knowing destruction of the life of an unborn child," and that the unborn child was defined as "the individual human life in existence and developing from fertilization until birth." Throughout the pews, people shook their heads while others clucked their tongues in disgust. Cotter talked about the "killing rate," that 10,000 lives alone were lost at Preterm each year. His language was strong. Fetuses were babies or children. Abortion clinics were abortion mills or abortuaries or killing centers. Doctors who performed abortions were murderers.

Cotter applauded Rescue's efforts, claiming that soon the jails and courts would be so full of rescuers and their trials that the only solution would be to "outlaw abortion." The crowd cheered. Cotter accepted his applause with a nod, his expression grim as he retreated from the lectern to make room for another speaker.

•   •   •

Bill Cotter first discovered his strong feelings about abortion during a debate on abortion's morality in a high-school social studies class. The

teenage Bill Cotter didn't understand why there was
Abortion was murder. Abortion was wrong. Aside fron
sional contributions to various antiabortion groups, he
was, in his own terms, an "armchair right-to-lifer" fo
decade. It wasn't until after he walked in the annual Ma
Washington, D.C., in January 1983 to commemorate *Roe*
anniversary that he began picketing Boston-area abortion clinics. He
would arrive at Preterm or Gynecare or Repro at six o'clock in the
morning and leave three hours later for his job as a software programmer. On Saturdays, he often stayed until noon.

Occasionally, he tried a more aggressive approach. In 1985, he and
eleven other protesters chained themselves to fixtures and equipment
on Preterm's fourth floor. A few months later he and four others did the
same at Repro Associates. That same year, he was arrested at Gynecare
for trespassing and at a Planned Parenthood clinic in New Haven,
Connecticut, for occupying an operating room.

"Abortion," he would say, "was killing babies and it was imperative
that I had to do something."

To outsiders, there had to be a deeper reason, something personal
that motivated Bill Cotter to invest so much energy in persuading
women to continue their pregnancies. One prochoice woman who had
infiltrated Operation Rescue said that Bill Cotter had a great need to
suffer, to be a martyr. Some of the police wondered if Cotter's activism
stemmed from a fear of women, that asking women to become mothers
somehow made females less threatening. Yet there was little in Cotter's
background—or in what anyone knew of Cotter's background—to
draw definite conclusions. The oldest of three boys, Cotter grew up in a
religious household, but he hadn't attended parochial schools. He'd
lived at home while earning a bachelor's degree in electrical engineering
and a master's degree in math from a technical college in nearby
Worcester. Although former computer company colleagues had reported to prochoicers that Cotter had lectured them at work about the
evils of abortion, Cotter hadn't seemed much different from any other
electronics engineer.

The only event that raised eyebrows was the death of his middle
brother over thirty years ago. At age one, the little boy had been run
over by a train after he wandered onto some railroad tracks near a
summer cottage where the Cotter family was vacationing. Bill Cotter
said that his prolife activity had nothing to do with the tragedy, but
others wondered if perhaps he felt guilty for living and therefore had to

sacrifice. Or perhaps he felt that all babies—whether zygotes, fetuses, or toddlers—were the same, and could come to no other conclusion: Abortion was murder and consequently must end.

Bill McDermott liked to play psychologist as much as anyone, but he wasn't sure that a sibling's death propelled Billy C. out of bed at 4 A.M. on Saturdays. McDermott believed that Cotter was motivated by one emotion and one emotion only: ego. "Wherever there's a TV camera, there's Bill Cotter," McDermott would say. Cotter had found a crusade that placed his face on the evening news, his name in *The Boston Globe*, and a crowd of followers who did as he bade.

When Cotter first heard about sit-ins being conducted in front of abortion clinics by a group called the Pro-Life Action Network (PLAN) out of Chicago, he wasn't sure that the idea would catch on. Was it possible to gather 100 people to blockade a clinic? It wasn't until 1986 when Cotter had actually witnessed sit-ins in Washington, D.C., St. Louis, and Pensacola, Florida, that he became a believer in what the antiabortion movement called "direct action." The sit-ins created enough confusion to give the sidewalk counselors more time to try to convince patients to find alternatives to abortion.

Direct action began in 1985, when a man named Joe Scheidler published the book *Closed: 99 Ways to Stop Abortion*. Frustrated with the poor results of political lobbying, Scheidler instructed his followers to stop abortion by physically confronting clinic personnel through whatever means possible: picketing the homes of doctors, tying up telephone lines, or filing legal suits. Scheidler formed the Pro-Life Action Network and led "sit-ins" around the country.

In 1987 at the annual PLAN convention, Randall Terry, a used-car salesman from Binghamton, New York, introduced the idea of blockading multiple clinics in major cities with hundreds, even thousands, of people. Without action, Terry said, the United States was doomed: God would destroy a civilization that killed its children. Borrowing from the Biblical phrase "Rescue those being taken away to death" (Proverbs 24:11), Terry called the blockades "rescues." The way Terry saw it, the "rescues" would not only stop "childkilling" for the day, but also would lead to arrests that would overwhelm the police and the jails, as well as to trials that would overwhelm the courts. The politicians ultimately would cave in to taxpayers' pressure and abolish abortion. Rescues, he said, would produce the social tension necessary for political change. Terry compared his movement to that of civil rights, despite the fact that civil rights leaders, including the Reverend Jesse Jackson, had formally denied any similarity, arguing that Martin Luther King, Jr.'s goal had been to provide equal rights, not deny women their reproductive rights.

For the next year, Terry plotted. In November 1987 he conducted a dry-run rescue in Cherry Hill, New Jersey, where 211 people were arrested. The following May, he descended on New York City with his flock for a week of clinic blockades that led to more than 1,300 arrests. Rescues in Pittsburgh, Philadelphia, and Jackson, Mississippi, followed, but Operation Rescue didn't hit the big time until the summer of 1988 when Terry led a convoy of three buses and twenty cars to the Atlanta Surgi-Center during the Democratic National Convention. Within ninety minutes the Atlanta police had arrested 134 protesters, using headlocks and vise grips, as television cameras captured the scene and replayed it to the nation. From July 19 through October, Terry and his followers blockaded Atlanta clinics relentlessly, securing themselves with Kryptonite locks to doorways and vehicles—doing anything they thought would delay arrest and, therefore, delay procedures.

Although many in the antiabortion movement, including the National Right to Life Committee, didn't condone the confrontations in front of the clinics, others found Operation Rescue the right movement at the right time. After sixteen years of trying to outlaw abortion through lobbying politicians and submitting bills, the antiabortionists had yet to gain much ground. For many, direct action—physically doing something to end abortion—seemed like a logical move.

Adding to the appeal was a new political tenor. For eight years the abortion foes had listened to President Ronald Reagan's promise to overturn *Roe v. Wade*, and for eight years *Roe v. Wade* had stayed intact. When George Bush became President, however, hope surged. Complementing the Bush administration's desire to overturn *Roe v. Wade* was a new Supreme Court. While in office, Ronald Reagan had replaced retiring liberal Supreme Court justices with conservatives—Sandra Day O'Connor, Antonin Scalia, and Anthony Kennedy—creating a divided court on the abortion issue. Justice O'Connor held the pivotal vote. For the first time in sixteen years, the antiabortion forces felt that they could successfully challenge the constitutionality of the right to an abortion. Their first chance would be in April 1989, when the Supreme Court would hear *Webster* v. *Reproductive Health Services*, a case that challenged a Missouri law restricting abortion. If the Missouri law were upheld, all states, in effect, would be free to determine their own abortion regulations.

In response, Operation Rescue satellites began sprouting up in major cities across the country. In Boston, Bill Cotter merely blended

Operation Rescue with his existing group, a chapter of Scheidler's Chicago-based PLAN. Cotter took charge. He had the experience. Not only had he invaded clinics in Massachusetts, but he also had accompanied Terry to Cherry Hill and New York. Cotter hoped that Operation Rescue:Boston could be big, really big. He could have the support of very Catholic Boston to invade very liberal Brookline, home of the clinics responsible for nearly one-quarter of all New England abortions and home of other noted liberals, such as the Democratic nominee for President of the United States, Michael Dukakis, and Congressman Barney Frank, known for his quip, "To the right-to-lifers, life begins at conception and ends at birth." What better bait to lure hundreds of abortion foes to Beacon Street?

•   •   •

Now, at St. Agatha's, a second priest, round and jolly, stood at the altar surveying the rows of faces, saying that the efforts of these soldiers of God to save babies would be rewarded, that "the line for heaven would be 'as long as a line at Bradlee's during a sale.' " When it was time for the offering, the priest asked those soldiers to "dig deep."

"If you dig for ten dollars, go for twenty dollars," he said. "If you grab for twenty dollars, get fifty dollars." Pocketbooks clicked open. Men flipped through wallets. Children plunked dimes into the plastic buckets being passed from hand to hand.

It was a heady time for many in St. Agatha's sanctuary. In Rescue they had found a family of like-minded souls, people who believed as they did. For many, abortion represented not only an insult to their church's teachings on the sanctity of human life but it also posed a challenge to traditional family values, the core of their belief system. Abortion became symbolic of modern society's social evils: premarital sex, promiscuity, divorce. If women could kill their own children, any kind of hell was possible. Although there was no party platform on birth control, Rescue's creator, Randall Terry, believed that contraception interfered with God's plan; that if a couple didn't want to procreate, then they shouldn't recreate in bed.

Antiabortion observers claimed that Operation Rescue was filled with women who had raised a herd of children and felt that women choosing against motherhood made a mockery of their lives. Others argued that Rescue comprised large numbers of men in their twenties and thirties who had not fared well in the past decade. Jobs that would have been theirs twenty years before had gone to women. The affluence of the 1980s had evaded them, and they found themselves earning significantly less than their fathers. They couldn't afford to buy their own homes, and if they could, their wives often had to work to help pay the mortgage. Preying on others, such as women entering abortion clinics, made them feel masterful, especially since they could claim that they were protecting the ultimate in vulnerability: the innocent unborn child.

Yet those who comprised the bulk of Operation Rescue:Boston could not be so easily stereotyped. Among the crowd in St. Agatha's sat bank auditors and brick masons, professional fund-raisers and waitresses. Their only common denominator was their drive, for whatever reason, to end legalized abortion.

In one pew sat Fred Pulsifer, a retired janitor for the city of Melrose, a Boston suburb. Catholic, he said that a woman in his church had convinced him to help "save the babies" six years ago. Ever since, he had stood in front of Repro and Preterm in rain and sleet and blazing sun, holding plastic fetuses in his palm, slyly hiding the miniature dolls when the police detail watched him. He wore his gray hair in a wiffle cut and smiled only enough to expose his front two teeth. Fred had added to his signature the initials SLE, which stood for "Sanctity of Life Effort." He hoped that whoever saw the initials (a supermarket clerk, for instance) would ask their meaning, giving him the opportunity to regale them with talk about his work to end abortion and to hand out antiabortion literature. Fred didn't have any children of his own and had never married. He participated in Operation Rescue, he said, because he believed that abortion was murder and therefore he should act as if it's murder.

On Friday mornings, Fred usually could be found in front of Preterm accompanied by two women: Jean and her best friend, Alice. Jean was blonde and Alice was brunette and often they wore matching pink Reebok sneakers. Long before they joined Operation Rescue, the two women had picketed abortion clinics, hospitals that performed abortions, and even porn shops. Jean was inspired to become active five years ago after the death of her parish priest, who had been deeply involved in the prolife movement. Although Jean worked as a teacher's aide for disabled children and had a twenty-three-year-old son with Down's syndrome, she didn't credit her experience with the physically challenged for her motivation. Instead, she said that humans were responsible for one another, and that the unborn needed protection.

Alice had started picketing five years ago after she had seen photos of babies dismembered by abortion. Since her three children were grown and she didn't work outside of the home, she was free in the mornings to try to talk women out of their abortions. She sent away for a lapel button showing a pair of tiny feet, which represented the feet of a ten-week fetus, and wore it everywhere. She believed it was insanity to give a mother the choice of which child to kill. When she discovered that her neighbor's teenage foster child was pregnant, she brought the girl to a prolife doctor and asked the girl to move in with her own family for the duration of her pregnancy. Now, five years later, the "baby" was entering kindergarten. The mother, said Alice, had her "ups and downs" as a single parent.

To Alice and Jean and their prolife peers, there were no good reasons to abort a pregnancy. If the pregnancy resulted from a rape, why should the innocent fetus be a second victim of violence? The same theory held true for incest. If the woman's husband or boyfriend had left her, God would provide and help her through single parenthood. The abortion foes often labeled women who said that they didn't have the money to raise a child as being "selfish." "We are a generation of hedonists," wrote one minister involved in Rescue. "We want comfort. We want more money to buy ourselves more comfort." "Everyone wants the best car, the best boyfriend," Alice would say. And even if the pregnant woman were truly impoverished, giving the child up for adoption was an alternative.

To patients entering the clinics, both Jean and Alice passed brochures listing options to abortion. Most of their resources were referrals to public agencies, such as Medicaid, designed to offer medical or financial assistance. Some of their literature included names of group homes for unwed pregnant women, but beds there were in short supply. The prolife organizations were always on the lookout for people who would take in indigent pregnant women.

Some of the women within Rescue claimed that their motivation stemmed from the horror that had followed their own abortions. Constance Smith, who was Rescue:Boston's executive director, had traveled to New York twenty years earlier at age nineteen to end her pregnancy. Five years of hell had followed, she would say: five years of drinking and smoking pot and feeling as if there were a cavern where her heart had once been. She didn't feel whole again until she moved from Pennsylvania to San Francisco, where she joined a religious order she described as right of Roman Catholicism. Born Catholic and raised Methodist, Constance took vows of purity, poverty, humility, obedience, and service when she became a sister in her new church.

For the next ten years, Constance bounced from city to city, coast to coast, answering crisis lines for abused women and children and working in soup kitchens. In 1985, she decided to enter the Third Order of her church, which meant she could live on her own, perhaps marry, and not relay her every move to her church superiors. She moved to Boston and instead of opening a shelter for unwed mothers (a dream she said she had harbored ever since realizing that she had "killed her own child"), she joined a group called Sanctity for Life. For income, she became a nanny for a wealthy Boston family. For spiritual fulfillment, she stood in front of Gynecare, asking abortion patients to reconsider their decision; telling them that they didn't know the desperation they would feel afterward.

Three years later, in 1988, she met Bill Cotter, whose PLAN booth was set up next to Constance's Sanctity of Life booth at a Christian conference in Boston. Constance thought that her sidewalk counseling would become more effective under Cotter's tutelage, and she joined PLAN. Tall and slender with waist-length brown hair, Constance soon became as much a presence as Cotter in front of the clinics. When Cotter started Operation Rescue:Boston, Constance was at his side. She didn't like the physical part of rescues—of being dragged into a police van and sleeping on police-station floors—and she abhorred the feeling of incarceration, but if she could save one baby, one life, by blockading, she said that her sacrifice was worthwhile.

Bill McDermott believed that Constance was genuinely motivated by her religion and feelings of right and wrong. The sergeant's sources within Rescue adored her. She was gentle and good, a crusader for the underdog. At St. Agatha's, rescuers and would-be rescuers beamed at Constance as she sailed up and down the aisles, smiling broadly, spending only a few minutes at the microphone to praise those in the sanctuary for their dedication to saving children.

Darroline Firlit was not as visible at St. Agatha's, or at any rally for that matter, as were Constance and Bill Cotter. Darroline's strength lay in strategizing the rescues, not socializing with the followers. She would nod to friends in the crowd, maybe even embrace a few, but for the most part, Darroline stood to the side, counting heads and analyzing. Always analyzing. Out of Rescue's three leaders, Darroline came across as being the toughest and the most determined. "How many people would stand by if the Supreme Court said all teenagers should be killed?" she would say when justifying her more than twenty arrests from Atlanta to Brookline.

Darroline claimed that she first realized that abortion was evil after she had encouraged a friend of hers to end a pregnancy. The year was

1975, her friend had five children and an alcoholic husband, and Darroline thought that a new baby would be too much for her friend to handle. Darroline said that she had escorted the woman to a Planned Parenthood clinic in East Providence, Rhode Island, where her friend aborted a twenty-two-week-old fetus. Two months after the abortion, the friend tried to commit suicide, later telling Darroline that she hated her for talking her into killing her baby. The next time Darroline faced a woman bearing a crisis pregnancy, she steered the woman to a prolife organization. She became an ordained minister through correspondence courses and soon began preaching to prostitutes, taking pregnant hookers home with her to make sure that they didn't abort. At one point, seventeen women lived in Darroline's home with Darroline, her husband, and two daughters. Her work brought her in touch with Massachusetts Citizens for Life, which put her in touch with Bill Cotter. Like Constance, when Cotter began Operation Rescue:Boston, Darroline was ready.

A powerful story, to be sure, except that there had never been a Planned Parenthood in East Providence. Planned Parenthood had a clinic in Providence, a separate city, but abortions there were performed only up to twelve weeks.

Darroline's critics might have been able to shrug off these mistaken details as oversights or as mere exaggerations. But there were so many exaggerations in Darroline's self-described history that it was difficult to discern fact from fiction.

Darroline, now thirty-five, said that her motivation sprang from her belief in doing God's work, that she had seen His power when he rescued her from drug addiction. Cocaine, angel dust, heroin—you name it, she would say, she tried it. Darroline said that she had begun experimenting with drugs at age sixteen, about the time she dropped out of high school. The oldest child of a military family, Darroline had moved constantly throughout her youth, falling so far behind in her studies that instead of repeating a year, she left school to sew shoulder seams at a shirt factory near Fall River, a faded mill town in southern Massachusetts where her mother had grown up and where her grandparents still lived. She met Ernie Firlit, who was three years her senior, at the company Christmas party, and married him the following July. She was seventeen. Thirteen months later their first daughter was born, but since Ernie was in the Army and stationed in Germany, Darroline had to learn motherhood by herself. Despite her heavy drug use, Darroline claimed that her pregnancy was healthy and that she was a good mother. Shortly after Ernie returned home from Germany later that year, Darroline and Ernie were invited by Darroline's drug dealer, who had been Born Again, to attend a service at a Fundamentalist church. During the service, Darroline felt God talking to her through the minister. Ernie, too, felt the power. Together, the Firlits walked out of the church ready to serve God.

McDermott didn't buy the drug story. A former woman convict he had talked to had known Darroline in her early Fall River days. Darroline had been a heavy drinker, the woman said, and if she had used drugs, they were probably prescription, not heroin or cocaine. Darroline said that her arms were free of track marks because she had shot under her tongue and in her groin, but McDermott knew from his years of work on the streets that addicts chose those spots only after all the other veins had been used up.

Nonetheless, if put through a lie-detector test, Darroline would pass, Bill McDermott claimed. She had told her story so many times that even she believed it. And it was a good story to tell the public, McDermott would say—the woman who crawled from the gutter of heroin addiction, the worst of all evils, to save babies. Darroline had found a cause that gave her a title and an office and reporters calling her for quotes. Without that cause, McDermott wondered, what would Darroline have?

Besides whether or not she were telling the truth didn't really matter. Her people believed her, admired her, were inspired by her dedication. The fact that Darroline had taken fetal remains from an abortion clinic to give "the children" a proper funeral was more important than how she had taken the fetal remains. Darroline claimed she had found "the children" in jars in a clinic dumpster. The clinic staffers, however, had noticed that the remains—or products of conception as they were called—were missing from the vault outside from which the medical laboratory picked up the tissue. Darroline said that she would bury the seven "children" in a cemetery with a gravestone after her husband had built each of them a casket.

Of one fact McDermott was sure: Darroline was a force within Rescue to be reckoned with. McDermott wasn't certain how far Cotter would go for the cause, but the detective believed that Darroline had no limits.

• • •

"We are nonviolent," Bill Cotter told the congregation at St. Agatha's. He was back at the lectern, this time to explain the details of a rescue.

At a rescue last fall, someone had grabbed the patient list from the hands of a clinic staffer. That behavior, Cotter said, would not be tolerated.

He explained that you could be a prayer supporter and stand to the side and pray without fear of arrest, or you could be a rescuer, laying your body down in front of the clinic. Preferably, all would blockade; what better way to prevent murder than 500 or more bodies crushed together in front of the closed clinic doors? Cotter also encouraged those who were arrested not to give their identity or pay bail: A weekend in jail was a small sacrifice to make for proving their sincerity to the public. On Monday they would be arraigned in court, where they would demand jury trials—another effort to clog the system.

To prepare for the rescue, both rescuers and prayer supporters were advised to drink no liquids to avoid the need for a bathroom during the demonstration. They should dress for extreme cold in durable clothing and they should bring no identification if they planned to risk arrest. Signs would be provided and umbrellas were discouraged; they dripped on your neighbor.

Obedience was the key. Operation Rescue boasted a pyramidal military structure with Cotter at the top, Darroline and Constance beneath him, and a handful of marshals who would orchestrate the actual blockade, telling people where to go. The masses who formed the pyramid's base were expected to obey the marshals, who would obey the leaders. A blockade was no time to question authority.

At the rescue site, Cotter told his audience either to pray and sing or to be quiet. Do not talk with the opposition; ignore their taunts. Do not speak to the women seeking abortions. The sidewalk counselors would talk to them. If struck by a member of the opposition, react passively and wait for a police officer or marshal to intervene. If the police remove you from the blockade, crawl under a barricade or around the police to get back to the entrance. The longer it takes the police to round up the demonstrators, the longer the clinic would be closed, and the more babies would be saved. At the police station, wait for direction from the leaders before you begin the fingerprinting and booking process. Those arrested must work as a group, not as individuals.

The rescuers were to meet at Our Lady Help of Christians Church in Newton at six o'clock Saturday morning. A mass would be held for Catholics upstairs, and a prayer service for Protestants downstairs. From there, maps would be disseminated and the rescue would begin. Cars should boast full gas tanks, although the rescue may be less than five miles from the church.

"How many of you have been arrested?" Cotter asked the audience. Hands shot up throughout the sanctuary. Cotter invited the veterans to stand at the altar. More than 150 men and women slid out of the pews and marched to the altar, as proud as graduates parading to the podium to receive their diplomas. The crowd clapped and cheered.

Heads bowed, the congregation uttered its final prayer. When the abortion foes emerged from the church at 9:45 P.M., the sidewalk was empty, clear of Bill Baird and other prochoice obstacles.

• • •

Forty-eight hours later, 227 people had been arrested for disorderly conduct at demonstrations in front of Brookline's three abortion clinics. One hundred and seventy-two of the arrested refused to give identification and post bail. More than fifty women spent the next two nights on the floor of the Lynch Recreation Center while their male counterparts slept on the cement floor of the Brookline Police Station's garage. To fumigate the stench of the rescuers' two-day-old clothes and unbathed bodies, the police kept the garage door slightly open, letting in the cold March air. When the high-school cafeteria ran out of supplies for peanut butter and jelly sandwiches, the police fed the prisoners hamburgers from McDonald's. On Monday morning, looking gray and tired and rumpled, the arrested stood before a judge in Brookline Municipal Court to hear their charges and to demand a jury trial for each and every one.

CHAPTER THREE

Bombarded from All Sides

THE weeks following the March 4 rescue weren't easy for anyone at Preterm. Although staffers claimed that the siege had reinforced their commitment to preserve reproductive freedom, a fierce undercurrent of anxiety flowed through the clinic. For two hours on that raw morning in early March, they had stood helplessly on Preterm's sidewalk, locked out of their place of employment by a mob of people who hated what they represented. Then, without a moment to collect their thoughts or express their feelings, they had been allowed inside to spend the next seven hours performing their jobs as if nothing extraordinary had happened.

Worried about how the staffers' repressed feelings would affect their mental health and job performance, Carolyn Wardell and her director of counseling had passed out a questionnaire the week after the siege. Staffers were asked to write anonymously about how they had been affected by Operation Rescue's attack. Fear—for themselves and for the future of abortion—snaked through the responses. One nurse wrote that she had felt confident that the "backdoor butcheries" of the past would never return—until she saw the throng of abortion foes in front of the clinic that day. A counselor said that her family worried that because of her work she would be stabbed or blown up, and that after the rescue she, too, was concerned. The antis were narrow-minded and evil, as intolerant as the Ku Klux Klan and the Nazis, others wrote. And with people that extreme, any kind of violence was possible.

The March 4 rescue had shattered Preterm's sense of security. What was once a threat was now a frightening reality. Anytime more than three protesters congregated in front of the clinic, staffers wondered if an invasion was imminent. Even today, Good Friday, almost a month after the blockade, Fran Basche wondered if the Way of the Cross procession would serve as a guise for another attack.

This was the second year in a row that the abortion foes were commemorating Jesus' journey to his crucifixion by following the Stations of the Cross in front of the three Brookline abortion clinics. Gathering on lower Beacon Street at 9 A.M. with their crosses and rosary beads, "STOP ABORTION" signs and color photos of decapitated fetuses, they prayed to the first five stations at Planned Parenthood, prayed to the second five at Repro, and concluded the ritual at Preterm with the last four.

Last year, Fran had felt sorry for the fifty antis reciting the rosary on the sidewalk. Wrapped in well-worn coats and windbreakers, their pink faces creased with age, the elderly protesters had looked to Fran more bedraggled than holy. They seemed frail, more likely to faint from the exertion of the two-mile walk than to storm the clinic doors. But with the advent of Operation Rescue and the hundreds of abortion foes it had spurred to action, this year's holy routine could explode with a fresh energy. Even the police questioned the procession's innocence. Last year, one private-detail cop had supervised the scene at each clinic. This morning, at least a dozen police patrolled Beacon Street, trailing behind the parade in cruisers or on motorcycles.

It was almost eleven o'clock when Fran spotted the first faces of the procession cresting the hill several blocks from Preterm. Two by two, then in clusters of four or more, the Soldiers of God tramped down the sidewalk on the last leg of their journey. Although staffers at the other two clinics had reported to Preterm that the protesters had been peaceful this morning, Fran dashed from her lookout spot on the sidewalk in front of the clinic to the safety of the building's front foyer. She felt better with a glass door between her and them.

Carolyn Wardell, on the other hand, chose to stand outside on the front steps of her clinic. She didn't feel as threatened by this troupe as Fran, and doubted if the religious routine would end in an attack. Raised Catholic, she was curious about how the abortion foes would perform the familiar litany. During her childhood, she had attended church regularly and had relished the peacefulness and the feeling that someone was watching over her. But as she grew older, she began questioning the church's position on birth control and sexuality and, eventually, stopped attending mass. Sex and Catholicism didn't jibe. As years passed, she grew further and further away from her religious roots. Now she had no tolerance for her church and its rigid stand on issues that she considered to be private.

Despite the clouds covering Brookline and the raw air that felt more like Thanksgiving weather than Good Friday, the Way of the Cross crowd had doubled this year. More than 100 people had gathered to pray in front of Preterm. Some of the faces looked familiar to Fran, faces she thought she'd seen blockading Preterm's doors on March 4. Would they try anything today? she wondered. Had one of them called in any of the four bomb threats that Preterm had received a few Saturdays ago? Had one of them mailed Preterm the latest anti-Semitic postcard that said "lynch the lousy Jew doctors" and "pray for another Hitler"? Picketers were forever shouting about Jewish abortionists, as if a Christian physician never crossed the clinic's threshold.

These people, though, didn't even venture near the clinic, choosing instead to obey old Bill Clarke as he directed them to line the sidewalk and keep the entrance clear. Once in place, they froze, their heads bowed, hands clasped before them. Four men carried a baby's casket bearing a red rose on a satin pillow and a "Love Life" button on the lid.

"Station Eleven," the priest announced. "Jesus is nailed to the cross." They genuflected. "Hail Mary, full of grace," the crowd murmured, reciting the rosary. "Our Father, Who art in Heaven," they continued.

While Carolyn stood transfixed on the front steps, Fran maintained her distance behind the door. They look passive enough, Fran thought, her fear of an attack fading with each "Hail Mary"—but what hypocrites.

Although Operation Rescue and other antiabortion groups claimed that their outfits comprised people of all religions, most members were, in fact, either Roman Catholic or Protestant. Since the Stations of the Cross is a Catholic ritual, it seemed safe to assume that most of the people reciting the rosary in front of Preterm were Catholic. To Fran, however, who was Jewish, whether the protesters were Baptists or Methodists or Catholics didn't matter. What mattered was that before her stood people who called themselves Christians, people who supposedly lived by the creed of "do unto others as you would have them do unto you," but who were using their religion as a weapon to make others feel guilty. Since nearly one-third of Preterm's patients were Catholic, some of the women entering the clinic this morning probably

had performed the Stations of the Cross themselves in church and felt that the protesters were talking directly to them. On ordinary picketing days, patients had rushed to Sonia's desk in tears, sobbing that a protester had flashed a cross at them or alluded to God's love for all Christians, including the unborn. If one picketer could incite such anguish, Fran wondered, what would a crowd of religious warriors do?

"And the Prayer of the Unborn Child," the priest intoned. "My grave will be a garbage dump, or an incinerator. My parents will admit that they killed their own flesh and blood."

These people are too much, Carolyn thought from her perch on the steps. They were not reciting the proper litany, but rather were creating their own, justifying every twist of words as God's will to help the world understand that abortion was murder. Carolyn often said that what infuriated her most about the abortion foes was that they viewed the world in absolutes, in black and white, refusing to see life's complexities.

Carolyn had seen life's complexities, or at least the complexity which had brought the protesters to Preterm's steps: She had had two abortions of her own. After years of unprotected intercourse with her first husband, she had thought that she had the rhythm method down pat. She learned otherwise when she slept with someone else after she and her husband separated. She wasn't in love with the father, nor was she ready to be a single parent. Working full-time and attending night school to earn a bachelor's degree, she couldn't afford to feed and clothe a child, let alone pay for day care. Her second pregnancy had resulted from a diaphragm failure. Her paramour already had two children by a previous marriage and didn't want more. Carolyn had considered continuing the pregnancy, for she would have liked a child, but money was tight and she still felt unequipped to assume alone the daunting responsibility for another person.

During Carolyn's second marriage, Lorena had been born, and even though the marriage hadn't lasted beyond her daughter's infancy, Carolyn had been better prepared—financially and emotionally—to nurture this child. Glaring at the people below her on the sidewalk, Carolyn felt a wave of scorn. How could these people presume to know when it was right for everyone to be a parent?

From her lookout several feet away, Fran, who had never had an abortion, felt the same scorn. Standing behind the glass door along with a handful of other staffers, Fran was reliving her fury of the Sunday before, Palm Sunday. A group of antis had picketed All Saints Episcopal Church in protest of the church's sheltering Preterm patients during the March 4 rescue. Singing their hymns and carrying their signs, one of which portrayed Jesus holding a dead baby, they circled on the sidewalk. Fran's anger built as she drove down Beacon Street, exploding when she reached the house of her boyfriend's mother. Flailing her hands, ranting about religious intolerance, she asked Peter's mother, "Can you imagine arriving at church to find people picketing your services?"

Winston Churchill once defined a fanatic as one who can't change his mind and won't change the subject. If that were the case, these people personified fanatic to Fran. They had no respect for anyone else's beliefs or religion, she fumed. They couldn't accept that the American Baptist Church, the Episcopal Church, the Central Conference of American Rabbis, the Presbyterian Church, the United Methodist Church, even many Catholics, supported a woman's right to become a mother by choice.

Abortion wasn't positive to Fran; it was an acceptable solution to a problem. Fran would be happy if there were no need for abortions, if birth control always worked, and if men and women always used it properly. But after a year and a half at Preterm, she knew that even the Pill wasn't foolproof and that too many people never learned how to insert a diaphragm correctly or use a condom properly. There were as many reasons to have an abortion as there were women, and Fran believed that no one but the woman involved should make the choice. The woman, after all, was the one who had to live with the decision, not the protesters.

"What would any of these people do if their sixteen-year-old daughter got pregnant?" Fran said to the cluster of staffers beside her.

As the crowd mumbled its last prayer, Fran turned and headed back toward her office. For months, she had been frustrated with the media's coverage of the abortion war. Photographers clicked shot after shot of protesters being dragged by police or elderly women deep in prayer. The antis made great visuals, and the publication of those visuals granted them legitimacy, Fran felt. But the papers and television cameras weren't showing what the public needed to know: that these people were using their religion to abuse others who didn't share their views. Carolyn agreed to Fran's suggestion to write a letter to *The Brookline Citizen*, one of the town's two weekly newspapers. "You know Fran," Carolyn would say. "She will speak."

After lunch that day, Fran sat down at the computer next to the secretary's desk and began to type frantically. "I am not naive," she wrote, "but I thought maybe there was such a thing as religious tolerance in our democracy, and that we as a society had grown more open-minded since the 1960s. And I always thought that places of worship were considered sanctuaries in America and throughout the world."

She mentioned the anti-Semitic postcards and the bomb threats and compared the antis' intolerance to that of the Spanish Inquisitors. "Judge not," she wrote, "lest ye be judged. Apparently, these people think they have a right to judge the private actions of others. But I have a feeling that they too are being judged. The citizens of Brookline and the Commonwealth of Massachusetts will not—and should not—accept religious intolerance, whether it comes in the form of Palm Sunday picketing or a vile postcard."

Fran felt good about the letter, but thought she should let it sit for the weekend before she mailed it. She wouldn't be quite so angry next week and it might need toning down.

When she returned on Monday, however, she was seething. Twenty protesters had picketed All Saints' Easter Eve service, again in protest of the church's housing Preterm patients during the March 4 rescue. "The word of God says you will know a church by its fruits," one picketer told *The Boston Globe*. "Murder is against God's will."

Carolyn okayed Fran's letter, agreeing that what Fran had written needed to be said. On her way home from work that Monday, Fran dropped the letter off at *The Brookline Citizen's* office. She was told that it would run the next Thursday, March 30.

•   •   •

Like most abortion clinic staffs across the country, the Preterm staff had endured over the years its share of bomb scares and threatening letters and picketers swarming around the neighborhoods of doctors, plastering car windshields and stuffing mailboxes with photos of fetuses in garbage bags. Yet no one, not even Sonia Lewis, who had begun counseling at the clinic before the carpet had been nailed down, could remember a time as tense as the spring of 1989.

The antiabortionists were relentless. If they weren't picketing in front of clinics—or churches—they were gluing the inside of clinic door locks, calling in bomb threats, or plotting blockades. Despite the federal lawsuit that the town of Brookline had filed against Operation Rescue several weeks after the March 4 attack, an Operation Rescue:Boston newsletter landed on Fran's desk announcing another blitz on April 29. Charging that Rescue's efforts to shut down clinics violated the Racketeer Influenced and Corrupt Organizations Act, also known as RICO, Brookline hoped to recoup the $75,000 it had spent on police overtime for the past three rescues. But Bill Cotter and Darroline Firlit contended that the lawsuit meant nothing and that they would continue to follow "a higher law." This meant that energies within Preterm would again be diverted from improving patient services to preparing for an attack.

Around the country, protesters in front of clinics were chaining themselves together or to rows of tires or to 150-pound cement blocks. It seemed to the Preterm staff that it was only a matter of time before the local "muffins," as Sergeant Bill McDermott called Cotter and his friends, tried something similar.

The most overwhelming threat of all, though, was the one over which Preterm, and all abortion providers, had the least control: *Webster* v. *Reproductive Health Services*. "Webster" was William Webster, Missouri's attorney general, who had defended the 1986 state statute that banned the use of public facilities and employees in providing abortions, or even discussing abortions with women. The statute also required fetal viability testing if the doctor suspected that the woman was twenty or more weeks pregnant and stated in its preamble that human life began at conception. Reproductive Health Services was the St. Louis clinic that originally had challenged the statute's constitutionality.

At best, the Supreme Court, which would hear the case on April 26, would uphold the appeal and lower courts' rulings, and *Roe* v. *Wade* would escape unscathed. At worst, the Supreme Court would use the case to overturn *Roe*. Most likely, the Court would use *Webster* to chip away at *Roe*, allowing states to determine their own abortion laws. Abortion rights advocates feared that this would create a patchwork effect for reproductive rights. Women of means could travel to states where abortion was legal; poor women couldn't. Reproductive freedom would be a luxury of the haves and a memory for the have-nots.

For the first time in sixteen years, the right to reproductive choice, which had seemed unassailable, was vulnerable. To the thousands of doctors, nurses, counselors, medical assistants, and admitting officers at the nation's abortion clinics, legal abortion spelled empowerment: the ability of women to take control of their lives; to finish school, find a job, get off welfare, achieve goals other than raising a child they didn't want.

Not since *Roe* v. *Wade* had a Supreme Court abortion case ignited the nation's passions like *Webster* v. *Reproductive Health Services*. The Court's switchboard was jammed with calls and its mailroom was virtually incapacitated by the 10,000 to 15,000 letters that arrived daily from people on both sides of the issue. A record-breaking seventy-eight friend-of-the-court briefs had been filed by state attorneys general, members of Congress, Nobel Laureates, historians, doctors, bioethicists, clergy members, and citizens. The longest brief was 225 pages and was signed by 2,887 women who had had abortions and who supported the right for other women. Although the high court had heard fourteen other abortion cases since *Roe*, repeatedly ruling against severe abortion restrictions, *Webster* loomed as a dazzling hope for abortion foes and a potential tragedy for abortion rights supporters.

The Supreme Court that had voted seven to two in 1973 that a woman's constitutional right to privacy included her right to decide, in consultation with her doctor, whether or not to bear a child, was not the same Court that would hear *Webster*. Three of the original justices were gone, replaced by three conservatives: Sandra Day O'Connor, who had written that *Roe* was on a collision course with itself and that states should have more power to regulate abortion; Antonin Scalia, who was thought to be hostile toward *Roe* and the idea that abortion was covered by the Constitution; and Anthony Kennedy, who had not yet spoken on abortion, but who had voted conservatively since joining the Court. Byron White and William Rehnquist, *Roe*'s two dissenting votes, remained on the Court. Since *Roe*, Rehnquist had become the chief justice.

If the Court returned abortion legislation to the states, Massachusetts seemed safe—for the short-term. Although the state's House of Representatives was overwhelmingly antiabortion and the Senate had a prochoice majority of only one vote, Governor Michael Dukakis was deeply prochoice. He had vetoed, and promised to continue to veto, all antiabortion legislation. If polls were accurate and the defeat of a 1986 referendum to adopt a constitutional amendment to ban abortions were any indicators, the state's population was also in favor of abortion rights.

But Dukakis's reign would end in 1991, and only one of the potential gubernatorial candidates stood firmly prochoice. Moreover, it was difficult for the prochoice movement to ignore the state's history. Massachusetts had been the first state in the nation to outlaw abortion in 1847 and the last to legalize contraceptives for unmarried women in 1972. It had been the first state to require a teenager to get either parental consent or a judge's approval to have an abortion. And although Massachusetts was one of the fourteen states that provided public money for abortions, it did so only because of a lawsuit. Prochoice groups had challenged a 1977 amendment to the state's budget which would prohibit the use of state funds for Medicaid abortions except in cases of rape or incest or when an abortion was necessary to save the life of the mother. The state's Supreme Judicial Court had ruled in *Moe* v. *Hanley* that restricting funding placed an impermissible burden on low-income women, which would violate their rights guaranteed in the state constitution.

So while Fran and Carolyn shook their heads, saying, "it can't happen here," they couldn't help but wonder what would happen in Massachusetts if a law similar to the Missouri statute were implemented. Although the law forbade public employees and public facilities from performing abortions, "public" had not been defined. Would a hospital or facility be considered public only if it received total state or federal funding? What if a hospital received *some* public money, say a federal grant for AIDS research? Would that hospital be forbidden to provide abortions? If so, where would doctors be trained to do abortions? Most residents learned the skill in a hospital setting.

And what about the patients? Although the vast majority of abortions were performed in outpatient clinics—only 13 percent of all Massachusetts' abortions were done in hospitals—women who sought a hospital for the procedure truly needed it. Women who were prone to seizures, whose blood didn't clot well, or who had complicated drug histories, for example, could require blood transfusions, cardiac monitors, or emergency drugs, none of which was available at freestanding clinics. Performing procedures on higher-risk patients was often technically more difficult and demanded general anesthesia. Most clinics offered local anesthesia and IV sedation. General anesthesia was riskier and usually unnecessary.

In *Roe* v. *Wade*, Justice Harry Blackmun wrote that if philosophers and moralists couldn't determine when life began, then the state shouldn't. But what if the new Court recanted and upheld the Missouri preamble stating that life began at conception? Would fertilized eggs in petri dishes have the same rights as living, breathing human beings? Would the IUD and certain birth control pills—contraceptives which didn't allow the fertilized egg to plant itself in the uterine wall—be made illegal?

• • •

City Hall Plaza was nearly deserted when Fran arrived a little before five o'clock on the afternoon of April 26. On one hand, she was disappointed. She wanted the entire city to fill this outdoor brick amphitheater in downtown Boston and cheer on abortion rights. On the other hand, the fewer people there were to listen to her speech, the less nervous she'd be. Fran had felt honored when the Boston chapter of the National Organization for Women had asked her to speak at its abortion rights rally, one of fifteen similar rallies going on across the country, on this day of the Supreme Court's hearing of *Webster*. But she had never spoken in front of more than fifty high-school students, so the image of thousands of people listening to her was daunting. Would her voice crack? Would she make sense? Would they applaud?

Fran certainly had plenty of practice discussing *Webster* and its implications in the past weeks. Everyone was talking about abortion. Since Fran was community relations director at an abortion clinic, everyone wanted to talk to her. At work, the telephone seemed a part of her ear. What's the mood of the clinic? reporters asked. Is the staff upset about *Webster?* The staff, in turn, asked her if they would still have jobs in July, and how did Fran think Sandra Day O'Connor would vote? At the hairdresser, a woman asked Fran if abortion would become illegal. Even at dinner parties, she was the focal point. Fran's boyfriend said he was sick of talking about THE subject, and often she was, too. But she felt that she owed the public information and that she was part of something greater than herself, almost as if she had been elected to public office.

The skyscrapers of Boston's financial district blocked the late afternoon sun, and an early spring breeze blew cold off the harbor. Fran buttoned her red raincoat as she strolled around the plaza, looking at the upper level where she would soon sit with the other speakers on the built-in benches. The crowd would stand below on the steps and in the courtyard. In less than an hour, she reminded herself, her final responsibility of the day would be over. From the minute her alarm had buzzed this morning and she had realized "It's *Webster*," this Wednesday in April had been crazy.

Between the press calls and rehearsing her speech, Fran had barely had time to turn on the radio for snatches of news on what went on inside the Supreme Court building this morning. She had been heartened to hear that Sandra Day O'Connor, who was perceived as the pivotal vote, had said that if the state could restrict abortion, could the state also force women to have abortions? Fran's favorite line of all, though, was uttered by Frank Susman, the attorney representing Reproductive Health Services. When Charles Fried, a former solicitor general speaking on behalf of the Bush administration, stated that he was not asking the Court to unravel the fabric of privacy rights, but to "pull this one thread," Susman rebutted, "It has always been my personal experience that when I pull a thread, my sleeve falls off."

As Fran continued circling the plaza, the five o'clock whistle blew and people began to arrive, not in twos or threes, but in clumps of ten and twenty, like baseball fans streaming into Fenway Park. Women skipped down the steps leading to the courtyard swinging their briefcases, chattering to each other, their leather pumps replaced by white Reeboks. Pastel blazers and flowered dresses popped up against the blue and gray suits worn by the Boston businessmen in the crowd. Although abortion rights demonstrations always lured more women than men, Fran was pleased with what looked like a lot of male faces. Since no seats graced the courtyard, the crowd, which seemed to blossom by the hundreds with every heartbeat, stood expectantly, facing the upper tier from which Fran would speak.

By 5:30 P.M., starting time, the plaza was full. There are 2,000, maybe 3,000, people here, Fran thought as she climbed the stairs to the speakers' level and sat down on a bench behind the podium. These were people who were looking to her for inspiration, or perhaps for information that they could use in their own arguments on why the right to choose should be preserved.

"Don't screw up," Fran warned herself as she looked at the blur of faces below. She wondered how many people she knew down there. Carolyn was at home with Lorena, but a few other Preterm staffers had said they would come, as had some of her friends.

Fran had planned to rehearse her speech mentally while Barbara Neely, from Women for Economic Justice, and Anna Ortiz, who represented a Puerto Rican women's group, spoke. But the minute Barbara Neely, a black woman wrapped in a loose-fitting outfit, stepped to the podium, Fran's attention was riveted. Women would not be economically free, Neely told the audience, unless they could control their fertility. She's so articulate, thought Fran. And her voice is so rich. She seemed ageless to Fran, and powerful. Barbara Neely had captured the crowd by the end of her three-minute speech.

Anna Ortiz was next. In Latin countries, 40 percent of the women of childbearing age have been sterilized, explained Ortiz, a large woman with dark hair. Many of the operations were done after childbirth without the woman's knowledge by doctors under pressure from the government to cut the population. Choice, Ortiz said, means the power of consent.

How can I measure up? Fran thought. These women are fabulous, far more experienced and knowledgeable than I. But mingled with Fran's fear was excitement, a ripple of pleasure that she would share the microphone with such powerful women.

"And here is Fran Basche from Preterm Health Services," Boston NOW's president Ellen Convisser announced, "to tell us what it is like on the front line."

What? Fran thought frantically. She had been told to talk about what choice meant to patients, not Operation Rescue. Don't panic, she told herself. Do the best you can. She didn't falter as she walked to the microphone, but she felt surreal, as if she were watching a movie of herself. All those people staring at her, waiting for her to say something.

"As the community relations coordinator for a facility performing abortion, I am often put to the difficult task of finding ways to tell our patients' stories," she said, her voice weak. "This is nearly impossible for two reasons. We place a high premium on confidentiality and secondly, abortion is an emotionally charged issue not easily distilled for the nightly news."

They were listening. She began to feel a little stronger. "There is, however, one simple phrase that I've started using. It's too long for a bumper sticker, and not catchy enough for a twenty-second sound bite, but it captures the essence of an abortion patient's dilemma and decision.

"Women make the best moral choices they can, given the complex circumstances and options in their lives."

They were still listening. In fact, the faces she could see from her perch even looked interested. Her voice grew firmer, louder. The 16 million women in this country who have had abortions agonized over the decision, Fran said. "Not only is this a difficult choice, but we find that for many of our patients it may be the first time in their lives that they have actively made *any* choice.

"This isn't surprising, really. Economics, sex discrimination, violence, peer pressure, racism, lack of education, low self-esteem, and inadequate access to safe and effective contraceptive methods all conspire to rob women of their choices."

The crowd was hers, rumbling when she said that the average woman who is sexually active would become pregnant fourteen times in her reproductive life if she did not use contraception. Add to that effective but high-risk birth control, safer but less effective birth control, and a backdrop of television sex combined with school systems and parents who don't teach their children about sex and contraception "and it's easy to see why women heading into the 1990s are still having trouble controlling their fertility," said Fran.

"Not me," someone yelled from the crowd.

Fran grinned. "Good," she said. "We like people like you."

The crowd whistled and clapped long after Fran had returned to her seat. Before the rally, she had told herself that she would consider her speech a success if her words touched one or two people. Afterwards, she knew that they had. As Fran wove through the dispersing crowd in search of her Preterm colleagues, several women stopped her to say how much they appreciated what she had said about patients making moral choices. If women felt that abortion was a moral choice, they would vote to keep that choice legal and available, Fran thought. They could persuade political leaders, maybe even the Supreme Court, to uphold a woman's right to decide her own fate.

For a moment, the future of abortion didn't look so grim.

•   •   •

Three days later, Fran was visiting her boyfriend at his home in Albany, New York, recuperating from her hectic week. She was a little disappointed to miss the April 29 rescue, but not so disappointed that she chose to hang around Brookline. Besides, there was no guarantee that Operation Rescue would hit Preterm, although Carolyn Wardell was confident that it would. After the March 4 rescue, she said, Cotter knew that he could jam Preterm's entrances with fewer than 150 people. There was no telling what he could do with more. And if the prochoice moles' estimate was correct of how many abortion foes had gathered at the pre-rescue rally on Thursday, the day after the Supreme Court heard *Webster*, the chosen clinic could expect 500 or more protesters the next Saturday.

This time Carolyn felt prepared. She had only been able to guess what she needed to do to get ready for the March 4 rescue, but now that Preterm had been attacked, she could plan accordingly. Fran had trained volunteers to escort patients, enabling staffers to save their energy for their real jobs later that day. The identifying pinnys to be worn by the escorts had not arrived—Fran and Carolyn wondered if the man responsible for forwarding their order to the manufacturer were antichoice—so Fran had spent Friday afternoon sewing blue vests and stenciling "ESCORT" in white across the chest. While the home-made blue bibs didn't look professional, they were distinctive enough for patients to spot. During the March 4 rescue, antichoice protesters had told patients that they were escorts and that the clinic was closed for the day. Most of the patients had caught on to the ruse, but Carolyn had worried that some of the twelve "no shows" on March 4 had believed the impostors.

And this time, Carolyn vowed, she would be outside her clinic, not locked inside.

It was only a few minutes after six o'clock on this Saturday morning of the slated rescue, but Carolyn had been parked across the street from Preterm for over half an hour. Reading her novel, sipping her Dunkin' Donuts coffee, she waited calmly for the first wave of rescuers. On the car seat beside her was a walkie-talkie. If Rescue successfully blockaded the doors, she could communicate with someone inside who was holding the other walkie-talkie. Already a handful of staffers sat in the phone room, ready to call the volunteer escorts and calm confused patients if Preterm were hit.

The police, too, seemed better prepared. Since detective George Driscoll was vacationing in Jamaica, McDermott alone had plotted the defense. This time, the barricades and police would be in place before Rescue arrived so that patient access would be guaranteed. The police had already arranged the black metal dividers, which stood about three feet high and looked like sturdy bicycle racks, into a square corral in front of the steps. Plastic handcuffs and chains linked the dividers. Inside the corral stood fifteen policemen chewing doughnuts and reading *The Boston Herald*'s sports page. Once Rescue descended, all available cops would be sent to the designated clinic. Bill McDermott hoped to have at least sixty officers working this rescue, but the cops were tired of lugging antiabortion protesters and even overtime pay wasn't enough to lure many of them in on their day off.

Carolyn felt the same excitement she had felt in March, but this time she wasn't beleaguered by guilt about her daughter. Lorena had whined a little when Carolyn left her at her day-care provider's home last night, but she hadn't been hysterical. She was in familiar surroundings and Carolyn knew that when she called later in the morning, Lorena would be playing contentedly.

The April morning was sunny and promised to be warm. Carolyn liked the early morning, an affection left over from her days in Nevada as a bookkeeper in a produce company when her shift started at 3 A.M. so she could push the orders out by midmorning. Carolyn had loved watching the sun rise and getting a head start on everyone else. During that time, she hadn't had a clear idea, or any idea for that matter, of what she wanted to do with her life. Certainly, running an abortion clinic hadn't been in her five-year plan. But, considering her background, no one could have predicted her career path.

In their hometown of Baltimore, Carolyn and her four siblings hadn't been expected to attend high school, let alone college. Their mother had attended high school, but their father, a frequently unemployed housepainter and an alcoholic, hadn't gotten past the sixth grade. While Carolyn's siblings had left school and started working at sixteen, Carolyn, the youngest, was encouraged by an eighth-grade teacher to go on to high school. Her parents agreed, but only if Carolyn would concentrate on vocational skills, not academic subjects.

After graduation, Carolyn became a secretary and began dating a Vietnam vet who lived on the nearby army base. When he said that he would soon return to his hometown of Lynn, Massachusetts, Carolyn said that she wanted to go with him. She figured that if they didn't marry and broke up, her Catholic family—appalled that she had lived with a man who wasn't her husband—wouldn't take her back, so she married him and moved to the industrial city just north of Boston. Her husband enrolled in college and so did she, immersing herself in political science and history and psychology. For the first time, she felt like her own person.

As she began to find her sense of self, however, Carolyn's marriage crumbled. Her husband had become addicted to liquor and to the amphetamines prescribed to combat his chronic fatigue. When he drank, he became abusive. A man twice her size, he once choked her until she thought she would die. Carolyn knew that she had to leave him, but she couldn't. She'd never been on her own, and she worried about what would happen to him without her.

Instead of leaving, Carolyn quit her job and her classes, and went to bed. She figured that if she lay there long enough and didn't eat— or didn't eat much—maybe she would die. After two months, she thought, "This is stupid. You'll either spend your life in bed, or you'll get up and do something." She got up and entered therapy, where she realized that her only option was to move out and end the relationship.

Although her husband had pounded on her apartment door demanding reconciliation, Carolyn eventually divorced him, earned a master's degree in counseling, and learned that she was more interested in mastering the politics of the system—in helping people find the housing, food, and help they needed—than in individual counseling. From her job as an office manager at Boston City Hospital, she learned that she had a great aptitude for organizing and getting things done. From a brief job with the Sheraton Corporation, she had also learned that she

loathed for-profit business; that when money is the only motivation, people get stepped on. She would stick with nonprofits, where the purported objective was to improve the quality of life for others.

It was only natural that Carolyn would apply at Preterm in January 1984. She had just returned to Boston after her year out West, newly married to a man she had met in Nevada. She had mailed résumés to a variety of nonprofits, but her first choice was Preterm. She had had her two abortions at the clinic years before and had found the staff to be warm, supportive, and nonjudgmental. Carolyn wanted to work among people like that.

"There's no guarantee of promotion," she was told when she was hired as Preterm's administrative assistant. Two months later, Carolyn became office manager. Lorena was born in November of that year, and after her pregnancy leave, Carolyn returned as Preterm's director of counseling. Within months, she was promoted to coordinator of the abortion clinic and then to assistant director of all of Preterm's services, before she finally took over as director in January 1989. Carolyn could fix a problem before most people could detect it, the outgoing director told the board of directors. Even while struggling with a failing marriage, Carolyn had been able to concentrate on her job and had stabilized patient flow in the abortion clinic so that patients would be kept, on most days, to the promised three- to four-hour stay. Carolyn would grow with the job of director, her predecessor promised, even with the added burden of dealing with Operation Rescue.

In January, four short months ago, few people had thought that Operation Rescue would last beyond the winter. But here Carolyn sat under a spring sky, the oak leaves bright green in their rebirth, feeling a little like a detective waiting for a suspect to show. So far, all she'd seen was a bumper sticker that read "THE RIGHT TO CHOOSE IS BEING ABUSED" on a car parked not far away on Beacon Street. But that car had already sped off.

Then, just before 6:30 A.M., Carolyn noticed a group of college-age women strolling toward the clinic. They didn't carry signs or banners. Were they patients? Another car parked and six people popped out, crossed Beacon Street, and headed toward Preterm. Carolyn tensed. They definitely weren't patients. Was this it?

Sure enough, they knelt before the barricade.

"It's gonna happen," Carolyn told herself. She hopped out of her car and ran across Beacon Street onto the median strip, freezing in the middle of the trolley tracks. Now what do I do? she thought. The clump of protesters hadn't tried to charge the barricades to get to the door. They just knelt there with their heads bowed, ignoring the row of tight-lipped policemen who stood before them behind the barricade, arms crossed. Carolyn wondered if she should try to contact the staff inside with the walkie-talkie. No, she was too far away to make a clear connection. If she moved closer to the clinic she wouldn't be able to see the troops arrive—if more did arrive. She stayed planted on the median strip and watched.

Protesters trickled in. A man with a video camera. A young woman in a pageboy haircut. A short fellow with a limp. Two by two, people walked up to the front barricade facing Beacon Street and slowly dropped to their knees in prayer. Others positioned themselves on either side of the barricade and, holding up song sheets, began to sing. Those were the prayer supporters, Carolyn knew. But where was Bill Cotter? Where were the masses that had attended Thursday night's rally? Carolyn turned to face the inbound stretch of Beacon Street.

"Oh my God," she gasped.

Marching toward her was not a line of people, nor a throng of 100 people as she had seen in the Way of the Cross Procession, but hundreds upon hundreds of people. Five and six abreast they thundered down the sidewalk toward Preterm, an army of Christian warriors dressed in sweatshirts and dungarees. No one smiled. No one talked. Grim faced, they stared ahead at their target, the signs they held of fetuses tossed in garbage bags swaying slightly in the breeze. A brightly colored poster portraying a blackened fetus against the red, white, and blue of the U.S. flag bobbed high above their heads. When they reached the corner of Englewood and Beacon, the final corner before Preterm, they stopped. On cue, they began singing "Amazing Grace." At the beginning of the second verse, row by row, they stepped off the curb and marched to the barricade.

Carolyn had no allies in sight. Prochoice demonstrators had probably just begun to start calling their recruits on the phone tree. She hoped that her phone counselors had alerted the clinic escorts. In any case, she wouldn't have much support out here for at least twenty minutes, just about the same time that the seven o'clock patients would begin to arrive. All she could do was wait, watch, and hope that the police could clear the place quickly.

That didn't look likely. Operation Rescue was everywhere. The prayer supporters stood twelve deep on one side of the barricade, singing at the top of their lungs—"His Name Is Wonderful," "What a Mighty God We Serve," "I Exalt Thee"—whatever song the priest with the bullhorn shouted. In front, those begging arrest had knelt

down, creating a sea of torsos from the barricade into Beacon Street, spilling down the sidewalk. Racing around the edges of the kneelers, shouting directions, was Bill Cotter dressed in his rescue wear of a blue workshirt, jeans, and sneakers that McDermott claimed had been bought at Osco Drug. Darroline, too, hovered at the edge, ordering her people into position, her arms pointing to holes in the crowd.

Then, like insects heading toward a carcass, the kneelers began to creep on their hands and knees toward the barricades. Those in front struggled to worm themselves under the metal dividers while others tried to slip between them. Up and down, the police bobbed, pushing a head back here, a shoulder back there. The effort seemed futile; as soon as one head retreated, another popped forward. "Do you believe this shit?" a cop hollered to the rest of his colleagues.

Carolyn watched from the safety of the trolley tracks, impatient for more of her staff and the clinic escorts to show. She worried that patients would soon start to arrive and not know what to do. Preterm's phone counselors had explained to the patients scheduling appointments for today what to do if they saw a crowd in front of the clinic. But Carolyn knew that patients would, most likely, panic at the scene and forget everything the counselor had told them. White-and-blue cruisers screamed down Beacon Street as the officers left the other two clinics to defend Preterm.

A car stopped in front of the clinic and Marian Wolfsun, Preterm's director of counseling, stepped out. A woman of imposing stature and long dark hair, Marian marched forward, trying to ignore the kneeling rescuers closing in around her. Two policemen reached across the pool of bodies for Marian's hands and pulled her through, helping her step over the demonstrators' backs and hop over the barricade.

Sonia Lewis arrived next. Like fish darting into water, protesters threw their bodies down in front of her.

"Are they preventing you from getting to work?" a policeman asked Sonia.

"Yes, officer," she said.

The arrests began. Among the first to go was Fred Pulsifer, the janitor-turned-picketer who added SLE (Sanctity of Life Effort) to his name, and Barbara Bell, a large black woman who sang so loudly outside of Preterm on Saturdays that she was heard on the fourth floor. Darroline was nabbed minutes later, followed by Bill Cotter. Handcuffed in front, eyes downcast, Cotter grimaced slightly as he was dragged to the prisoner bus, a policeman at either side holding an arm and leg.

Just as the police started slapping on plastic handcuffs, the prochoice forces began arriving. Vans and Volkswagens parked up and down Beacon Street, their passengers pouring out into the fresh air carrying blue-and-white "STAND UP FOR CHOICE" signs. Within minutes, it seemed to Carolyn, the crowd had doubled. There wasn't an inch of empty sidewalk from the corner of Englewood on the right to well beyond Preterm to the left. Carolyn couldn't see the clinic steps through the people. And it was only 7:30 A.M.

At the barricade, one woman's shoulders had become wedged under the divider's metal bar as she had tried to creep underneath. Her head and arms lay stranded on one side of the barricade while her rump and legs splayed on the other, lost in the crowd. A patient, the first to arrive, jumped on the woman's back as the woman tried to wiggle through. "She's stepping on me," the rescuer cried. Using the woman's back as a springboard, the patient hurdled the barricade. Once the patient was safely inside the clinic, the cops pulled the rescuer through, slapped handcuffs around her wrists, and let her lie, like a seal on a rock, in the middle of the pavement inside the corral.

Moments later, the clinic's volunteer escorts arrived, flushed with excitement. Half would stay at the clinic to direct patients to walk to the Star Market a few blocks up Beacon Street. The other half would escort patients from Star Market to All Saints Episcopal Church, which, despite the Palm Sunday and Easter pickets, once again was allowing the patients to wait out the rescue in one of its rooms. Carolyn had added Star Market to the route to confuse the antis, although she realized that the effort was probably wasted; the antis always seemed to figure out her plans, whether it was changing abortion clinic hours or rerouting patients.

Now that the arrests had begun and the prochoice support had arrived, Carolyn, too, could bolt into action. Donning her own blue-and-white escort pinny, she crossed Beacon Street and swam through the crowd, shouting orders to the escorts and to the counselors, medical assistants, and nurses who had just arrived. Staffers were sent to the church, to Dunkin' Donuts, or wherever else they wanted to go to escape the hubbub. Many chose to stay and shout for abortion rights or help patients. Standing outside the phone room on the sidewalk, Carolyn tried to communicate via the walkie-talkie with Marian, who stood inside the phone room. But every time Carolyn picked up the walkie-talkie, a group of protesters swirling around her like blackflies began shouting, "You're killing babies!" Carolyn gave up.

By the time she returned to the crowd in front, arrests had ground to a halt. A man had slithered under the police bus and fastened himself by the neck to the driveshaft with a Kryptonite lock. If the bus couldn't move, the police couldn't transport the arrested and consequently had no place to put the newly arrested. That meant more time blockading the clinic, which, in Rescue logic, meant more saved babies. If women couldn't get inside the clinic, they couldn't have an abortion—or at least they would have extra time to reconsider their decision. Bill Cotter stood in the back of the stranded bus, hands still cuffed together, shouting to rescuers already handcuffed and lying on the ground to crawl back to the barricade. Keep the police busy.

Carolyn worried that this new driveshaft tactic would delay Preterm's opening for hours. The protester had locked himself too close to the gas tank for the cop to drill the lock open. One flying spark and kaboom. The next option was to remove the man by removing the driveshaft. "You are a fucking asshole," the cop hissed at the protester, as they both lay under the bus. "You're gonna be arrested as soon as you're out of here."

"God bless you," the protester said.

"He better bless me," the cop yelled to the man, whose eyes were closed in prayer. "And you, too. 'Cuz if anything happens here, I'm gonna shoot you."

The barricades began to throb with pushing demonstrators. As prochoice supporters snaked through the crowd, the antis squeezed tighter together. A child, pressed against the metal bars of the barricade, screamed.

"You're hurting your own people," a policeman bellowed. "Don't push."

Bill McDermott, who had patrolled Beacon Street until he was sure that Rescue didn't have plans for hitting either of the other two clinics, was stunned by what he saw in front of Preterm. The crowd had swelled to more than 1,500 people. Wooden sawhorses cordoned off Beacon Street in front of Preterm, forcing traffic to detour down Englewood and allowing the crowd to spread onto the road. The air was filled with cardboard signs—signs calling abortion murder, signs calling abortion a right, signs showing blonde-haired babies, signs showing women in chains, a symbol of lost reproductive rights. One woman, a prayer supporter, nursed her baby as a young man representing the Young Socialist Alliance passed out his organization's newsletter. These demonstrations lured all kinds of activists, McDermott noted. There were union people here for Chrissake, passing out buttons defaming Eastern Airline's owner, Frank Lorenzo, in support of

Eastern employees' monthlong strike. This is like a carnival, McDermott thought. All it needed was a Ferris wheel. He thought he'd go deaf from the noise. "Operation rescue, that's a lie. You don't care if women die!!" the prochoicers chanted at the top of their lungs.

"Number fifteen on the song sheet," hollered the priest through his bullhorn. "Kum Bah Yah."

One rescuer, his hands cuffed to barricade bars, his head stuck between the clinic's cement step and the barricade's bottom bar, his feet dangling below into the rhododendrons, looked like a prisoner hanging from the stocks. "We've got a live one for you, Billy," one of the cops yelled to McDermott.

"Beauuuutiful," the detective said.

Arrests had resumed with the arrival of a new bus, and McDermott ordered the cops to clear a path through the thinning crowd of crawling rescuers. He found Carolyn and told her to escort the first group of patients and staff from the church.

By the time Carolyn and her band neared Preterm, the cops had managed to move the barricades to create an L-shaped alley from the front entrance down the sidewalk, bearing right on Beacon Street. The tough part was weaving the human chain of staff and patients safely through the crowd to the shelter of the barricades. Although prochoicers outnumbered the antis by three to one, the 100 or so abortion foes left were determined, throwing themselves in front of Carolyn and those who followed her. Police strode into the melee, pushing the interlopers back into the crowd. Carolyn was terrified. This can't be my life, she thought. A group of protesters dropped to their knees as the patients walked by. "Christ have mercy!" a man boomed.

"Operation failure! Operation failure!" taunted a group of prochoice women.

Inside Preterm, Marian told Carolyn that as soon as the staff had set up the procedure rooms and the doctors arrived, business would start as usual. If the prochoice people left, Carolyn thought, the antichoice people might leave. One side fed the fury of the other. "We're open," she told the prochoice leaders. "You can go. Thanks for coming."

"We can't go," a leader said. "If we go, they'll blockade again." The chanting continued.

"The police took my bullhorn!" the priest yelled. "We must sing together. We can't be stopped by people who steal."

Sonia led in the next group of patients. One fourteen-year-old girl looked terrorized. Sonia offered her a coat to shield her face from the cameras. "Why do I need that?" the young patient asked. "I'm not doing anything wrong." Sonia smiled at the girl's mother. "You have quite a daughter," she said.

"I know," the mother answered. "I know."

The second train of patients drove a wedge through the crowd, and again, a group of antis dropped to their knees. "Lord have mercy," one man wailed. "Pray for the girls inside," the priest implored, "for what they'll go through in the weeks to come, in the months to come."

With each train of patients, the antis became more frantic. They dived at the women's feet, hurling their bodies in front of the pack. "Murderers!" they screamed. "You're killing your child!" With each trip, Carolyn wondered if the group would make it through the crowd unscathed.

Marian stopped Carolyn on the front stairs. "We have a problem," she said. Three bomb threats had been called in to the police station, all saying that a bomb would go off at Preterm at eleven o'clock. A nurse and a medical assistant had spotted a suspicious-looking radio with little wires sticking out of its side in one of the fourth-floor offices. The police said to evacuate, and Carolyn agreed. Within minutes all of the patients and staff were crammed in the first floor hallway. Since the bomb threats were usually confined to the fourth floor and always had been false, Preterm rarely sent its staff outside. No patient had been dragged off the table in the middle of a procedure this round, but several patients were forced to dress and one recovered on the couch in Carolyn's office.

Doris Merrill, one of Preterm's nurses, trembled as she waited out the bomb search. When she looked outside all she saw were angry, twisted faces. There will never be a meeting on this issue, she thought. Doris had been alone in the room with the suspicious radio, working on statistic sheets. What if the radio were a real bomb and it had exploded? She began to cry. If she died, no one would mourn her loss as her husband would have mourned, for no one cared about her as he had. She had felt alone since his death the year before, but at this moment, her solitude was overwhelming.

Carolyn preferred to wait out the bomb search on the front steps so she could keep an eye on the demonstration. She looked at her watch. Five minutes of eleven. Four minutes. Eleven o'clock. Nothing. The fire department took the radio, and the patients and staff returned upstairs. "I can't work," a medical assistant said. "I just went through six hours of this stuff."

"You're a hero," Marian told her. "This can't stop you."

Outside, the prochoice signs bobbed at the barricade, which meant the police had arrested most of the crawling rescuers. The threat to Preterm was over. A few antis, elderly women, clung to their position in front, clutching their rosary beads, their lips moving in prayer, but most of the antis were either en route to the police station or on their way home.

"This rescue is flat," McDermott announced.

Carolyn was impressed with McDermott. When he was around, patients got in, protesters were arrested. When he left, action stopped. Carolyn had never had much contact with him; he usually called Fran for or with information. That was OK with Carolyn. To her, McDermott was a tough, blustery Irishman with a keen sense of story and rough manners. But he had worked hard at this rescue, kept things under control. She trusted him.

Shortly after noon, with the last group of patients safely escorted inside, Carolyn picked up a bullhorn and yelled to the prochoice crowd, "All of our patients are in. Thank you for coming." Within fifteen minutes the place had cleared. The singing priest guided his flock to the police station, where they would sing outside the garage which held 135 of their brothers and sisters. The prochoice people packed their signs into their vans and Volkswagens and left.

Carolyn surveyed the piles of crushed coffee cups and broken plastic handcuffs scattered like garter snakes on the pavement. The sidewalk looked like the morning after a New Year's party, but instead of cigarette butts and party hats, the leftover debris included crumpled pamphlets showing transparent fetuses in utero. Operation Rescue had dished out its best, Carolyn thought, and Preterm had survived. Forty-seven brave women were being offered a choice on how to live their lives, and almost that many counselors, medical assistants, nurses, and doctors were there to help them. The people of choice had won this round.

•   •   •

The weeks following Fran's literary outburst to *The Brookline Citizen* were so chaotic that she hadn't spent much time thinking about the impact of her prose. Days after she wrote the letter, she and Carolyn flew to the National Abortion Federation's (NAF) annual conference in San Francisco. At the end of the conference, Carolyn returned to Boston and her daughter while Fran jetted to Washington, D.C., where she hooked up with other Preterm staffers to parade down Constitution Avenue in the March for Women's Equality and Women's

Lives along with hundreds of thousands of other abortion rights supporters.

Still high from the NAF conference and the memory of shouting "Not the church, not the state, women must decide their fate," in front of the Supreme Court building during the Washington, D.C., march, Fran had returned to Preterm ready to tackle anything—until Stephen Bressler from the Brookline Human Relations Commission called just minutes after she sat down at her desk for the first time in over a week. He wanted to discuss an Op Ed piece in last week's *Brookline Citizen* in which the author had lodged a formal complaint against Fran with Bressler's commission. This individual wanted to make public what he considered an assault on Catholicism.

"I'll have to call you back," Fran said, hanging up the phone and running to the pharmacy next door for last week's *Citizen*.

"I thought that prejudice and bigotry had been erased from the enlightened community of Brookline, or does it depend on who the bigot is?" wrote David Coleman, whose picture portrayed a cheery man with glasses. He claimed that Fran had attacked Christianity in her letter, that her references to the Spanish Inquisitors reflected "centuries of hate pouring out of her pen."

Acknowledging that he was against "the destruction of the unborn," Coleman wrote that as a Catholic, he was offended.

Fran was horrified. She hadn't meant to assail Catholicism. She had simply meant to explain to the public how the abortion foes misused religion in the name of their cause. Who was David Coleman? Had Operation Rescue egged him on to write this scathing letter? She felt defamed, accused of something she hadn't done. That prickly heat— the same heat she had felt years ago in college when she had been falsely accused of shoplifting book labels—flushed her face.

She reread her letter to the *Citizen* and immediately regretted that she hadn't been more thoughtful about the examples she had chosen. She should have included names of religious zealots who weren't Catholic, she realized. Nonetheless, she didn't feel that she needed to apologize for the rest of it.

Fran called Stephen Bressler back. He said that he wanted to meet with her to determine if her letter was motivated by bigotry. If he felt that it was, the case would go before the full Human Relations Commission for a public hearing. What he didn't add was that the Human Relations Commission didn't want to get involved, that it felt that *Coleman* v. *Basche* was a no-win case. Fran wouldn't change her mind, and David Coleman, a devoted Catholic, wouldn't change his. To be fair to Coleman, however, the commission had to address his complaint.

Carolyn didn't think Fran should bother to meet with Bressler. Why did Fran have to excuse herself to a man in the community whose views differed from hers? Carolyn felt that the observations Fran had cited in her letter were legitimate. But Fran felt that if she ignored Coleman's complaint, the abortion foes would say that she didn't have the guts to face them. She didn't need to recant, she decided, just clarify.

For the record, but not for publication, she wrote a letter to Bressler, explaining that she did not perceive abortion to be a solely Catholic issue, nor were all of Preterm's protesters Catholic. But, she wrote, she had seen hate and prejudice from people who "admitted that their religion motivated their actions." She cited the anti-Semitic postcards, the March 4 rescue, and the Easter picket at All Saints. She ended the letter with a two-page list of harassments that the clinic had endured in the past year, ranging from the religious radio station suggesting that callers jam the lines of all abortion providers to a protester yelling "Don't let that Jewish doctor touch you" when a clinic physician attempted to treat a demonstrator who had been hurt during a rescue.

Fran met with Bressler the next day, presenting him with the letter, samples of the anti-Semitic postcards, and an oral defense. After listening to Fran and reading the postcards, Bressler said he would tell David Coleman that he felt Fran hadn't meant any harm. Relieved, Fran left Bressler's office hoping that the matter had been resolved.

It wasn't. A few days later, Bressler called with news that Coleman wanted to meet with Fran. She hesitated. Carolyn would tell her to skip it, that this episode had gone far enough. Fran felt badly that she had hurt David Coleman's feelings, but she also felt that he had over-reacted. Other Catholics whom she had contacted, including Sergeant McDermott, weren't offended by her letter. Then again, they were a liberal breed of Catholics. McDermott had told her that Coleman was of the old school, devoted to all of the teachings of his church.

Walking into the Human Rights Commission office several weeks later for the meeting, Fran kept hearing her father's voice saying, "Be a lady." This had always meant: Be nice, be thoughtful, don't stoop to someone else's level. She hoped she wouldn't cry; that would make her look guilty. She wondered if Coleman would listen to what she had to say.

He looked harmless enough. Balding and dignified, Coleman reminded her of a grandfather in a business suit, the kind of man who made a nice neighbor. They shook hands and took their places at the

conference table. Stephen Bressler, acting as mediator, sat at the head of the table, with Fran to his right and Coleman to his left. Coleman spoke first, briefly stating that he was insulted by Fran's letter and felt compelled to respond. He wanted Fran to retract her statements.

"If you were insulted or hurt by this, I apologize," Fran said. "I didn't mean to insult you or your religion, but I don't take anything back."

Fran admitted her mistake in using only Catholic examples of religious bigotry; that when you grow up Jewish in America as she had, you don't always make distinctions between Christian denominations. When Bressler suggested she discuss her motivation, she mentioned picketers spitting at staff nurses, following staffers up the street hollering about the "death business," and badgering patients until they dissolved into tears. She mentioned nasty phone calls and bomb threats in which the caller phones repeatedly, asking, "You haven't left yet?"

Coleman agreed that people were wrong to behave that way, even though he shared their philosophy. He said that while Fran wouldn't see him praying in front of the Preterm at a demonstration, she might see him standing across the street.

"I have no problem with that," Fran said. "You have every right to be there."

And that was it. They stood up, shook hands, and left. Fran felt vindicated; he had understood some of her reasons for writing that letter, and he didn't think of her as an evil person. But even as she savored what she felt was a small victory, she also knew that the attacks against her wouldn't stop here. Nothing happened that easily in the spring of 1989.

CHAPTER FOUR

Such a Simple Procedure

THIS time she would do it. This time she would really call. Colleen Dempsey picked up the telephone receiver. Seven, her finger dialed, three . . . eight . . . She thought of hanging up, just as she had hung up for the past two weeks every time she had started to dial these numbers. She fought the urge.

"Preterm Health Services," a voice on the other end of the line said. "How may I help you?"

Colleen took a deep breath. "I . . ." she said, fumbling for the words. "I . . . I . . . think . . . I'm . . . I'd like . . . to . . ." She paused to gather courage. "I'd like to make an appointment."

"What kind of appointment?" the woman asked.

"A . . ." Colleen couldn't say it.

For weeks, she had felt the symptoms—tender breasts, nausea, the frequent need to urinate. At first, she pretended that the missed period was a fluke, a momentary skip in her usually regular menstrual cycle. But after weeks passed and the period still hadn't arrived, she knew she couldn't ignore the possibility any longer. "I'm fine," she still had tried to convince herself when she bought the home pregnancy test at the drugstore. Taking the test was just a precaution. She wasn't pregnant. She couldn't be pregnant. Denial, though, couldn't change the fact that as she had stood in her boyfriend's bathroom, she watched her urine turn the pregnancy test's dipstick blue.

"Well?" Eamon had asked, entering the bathroom cautiously.

Colleen couldn't say it was positive. "It didn't say I wasn't pregnant," she mumbled.

Eamon was calm, as always. "These things happen," he said, reaching to comfort her, to make her realize that the pregnancy wasn't the end of the world. She stepped back, away from him.

Later that day, after she returned to the home of the ninety-two-year-old woman for whom she cared as a live-in nurse, the thoughts she had shoved away all afternoon beat against her temples. These things did happen, but why to her? Why now? She was only twenty-three years old. She didn't even have a place of her own. For most of the week, she stayed with her elderly charge; on her free days she crashed at friends' apartments. She had moved to Boston from Northern Ireland a year ago in search of adventure and work that she liked more than nursing in a suburban Belfast geriatric home that had reeked of disinfectant.

Where in the world would she house an infant? She couldn't afford $600 or more per month for her own apartment, and what roommate would want her with a baby? Boston's young Irish community was good for a couple of drinks and a lot of laughs—even for some cash if things got tight—but it was hardly hospitable to children. The thousands of native Irish in their late teens and twenties in the area were transients, unattached singles who moved to wherever they landed the jobs that they couldn't find back in Dublin and Cork.

Eamon had said he would support whatever decision she made. He would help her through an abortion or, if she chose to have the baby, he would stay with her. He said that he loved her very much and hoped that someday they would marry. She wasn't ready to talk about that yet; they'd known each other only for four months. She liked Eamon well enough. A plumber from Dublin, he was dark and lean with happy blue eyes and a sunny heart. But their relationship was too new to make long-term plans, and she didn't want to test it with a baby. Besides, Eamon barely earned enough in Boston to care for himself, let alone Colleen and a baby. No, Colleen thought, this has to be my decision. Mine alone.

For the next few days, Colleen tried to envision life with a baby. She'd have to quit her job. Although her elderly boss had a good sense of humor, she would not welcome an infant's wailing. Finding new work would be tough, perhaps impossible. Without a green card, Colleen was limited to minimum-wage jobs with employers who wouldn't report her to Immigration. How would she pay for an infant's clothes and food and medical care? No public assistance was available

for immigrants without green cards. And even if she found employment, who would care for the baby while she worked? At night, she
asked herself the same questions again and again, until she was so
exhausted she finally slept.

She was too far from home to call for help, but then her parents were
staunch Catholics who wouldn't help much anyway. Her mother didn't
even believe in birth control, and neither did her oldest sister, who at
twenty-five already had three children. She'll have kids till she drops,
Colleen thought. One of her younger sisters had started taking the Pill
after the birth of her second child, but that was extraordinary. Birth
control wasn't part of the Irish culture. In Colleen's hometown, contraception was evil; it interfered with God's plan.

Colleen didn't believe that. How could a religion tell women how
many children they could have? But she had never used birth control.
At home, people whispered nasty things about single girls on the Pill.
"She sleeps around," they would say. Taking precautions was proof that
you were sexually active, a sin in the eyes of the Church. Yet Irish
teenagers, just like teenagers everywhere, were human, had sexual
feelings. Most of Colleen's friends began having sex at age seventeen or
eighteen. Colleen had waited until she was nineteen, when she had
started going with Thomas.

Two Christmases ago, she had become pregnant and had considered
getting an abortion in London, where many Irish girls went because
abortion was illegal in their own country. Even though Thomas said he
wanted nothing to do with a baby, Colleen couldn't bring herself to
make the arrangements, not while she lived in Ireland where an abortion would bring instant shame to her family. Yet having the baby as an
unmarried woman would be equally disgraceful. She didn't know what
to do until nature finally did it for her. She cried with relief when she
miscarried.

Colleen's mum and dad would be mortified if she returned home
pregnant. Would they disown her? On a nurse's salary in Ireland, she
couldn't afford her own place. Even if her parents let her stay with
them, she still would need to scrape up enough money to pay for a
baby-sitter every day. No one in her family could care for her child;
everyone worked. Adoption was out of the question. People would
think her heartless and her family would be scandalized. And what if
things didn't work out with Eamon? She was fair and slim with an open
face and a sharp humor—she'd never had trouble meeting men. But
who would marry her with a baby?

A friend had had an abortion at Preterm and said that the people were friendly and kind. Colleen couldn't imagine why anyone would be kind at an abortion clinic. Abortion was wrong. They should make the women feel guilty. Then again, perhaps there were enough other people to make the women feel guilty. Colleen had seen the news coverage of massive protests in front of Brookline abortion clinics. Had the demonstration last month taken place in front of Preterm? She couldn't remember. She only hoped there wouldn't be a mob outside if and when she walked in for her appointment.

Days passed. Each time Colleen hung up in the middle of calling Preterm, she knew that she was postponing the inevitable. She couldn't raise a baby in Boston, and she couldn't raise a baby in Ireland. She tried to forget about the pregnancy, wishing it would go away, or that she'd miscarry like last time. Yesterday, a warm Sunday in May when ordinarily she would have been celebrating spring, she broke down and wept for the first time in Eamon's kitchen. When Eamon walked in, she stopped. She didn't like to share her feelings or depend on anyone for support.

Now, however, she had to share her feelings, or at least her suspicions, with Paula, the Preterm phone counselor, who asked again, "What kind of appointment would you like?"

"Abortion," Colleen whispered. There. It was out.

Paula took over. Had Colleen had a pregnancy test? she asked, her voice gentle and almost matter-of-fact. When was the first day of her last menstrual period? March 13, Colleen answered, to the best of her memory. Gestation is figured from the first day of the last menstrual period, even though conception occurs during ovulation, which is usually fourteen days later, and the fertilized egg doesn't implant in the uterus for another week.

"You're about nine weeks pregnant," Paula said, explaining that Colleen was in her first trimester, which comprises the first thirteen weeks of pregnancy. Preterm offered abortions until the sixteenth week, but second-trimester abortions were slightly more complicated and uncomfortable. If Colleen wanted an abortion, she should make an appointment in the next two or three weeks. Colleen wanted an appointment as soon as possible. This agony had to end.

"How is Thursday morning at eleven o'clock?" Paula asked.

•　•　•

In the weeks following the Supreme Court's hearing of *Webster* v. *Reproductive Health Services*, many women who found themselves unhappily pregnant also found themselves confused. Was abortion still legal? Would they be arrested as soon as they entered a clinic? While Colleen Dempsey understood that there were forces in the United States that threatened the availability of abortion, she took for granted that she would be able to find someone to help her. Even in a country like Ireland where abortion was illegal, women found ways to control their family size, be it in the back alley or by taking the night ferry to England. In America, all sorts of possibilities existed.

They always have. In the early years of this country, when the states followed English common law which allowed abortion until quickening (when the mother first felt fetal movement, usually in the fourth or fifth month of pregnancy), women ingested herbs and potions and endured probing cervical invasions, and anything else the abortionist prescribed. The practice was so common that newspapers were full of advertisements for abortion-inducing drugs. But as physicians sought more respect and legitimacy (until the mid-nineteenth century when the American Medical Association was formed, doctors practiced without certification or supervision), they began lobbying against abortions performed by lay healers. They claimed that their motivation was to protect public health, that only a doctor had the medical background to determine whether a woman should have an abortion, and that if she should, only a doctor had the skills to perform it safely. At the same time, the American birthrate was falling as the immigrant population soared. Americans feared that they would soon be outnumbered by large Italian and Irish families. Moreover, with the onset of the Industrial Revolution, all bodies were needed. In 1847, Massachusetts outlawed abortion except when necessary to save the mother's life. By 1900, all the other states had followed suit.

Yet women continued to terminate their pregnancies. They drank combinations of turpentine and quinine water, or ammonia and laundry detergent, hoping to harm their bodies enough to reject the fetuses. They douched with lye and herbal potions. Into their cervixes they injected knitting needles, coat hangers, pieces of glass, anything they thought would disrupt the pregnancy. As a resident at Harlem Hospital in the 1950s, Waldo Fielding, Preterm's medical director, watched women suffering from botched abortions flood the emergency room every day. (In 1962 alone, the Alan Guttmacher Institute, a nonprofit organization dedicated to researching reproductive issues, reported that Harlem Hospital admitted 1,600 women for incomplete abortions.) "I took out of the female vagina every possible thing that could cause abortion," Waldo remembered, from fragments of salt shakers to chicken bones.

Waldo had worked on women who had inserted potassium-permanganate tablets into their vaginas. The tablets often didn't spark a miscarriage by disturbing the pregnancy, but they ate their way into the abdomen, causing excruciating pain and often death. He had worked on women who had injected themselves with a soap solution, hoping to irritate the uterus into expelling the fetus, but instead causing the kidneys and liver to shut down. And he had worked on women whose abortions had been performed by anonymous "doctors" in darkened hotel rooms or on kitchen tables. These women arrived in the emergency room doubled over in pain and hemorrhaging, any one of a number of their organs having been perforated. Waldo once examined a woman who seemed to have an umbilical cord emerging from her vagina. The cord was her bowel, punctured many times by the abortion instrument.

It was impossible to determine exactly how many illegal abortions were performed in the decades before *Roe* v. *Wade*, since no numbers were officially reported. Estimates, though, ranged from 200,000 a year to 1.2 million a year. One study conducted in the 1940s by psychiatrist Alfred Kinsey found that 22 percent of married women had had one or more abortions before the age of forty-five, and that 88 percent to 95 percent of premarital pregnancies were terminated by abortion. Another study concluded that 699,000 abortions occurred nationwide in 1955 and 829,000 in 1967. New York City municipal hospitals reported twenty-three admissions for incomplete abortions for every 100 deliveries in 1969.

Estimating the number of illegal abortion-related deaths was easier, although hardly accurate. In 1930, abortion was listed as the official cause of death for almost 2,700 American women, or 18 percent of all maternal deaths. With the advent of antibiotics the mortality rate dropped, but in 1965, when the number of abortion deaths had fallen to 193, illegal abortion still accounted for 17 percent of all deaths attributed to pregnancy and childbirth, according to the Guttmacher Institute. Minority women suffered the most. Between 1972 and 1974, more than two-thirds of women who died from illegal abortions were not white.

It was these statistics, and stories from women who had survived the unspeakable, that in the 1960s prompted a variety of interest groups, including the American Medical Association, to press for abortion-law reform. Using as a model a recommendation by the American Law Institute (ALI)—which called for abortion to be legal when the pregnant woman's life or health would be endangered if she carried the pregnancy to term, when the pregnancy was the result of rape or incest, or when the fetus was diagnosed with a severe defect—as a model, states began loosening abortion restrictions. In 1967, Colorado adopted an abortion law based on the ALI's stipulations, and by 1972 twelve other states had approved similar laws. In the meantime, four states—Washington, New York, Alaska, and Hawaii—repealed anti-abortion laws, permitting an abortion if the woman and her doctor deemed it necessary.

In Massachusetts, thanks to a 1944 Supreme Judicial Court decision that a physician could perform an abortion if he believed it was necessary to save the mother's life or to prevent "serious impairment of her health, mental or physical," women could seek hospital abortions. All they needed was money (the procedure could cost $1,000 and up), and a convincing case that they would suffer an emotional breakdown, perhaps even attempt suicide, if forced to complete the pregnancy. A board of doctors would review the case. If they thought that the woman was indeed significantly troubled, they would approve an abortion. If not, she was left to her own methods. A woman's fate depended on the panel of doctors assigned to review pleas for abortions and their attitude toward abortion. In Catholic Boston, many women suffered.

With *Roe* v. *Wade* came the creation of hundreds of clean, professional outpatient clinics across the country. Safe from arrest, doctors could use high-technology equipment in sterile surroundings, and patients could end their dilemma without fearing for their lives. Today, abortion is one of the safest medical procedures available, with less than a 1-percent complication rate. A woman is eleven times more likely to die from childbirth than from an abortion.

Although the women who seek the 1.6 million abortions performed every year in the U.S. represent all socioeconomic, racial, ethnic, and religious backgrounds, some lines of commonality can be drawn. If a "classic" abortion patient could be described, it might be Colleen Dempsey: She's twenty-three (According to the National Abortion Federation, 33 percent of all abortions are performed on women aged twenty to twenty-four); she's nine weeks pregnant (90 percent of women obtain abortions in the first trimester); she's white (nearly 70 percent of U.S. abortion patients are white, although black and Hispanic women have higher rates of abortion); she's single (81 percent of the women were unmarried at the time of their abortion); and like nearly one-third of all abortion patients in the U.S., she's Catholic.

Yet even if Colleen Dempsey acknowledged that there were thousands of other young women like herself wrestling with the same dilemma at the same moment, she would hardly take comfort. An unwanted pregnancy is a private crisis. There is no lonelier person than a woman facing an abortion.

•   •   •

On Thursday, Colleen woke early. Ever since making the appointment three days ago, she had tried not to think about the abortion. When she did, she just got upset and scared. She had never had much contact with doctors except for an occasional Pap smear. During routine checkups, she had always felt totally vulnerable as she lay on her back with her legs spread, her feet in stirrups, while some stranger poked and palpated her most private parts. How would she feel when a doctor began vacuuming out her insides? How much would it hurt? Would she be OK afterwards? Would she be sick? Would she ever be able to have children again?

"Are you nervous?" Eamon asked her as she stepped into his car. Often when she was anxious or tense, Colleen laughed. She didn't know why. She just did. Now, driving to Brookline from South Boston on this May day when the tree buds were about to burst and she was about to end the life inside her, she giggled uncontrollably. Eamon didn't know what to do, so he held her hand.

Colleen had followed Paula's directions to the letter. She wore a short-sleeved shirt and loose-fitting pants (Paula had told her to dress in a two-piece outfit since she would only strip from the waist down). In a plastic bag she carried two sanitary napkins, an extra set of underwear, and a sample of her morning urine. Paula had told Colleen on the phone to expect a few picketers out front, but that she could enter through the back door to avoid them.

Colleen knew they had arrived at Preterm when she spotted the old man with the wiffle cut—Fred Pulsifer SLE—pacing in front of the building's steps. I can handle just one of them, she told herself and suggested that Eamon park on Beacon Street, not out back. Still, her hands shook as she and Eamon approached the building.

"Remember what you are doing," Fred Pulsifer said, pulling a batch of pamphlets from the pocket of his oversize apron, the kind with deep pockets most often seen on men selling newspapers and magazines. Fred's voice was squeaky, like that of an adolescent. "Your baby was conceived in love."

Eamon swung his body in between Fred and Colleen, who stared straight ahead. But Fred was experienced in this kind of maneuver and quickly reached in front of the couple, thrusting a pamphlet and a scapular into Colleen's hands. "Your baby has arms and legs and a heartbeat," he said as they climbed the steps.

"Ignore him," Eamon said.

"Jesus loves you," Fred Pulsifer SLE squeaked, staring after them as they entered the building and shut the door. Outside, the cop on private detail stood guard to make sure that Fred didn't step over the private-property line—a crack in the sidewalk ten feet from the steps.

Colleen felt flushed and shaky. She had glanced briefly at what Fred had given her and was stunned to notice the scapular, two pieces of cloth encased in plastic suspended from a green string. On one piece of cloth was a drawing of the Virgin Mary. On the other was a cross and the words "Immaculate Heart of Mary pray for us now and at the hour of our death." Elderly people wore these scapulars around their necks to mass. How had he known that she was Catholic? Don't think about it, she told herself. Don't think about it.

Eamon guided her to the front desk at which sat a woman with high black hair, freshly rouged cheeks, and the longest fingernails that Colleen had ever seen. "Good morning," Sonia said to the couple, smiling brightly. "Why don't you have a seat here."

She directed Colleen to the chair beside her, and Eamon to the chair against the wall, facing Colleen. Their knees almost touched, they sat so close. To Colleen's left was an area about the size of half a basketball court, separated by fabric-covered dividers into clusters of soft couches and chairs. Before the partitions had been put up, visitors had faced each other, which had made the room feel like a doctor's waiting area. Sonia thought that her guests deserved a cozier setting. To lend a more living room–type atmosphere, the family room, as Preterm called it, was lit by lamps, and throw rugs were tossed over the wall-to-wall carpet. Magazines covered the coffee tables and novels donated by staffers lined a bookcase. A large overhead TV projected morning talk shows and afternoon movies, interrupted by occasional viewings of Preterm's video on the patient's experience.

"Do you want me to take those for you?" Sonia asked, pointing to the pamphlets that Colleen held.

Colleen shook her head. "I want to read them," she said.

Sonia reached for Colleen's medical chart stacked in the eleven o'clock pile, snapped it onto a clipboard, and explained to Colleen how to fill it out. She gave Eamon a visitors' information sheet outlining what his day and the patient's day would involve. "Will you have IV sedation?" Sonia asked Colleen. Paula had explained to Colleen that all patients receive a local anesthetic to numb the cervix, but that they also could have a sedative, a combination of Valium and Sublimaze, to relax them. Preterm had stopped offering general anesthesia years before, finding it too risky and unnecessary for such an uncomplicated procedure.

Colleen agreed to the IV sedation. Whatever she could do to avoid pain, she'd do. She hoped she'd be so out of it that she wouldn't notice what the doctor was doing.

"You can leave for the first hour," Sonia told Eamon. "But you have to be here after that. After Colleen's counseling session (before the surgery), I'll check to see if you are here. If you aren't here when she is ready for the procedure, we won't administer the sedation."

Even though a patient's day averaged three to four hours, it could drag on for five, maybe six, depending on the number of patients and staff available (the clinic figured a 10-percent no-show rate, but occasionally all patients arrived, which backed up flow). Still, Preterm demanded that an IV patient's partner remain in the clinic; too often in the past, the partner disappeared and the patient, still woozy from the medication, had no way to get home. Partners of patients receiving only local anesthetic could leave the clinic. Unaffected by sedation, those patients would be capable of driving home. Sonia kept a legal pad by her desk to jot down the names of partners leaving the family room, which was her domain.

"I'll be here," Eamon said, jerking his head toward the family room.

Eamon and Colleen retreated to a couch to complete the part of the chart dealing with the patient's medical history. Beside them a young man in jeans and a T-shirt dozed, his legs stretched out, *Sports Illustrated* opened across his chest. Another woman with gray hair and wire-rimmed glasses sat pensively, staring into space. Most seats were occupied. Colleen tried to be cheerful, but her hand shook as she circled "miscarriage" after the question about earlier pregnancies. She returned the chart to Sonia, who said that Colleen would be called shortly to head upstairs.

Back at her seat, Colleen opened the picketer's pamphlet. "This baby was killed by a salt poisoning abortion when his mother was 4½ months pregnant," read the caption beneath a photo of a blackened fetus in a petri dish. What am I doing reading this disgusting stuff, Colleen scolded herself, and flipped the pamphlet onto the coffee table. Those brochures should be illegal, she thought. Gently fingering the scapular, she knew she wouldn't throw away the religious badge. Although she rarely attended church and was skeptical of much of the church's teachings, she couldn't totally shake Catholicism's mystique. Colleen tucked the medallion into her breast pocket. What Colleen didn't know was that Carolyn Wardell, Preterm's director, had two scapulars hidden in her top desk drawer; she, too, had been unable to toss the picketer's gift for some vague fear of what might happen to her if she committed such a blasphemous act.

"Colleen D.," an admitting officer shouted. To ensure privacy, no one at Preterm, neither patient nor staffer, was called by last name. Eamon squeezed Colleen's hand as she left to be admitted.

To maintain a calm facade, Colleen struggled to concentrate on answering Erika's questions. Erika was the admitting officer, a striking black woman whose shoulder pad peeked out from underneath her blouse's neckline. Since Colleen had no health insurance, she and Eamon had pooled resources to come up with the $320 in cash that she handed Erika. Had Colleen been unable to pay the full fee, she would have been placed on the deferred-payment plan and asked to mail the remaining debt in monthly payments. Had she been unemployed and unable to pay anything, Preterm would have dipped into its Indigent Patient Fund, which was subsidized by a small grant and contributions. Preterm believed that every woman deserved quality health care, regardless of income. Twenty-five percent of the clinic patients received Medicaid benefits.

Colleen said good-bye to Eamon, then headed toward the elevator that would take her to the fourth floor, Preterm's medical area. The next time she saw Eamon, she told herself, it would all be over. She was scared as hell.

•   •   •

In the late 1960s and early 1970s, the term "clinic" conjured up a picture of impoverished women holding screaming infants in a grimy waiting room. Private doctors tended to those with means. Yet the sexual revolution and its resulting diseases, infections, and unwanted pregnancies placed new demands on women's health care—demands that many doctors were unprepared to meet. How could they help young women too shy to tell their family doctor that they were sexually

active, much less suffering from herpes or morning sickness? Besides, most private physicians didn't have the time—or didn't make the time—to discuss all birth-control options. Family planning wasn't lucrative or essential to an obstetrician-gynecologist's practice. Women were given pills and diaphragms, but not detailed instructions.

One Boston businesswoman, Jane Levin, recognized that those young women in hiphuggers and tie-dye T-shirts needed a medical facility that specialized in gynecology, one that would be clean, professional, and confidential. The clinic would emphasize birth-control counseling and information and would be accessible to all women, regardless of income. She envisioned quality care, not ability to pay, as the top priority; the clinic would be nonprofit, serving the public, not investors. After expenses were met, all income generated would flow back into the facility to expand and improve service.

Preterm opened in 1971 at 1031 Beacon Street in Brookline, the same spot which later housed Planned Parenthood. The clinic was named after the Preterm abortion clinic that Jane Levin's husband, Harry, had opened the same year in Washington, D.C. (Advertising executives had suggested Pregterm, for pregnancy termination, but Harry Levin had wanted a name that wouldn't mean anything, such as Kodak, so he shortened the title to Preterm.)

Preterm's genesis was a meeting in Geneva, Switzerland, in 1965 concerning world population which Harry Levin attended as a representative for the Population Council, an independent foundation for which he worked. At this meeting, Harry Levin learned that abortion was the most widely practiced form of birth management in the world, but that it was illegal in 75 percent to 80 percent of the world's countries. He found the Population Council reluctant to address the controversial issue because doing so might endanger opportunities to bring other forms of birth control to countries where abortion was illegal. Still, Harry Levin felt that if abortion were that important, somebody ought to do something—and the U.S. was a good place to start. His nation had among the toughest abortion laws in the world.

Washington, D.C., seemed the likely target; there, the proper abortion clinic model could have an impact on the U.S. legislature and judiciary, Harry hoped. More important, he discovered that various abortion lawsuits still jammed in the judicial system had left Washington, D.C.'s abortion laws in a state of limbo. (Only Alaska, Hawaii, New York, and Washington state offered unrestricted abortion at the time.)

Challenging the district's vague laws, Harry Levin opened Preterm in 1971, aiming to soften a woman's abortion experience. At his clinic, women would not remove all of their clothes, which Harry felt was dehumanizing, but would take off only the garments necessary for examination and treatment. Women would discuss their decision with a peer counselor who would listen and respond, but who would not influence. All options would be discussed, from abortion to adoption to keeping the baby. Counseling would be key, not only for the abortion decision, but also for birth control. The only way to decrease the need for abortion would be to improve women's contraceptive use.

Four hundred miles away in Boston, Jane Levin didn't think of challenging Massachusetts law by offering abortion services at her Preterm. While Washington, D.C., police merely surveyed her husband's clinic suspiciously, Brookline police would shut her down faster than she could pick up the phone if she so much as mumbled the word abortion. Her clinic, after all, operated in a Catholic state, although Brookline itself was predominantly Jewish and liberal. As it was, her landlord continually tried to evict her. He didn't like the idea of all those young women trooping into his building for birth control. But when the Supreme Court legalized abortion, Jane decided to offer the procedure. By August, she had moved Preterm down Beacon Street to a new medical building which provided the necessary space for her expanded services.

Jane's clinic required two floors: one for admitting and administration and another for gynecology and abortion services. Operating the medical services on the second floor would be convenient, but it wouldn't allow Jane to install the special airflow system she wanted to remove clinical odors. Medical services then moved to the fourth floor, which could accommodate the ventilation. The floor offered five rooms for gynecology, five rooms for abortion, a waiting room, laboratory, medical center, recovery room, and a variety of other offices and operating rooms to be used for sterilization.

It was on this floor that Colleen Dempsey stepped off the elevator, turned left, and faced the reality of the decision no woman wants to make.

• • •

The waiting was unbearable. Colleen had given her urine sample to the lab technician, who would run it through a two-minute pregnancy test. Maybe she wasn't pregnant after all. Maybe her home test had been wrong. A wave of nausea struck, squelching the hope.

Colleen studied the other patients in this waiting room with the floral wallpaper, amazed that so many women shared her crisis. Entering the clinic this morning, she had thought that she'd be joined by five, maybe ten, other patients seeking abortions, not fifty-three. Did all of these other women feel the same desperation? She couldn't ask—few words were exchanged up here, and eye contact was avoided. One woman sat, her book opened against her chest, staring at rooftops out of the picture window. Another picked up a magazine from the end table, flipping through the pages too fast even to catch a headline.

To reduce the confusion and the number of people on the fourth floor, partners were not allowed upstairs except to attend the counseling session or go through the procedure if the patient wanted them there. Most women didn't, Colleen among them. She didn't want Eamon to see her if she broke down. He hadn't argued when she'd said that she wanted to go through the counseling and procedure alone, that she needed privacy, even from him.

It was half past noon, and Colleen hadn't talked yet to a counselor, the last step before the surgery. She had had her blood drawn, and a nurse had taken her into a little room with an examination table and a wooden medical cabinet and asked her if she suffered from diabetes, asthma, anemia, or allergies, or had experienced difficulties after her miscarriage. The nurse asked where Colleen would go for her post-abortion checkup two weeks from now to make sure that she had healed properly. Preterm, Colleen said. She didn't have her own doctor. The nurse had been impressed with Colleen's low blood pressure and sense of calm. After jotting down Colleen's medical history, she had escorted Colleen back to the waiting room. Colleen thought she was very nice, that nurse.

Eamon had said to her earlier that morning that they had years ahead of them, that they could have hundreds of babies, but that now wasn't the right time. In her heart, Colleen knew he was right, but sitting here she had plenty of time to wonder. If I'm doing the wrong thing, she thought, staring at the scapular, God will forgive me. He knows that I have to do what is best for me.

A woman holding a clipboard rattled off some names. Colleen stood up as soon as she heard her own. "Hi," the woman said. "My name is Joan. We'll head down to the conference room for the group counseling session."

Some clinics offered only one-on-one counseling in which the counselor discussed everything from contraceptive options to the woman's decision. Others offered only group counseling, in which various issues as well as birth control were discussed between a counselor and up to eight patients. Preterm offered both, detailing birth-control options and a step-by-step description of the procedure in group counseling, and focusing on the woman's decision in individual counseling. Women who were especially nervous, who didn't speak English, or who were pregnant as a result of rape were allowed to skip the group and receive all their information in an individual session.

Joan smiled broadly as she led the group down the hall to a long room with a conference table, around which the seven patients sat. Joan was about forty, Colleen guessed, and fit, with her dark hair cut in a pageboy. Joan's voice was deep and she drew out the last syllable of each word.

"The medical assistant will take you into the procedure," Joan began. "She is there for you and will be with you the whole time."

Colleen listened carefully as Joan described the procedure. First a nurse would place an IV catheter in her arm, followed by a doctor who would inject the sedative. The doctor would perform a pelvic exam to check the pregnancy's gestation and would do a gonorrhea and Pap smear culture. From a basket in front of her, Joan picked up the abortion instruments—the speculum (a large, shiny metal device that looked like a duck's beak on legs) which opened the vaginal lips, little stainless steel rods called dilators that would open the cervix, the tenaculum (a scissorlike instrument with ends that curled toward each other) which would hold the cervix in place, and the cannula, which looked to Colleen like a plastic straw. The cannula would be inserted into the cervical hole and attached to the aspiration machine.

"At home you may have some bleeding, which can last from two to three days to two weeks," Joan said. "It is very important that you don't do anything too strenuous in the next two weeks. That may cause you to bleed too much."

Colleen had thought that after today, her worries would be over, but Joan explained that patients had to be careful for two weeks, that their cervixes will have been invaded and wouldn't close right away. Bacteria could easily float into the uterus and cause a raging pelvic inflammatory disease, which could result in sterility. To avoid infection, patients received a seven-day prescription of tetracycline and were warned not to put anything in their vaginas for two weeks—no tampons, no penises, not even douche.

"Complications are rare," Joan said, "but here they are." A patient could retain tissue and need to be reevacuated. Heavy bleeding and severe cramping were indicators of this. A patient could suffer from an

incomplete abortion in which the pregnancy was so small that it was missed. She, too, would be reevacuated. A patient's uterus could be perforated, in which case the patient would be monitored for several hours at Preterm, and, if necessary, be taken to the hospital where the puncture would be stitched. In most cases, the puncture healed itself. If a patient had any questions, she could call Preterm's emergency telephone number at any time, day or night, and talk to a nurse.

Without taking a breath, Joan launched into contraceptive options. Colleen and Eamon had discussed birth control, but it hadn't sunk in. This time it would, Colleen promised herself.

The IUD was effective but invasive. The diaphragm was messy and inconvenient. Colleen knew herself well enough to realize that she might not think to insert a diaphragm less than six hours before sex, or add more spermicide in the morning if they had intercourse again. Condoms and foam would be worse: no way would she remember to shake a can of foam and then apply it minutes before penetration. That seemed a bit awkward, and talk about ruining the moment. The cervical cap made sense, and Preterm was one of the few facilities in the area that offered it (the Food and Drug Administration had only recently approved its use in the U.S., although European women had used caps for years), but it was hard to maneuver and she was afraid she would give up before it was properly in place. She had considered using the sponge, which was available without a prescription and was advertised to be as effective as the diaphragm, but Joan said that Preterm didn't recommend them. The sponge comes in one size, and women aren't a standard shape. The sponge could flip over, slip out, even get stuck. Joan had seen too many sponge patients at the clinic. Joan also recommended against suppositories, withdrawal—preejaculatory semen could swim into the vagina—and using foams, creams, or jellies without the benefit of a condom. They simply didn't work.

"How many of you want the Pill?" Joan asked first, since that was most Preterm patients' method of choice. Colleen and several others raised their hands. Colleen didn't like the idea of ingesting extra hormones, but she felt that she would remember to take the Pill daily and she wanted something that she felt was effective. She didn't want to repeat this experience ever again.

• • •

It was 2:15 in the afternoon and Colleen was so bored and hungry that she had almost forgotten her fear of the operation that had brought her here. At least she had moved into another room. This one was smaller, closer to the medical center. When she heard a doctor's name called, she wondered if that were the name of the doctor who would perform her abortion. She looked around this square room at the four other women who sat there, all of whom had also complained of hunger. Since food and IV medication didn't mix, patients were warned to eat a light breakfast and not much else before the procedure. Listening to her stomach rumble, Colleen stared out the window at the neighboring rooftop and wished it were tomorrow.

Her individual counseling session had gone more smoothly than she had expected. Colleen had worried that the counselor would shame her for being so stupid, so irresponsible, especially after she'd been pregnant before. Instead, Kaylah, a pale woman about her age with short blonde hair and wire-rimmed glasses, had smiled and said that no one is perfect. Many of the patients she counseled felt conflicted about contraception, Kaylah said. The reason could be religious restrictions, fear, or ignorance. What was important, Kaylah emphasized, was that Colleen had taken control and seemed determined to take better care of herself. Since Colleen had chosen to go on the Pill, Kaylah explained the different kinds and how they should be taken.

As they discussed her decision, Colleen struggled to stay calm. A private person, she didn't want even a counselor probing her thoughts. Kaylah nodded as Colleen listed her reasons for ending the pregnancy, asking Colleen if she knew anyone she could talk to about the abortion afterward and what she would like her life to be like if she were to have a baby. Colleen said that she would talk to Eamon about her feelings, and she wanted to be married and financially stable before she started a family. Colleen surprised herself with her confidence. But when Kaylah asked Colleen how she would feel after the abortion, the answer popped out of Colleen's mouth before she could stop it.

"Not very good," she replied.

Kaylah's eyebrows shot up. "Let's talk about it."

Colleen regained her composure. She didn't expect Kaylah to understand the conflict between what she had been raised to think about abortion and what she thought was best for herself. Even she didn't understand it completely. All she knew was that she felt more strongly about making a good life for herself than she did about following her church's teachings. And that's what she told Kaylah, who accepted the answer.

A young woman with long dark hair and a friendly, round face appeared in the doorway. She wore green scrubs, the kind doctors and nurses wear in surgery. "Colleen D.?" she called, looking at each of the five faces in the room. Colleen jumped up, her hunger forgotten, her heart beating fast. Very fast.

"My name is Michelle, and I'll be with you during the procedure. Is this you?" she asked, holding up a medical chart and pointing to the name. Colleen nodded.

Colleen followed Michelle, the medical assistant, into a room that fit an examination table, a wooden medical cabinet with glass doors, a sink, a couple of chairs, and the evacuation machine, a tall, white box with a steel top from which sprung a long plastic hose. "Do you have any questions?" Michelle asked. Colleen shook her head. "Then why don't you step behind that curtain, undress from the waist down, and cover yourself with this sheet."

Colleen slipped off her sneakers and socks, her pants, then her underwear, wrapped the white sheet around her waist, and hopped on the table. The paper sheet underneath her crinkled when she moved. She lay down and stared at the ceiling, which had been painted a light blue—the color of the Irish sky in early spring. She clutched the sheet on top of her. This will be over soon, she told herself. This will be over soon. To take her mind off her beating heart, she asked Michelle if there had been any demonstrations lately.

"Not lately," Michelle said, rolling her eyes. "But you never know what Saturday will bring."

The door opened and a nurse appeared, explaining that she would place the IV catheter in Colleen's left arm and that the doctor would inject the medication. No sooner was the catheter in place and the nurse gone than the doctor arrived. He was an older man, in his late sixties, Colleen guessed, with a slight paunch and gruff manner. His greeting was more of a grunt than a hello. Colleen lifted her head enough to watch him as he donned the plastic surgical gloves, stretching his fingers for a better fit. He glanced at her medical chart, which lay open on a counter facing Colleen. The clock above the counter said 2:30.

Without a word, the doctor wheeled a stool to the foot of the examination table and sat down. Automatically, Colleen placed her feet in the stirrups, which were covered by oven mitts to keep patients' feet warm and comfortable. This doctor was certainly silent, Colleen noted, but that was just fine with her. She'd rather he concentrated on what he was doing and do it quickly than waste both of their time with idle chatter. His internal exam—the gentle probing of her uterus with his finger—was over almost before she knew it had begun.

"How ya' doing?" Michelle asked softly.

Colleen nodded OK.

"Relax your legs," the doctor directed.

Colleen felt the paper sheet fall across her inner thighs as she opened her legs wider. The speculum felt cool as it opened her vaginal lips. She felt something else inserted into her vagina and looked at Michelle, who said, "That's the Pap smear. Next comes the gonorrhea culture." So far, nothing the doctor did was painful or any different than what she had endured during routine gynecological checkups. The doctor then walked up to Colleen's left side, placed a syringe in the IV catheter, and shot the medicine into Colleen's vein. Within ten seconds, Colleen felt lightheaded, as if she were slightly drunk. "Whoa," Colleen said. "I feel high as a kite."

Michelle smiled. "It hits some people faster than others," she said. "You must have a low tolerance for drugs."

Colleen felt as if she were floating.

"Now the doctor will inject the local anesthetic into your cervix," Michelle said. "You should feel a pinch."

Staring at the ceiling, Colleen braced herself. She bit her lip with the first injection. The "pinch" was more like a series of bites as the doctor injected the lidocaine into several spots on her cervix. Then it was over. Colleen let out her breath and tried to relax, but the doctor was quick, immediately inserting the dilators, each one larger than the last, to open her cervix. The cramps began as Colleen's uterus contracted in response to the invasion. At first the pain was slight, a mild tugging in her belly just like the sensations she felt during the first few days of her period. With each dilator, however, the cramps intensified. Colleen felt as if a 200-pound man were dancing on her stomach. Michelle offered Colleen her hand to squeeze, but Colleen gripped the side of the table instead.

Not saying a word, the doctor inserted the cannula. Colleen gasped with the cramp that followed. The doctor attached the hose of the evacuation machine to the cannula and stepped on the machine's foot pedal.

"You'll hear some noise," Michelle told Colleen.

The whir of the machine was like that of a vacuum cleaner and it filled the room. Colleen didn't care about the noise. In fact, she wished she could concentrate on it. As the doctor suctioned out the pregnancy, she felt as if all of her was being sucked out with it. Never had she felt such cramps. The 200-pound man on her stomach had become a 500-

pound slab of concrete. She held her breath, praying that this would be over. It was, within moments.

"Your cramps should start subsiding in a few minutes," Michelle said. "You did great. How do you feel?"

Colleen nodded weakly.

"Just rest for a while. Then we'll get you dressed and we'll go into the recovery room."

Colleen glanced at the clock: 2:36. The whole ordeal, from pelvic exam to abortion, had taken fewer than six minutes. Colleen leaned back and let her legs rest straight, free from the stirrups. She placed her hands on her stomach, hoping that the pressure would ease the cramps. Slowly, like a heartbeat fading, the throbbing in her belly relented. She still felt lightheaded from the IV, but she wanted to get out of this room, out of this clinic, and home to something familiar.

Colleen had heard that some women had felt empty after an abortion, that even though they hadn't wanted the pregnancy, they felt as if they had lost something. Colleen didn't feel that way. Instead, she felt overwhelmed with relief. It was over. In half an hour, she could collect Eamon and they could go home, or go out and get a hamburger. She knew that she would never forget this experience, but she also sensed that she could live with it.

Colleen lifted herself up off the table, elbow by elbow. Michelle, who hustled around the room cleaning up after the doctor, smiled and asked if Colleen were ready to go to the recovery room. Colleen nodded.

Still feeling queasy, Colleen sat on a chair as she pulled on her pants. "Funny," she said to Michelle, "that such a simple procedure is such a big thing."

CHAPTER FIVE

Waiting for *Webster*

T HE Supreme Court had until Monday, July 3, the last day of the 1988–89 session, to issue its verdict on *Webster* v. *Reproductive Health Services*. Few expected the decision before June. Some didn't expect it at all this term, believing that the Court would hold the case over until the following fall for further discussion. As the calendar flipped from May to June and abortion headlines blared from every newsstand and television channel, the suspense inside Preterm Health Services became agonizing.

The Court announced its decisions at ten o'clock on designated mornings. Every morning that a decision was expected, Fran and Carolyn sat in Fran's office listening to WEEI, the all-news station, on Fran's boombox. They listened as the Court ruled that white men could more easily challenge affirmative action programs, that railroads could require workers to submit to drug testing, and that burning the American flag as a political protest was protected under the Constitution. Only the flag-burning decision seemed a hopeful sign to the two women; at least the Court had acknowledged some rights.

One Wednesday morning—rumored to be *the* morning—Carolyn and Fran sat, as usual, in Fran's office like anxious defendants awaiting a verdict. Carolyn, trying to defuse the tension, teased Fran about the dish of condoms she kept on her desk, right at the edge, directly in front of the visitor's chair. "Well," Fran said, grinning, "we have to push the fact that birth control must be talked about." Her grin evaporated with the news flash: "The Supreme Court announced today that states are free to impose . . ."

Carolyn's knuckles turned white as she gripped the arms of her chair. Fran's fingers froze on the sourball candy she was unwrapping. Both women held their breath.

". . . the death penalty on murderers who commit their crime at the age of sixteen or who are mentally handicapped."

The women exhaled. "This is so distracting," Fran moaned. "Even when they don't decide, I have a hard time concentrating on everything I have to do." Nodding, Carolyn stood up and, without uttering a word, returned to her office next door. An hour or two would pass before she, too, could fully focus on staff schedules and budgets, but even then, deep in her subconscious, she wondered "when?" When would they know abortion's future? When would they know the new battle lines? On one hand, no decision was better than a bad decision, but since some decision was inevitable, better that it be announced now and end the tension—especially the tension on Preterm's sidewalk every weekend.

Saturday prayer vigils were Operation Rescue's latest strategy. In an effort to diversify its tactics, the group gathered in front of Preterm, Repro, and Planned Parenthood to sing hymns and recite the rosary every Saturday, beginning the day before Mother's Day, May 15, and ending when the Supreme Court handed down the *Webster* ruling. This way, the abortion foes could demonstrate their dedication to saving the unborn without breaking the law as they did when they blockaded clinic entrances. Rescues remained the outfit's focus, but prayer vigils were an effort to gather more support from people who preferred not to spend weekends in cellblocks.

The first vigil at Preterm had been a bust, luring only seven antiabortionists and seventy-five abortion rights advocates. Patients and staff had entered the clinic without so much as a backward glance at the antis. The second vigil a week later, however, began what the Preterm staff called Saturday Madness, a weekly torment that placed the clinic and its patients in the crossfire as both the antichoice and prochoice armies exercised their anxiety over the uncertainty of abortion's future.

·   ·   ·

The prayer vigil had started off quietly enough that Saturday morning at the end of May, a morning so warm and sunny that men jogged shirtless down Beacon Street as cars sped by, loaded with sailboards and beach chairs. When Sonia Lewis opened Preterm's door shortly before 7 A.M., only six picketers stood under the sycamore tree in front, holding their signs and chattering amiably. Even an hour later, when a tall blond man arrived with a microphone, the procession remained peaceful. The protesters, about fourteen of them by then, walked in a circle on the sidewalk, softly singing "Kum Bah Yah" and reciting the Lord's Prayer, or whatever else the man with the microphone instructed. Flanked by clinic escorts, patients easily avoided the two sidewalk counselors who approached them with pamphlets and pleas of "You don't have to do this. We can help."

Sometime after 8:30 A.M., however, station wagons began arriving, spilling forth people carrying children and balloons and brightly colored signs warning of the Holocaust and human destruction. The sidewalk circle grew bigger and bigger: a moving wheel of elderly women holding rosary beads, young men carrying color photos of fetal heads, and parents pushing baby strollers. Heads bowed, the protesters sang hymns as they shuffled from the clinic steps to the end of the block and back again. One frail man, a faded baseball cap shielding his hairless head from the bright sun, prayed silently on his knees in front of Preterm's steps, his bony hands clutching a framed painting of the Virgin Mary.

The prochoicers, too, had gathered, though not in the numbers of the week before. This Saturday's group of twenty women and a sprinkling of men stood to the left of Preterm on the sidewalk, less than five feet from the tip of their opposition's circle. Dressed in brightly colored T-shirts and jeans or shorts, the prochoicers chanted to drown out the hymns and prayers. "Ho ho, hey hey, you aren't the only ones who pray," they taunted.

No response. Their chanting grew louder.

"You can pray all night and pray all day, but *Roe* v. *Wade* is here to stay!"

Standing at the top of Preterm's steps, Sonia watched the growing circus with disgust. How many patients would drive away when confronted by this sight? Sonia knew that most would reschedule—as they had after the past two rescues—but why did their crisis have to be prolonged just because the antis and the pros had chosen to blast their views in front of Preterm's steps?

Carolyn Wardell was also worried, not just that access to the clinic might be hindered for patients and staff, but also about the clients of the building's other tenants. Carolyn had heard rumblings that some tenants of 1842 Beacon Street were plotting to evict Preterm because of the increasing number of demonstrations, that their clients were sometimes followed to their cars by picketers branding them as murderers. One protester had shouted "Don't kill your baby" to a chemotherapy patient heading to the wigmaker on the second floor. Another had accused a twelve-year-old girl of lying when she said that she was going to have her braces tightened at her orthodontist's office. Although the building's owner had stated that Preterm was a good tenant and that its five-year lease would be honored and renewed, Carolyn couldn't relax on demonstration days. This morning, Lorena had had a gymnastics class at 9:30, but instead of lingering at home until the lesson, Carolyn had brought Lorena to Preterm so that she could monitor the prayer vigil for an hour. She needed to observe the protesters' strategies to figure out her defense.

"No honey, you can't play with those people," Carolyn told Lorena, who started to skip toward the children marching in the circle of abortion foes. Lorena, a wiry little girl with long blond hair and an impish grin, skipped back to her mother, who stood watching the show from the front steps.

Staring at the antis, Carolyn felt resigned. Picketers had always stood in front of the clinic, and would always stand in front of the clinic. They were annoying and obnoxious, but as long as you ignored them, they were, for the most part, harmless. Carolyn had no problems with the antis' expressing their beliefs on the sidewalk as long as they stayed away from the clinic. But she did have a problem with the prochoice activists.

As soon as they had heard that Operation Rescue had a Boston chapter, the prochoice organizations had begun debating how best to handle the blockades. Should they ignore the abortion foes or outshout them? Would counterdemonstrating give credence to the antis or overwhelm them? Should the prochoicers stand to the side or fight the antis for sidewalk space? At first, the prochoicers agreed to cooperate with the police, holding their signs and singing their songs a safe distance from the fracas. But simply watching the abortion foes clog the entrances of Gynecare, Repro, and Planned Parenthood last fall had frustrated the troops. They felt strongly about the injustice of the blockades and yearned to be more active, more of a threat to the antis. In the late winter of 1989, Ellen Convisser, president of Boston NOW, decided not to restrain her people anymore. She felt that it wasn't her position to corral her people if they wanted to challenge Operation Rescue's control of the sidewalk. The antiabortionists had declared war on women—on a woman's right to control her body—and since NOW represented women, Boston NOW would fight to defend that right. Unfortunately for the clinics, Ellen acknowledged, the battleground was their front steps.

As far as Carolyn was concerned, the prochoicers could wage their war as effectively on the median strip as on the sidewalk. Drivers zipping down Beacon Street would see the signs and hear the chants; the prochoice statement would be made. Left undisturbed, the antis would hum their songs, pray their prayers, and go home. But by blasting their rhetoric close enough for the antis to smell their breath, the prochoicers had antagonized their foes into a noise competition.

Now, minute by minute, the protesters' volume was rising from a steady drone to a cacophony that woke a woman two blocks away. When the prochoice demonstrators sang loudly, so did the antis. When a gray-haired woman wearing jeans and a white T-shirt commemorating the April 9 March for Women's Lives whipped out an electric microphone, a priest marching in the antis' circle began reciting the Lord's Prayer into a bullhorn. As a young man thumped a coat hanger against a sandwich board that said "FAGGOTS FOR CHOICE," the blond man who quietly had been uttering instructions to the parading antis invited his more vociferous peers to wield the microphone.

"We will, we will save babies, save babies," crooned one woman. Next, a chubby woman in a sailor cap shrieked what may have been a song but sounded more like wasps buzzing against a screen. Even the prochoicers stopped chanting to hold their ears.

As the noise soared, the clinic escorts, who an hour before had calmly walked up to patients to ask if they'd like help getting to the door, became frantic. As soon as a patient stepped out of her car, the escorts raced to her side, sidewalk counselors hard on their heels. Before the patient had even shut her car door, she was surrounded. From where Carolyn stood on the steps, it was clear that the patients didn't know who was on their side, only that a crowd had enveloped them as they were about to make one of the most private decisions of their lives. Most patients were frightened enough of what lay ahead of them that day, worrying that the abortion would be painful, wondering how they'd be treated, even wondering if they would survive the procedure. They didn't need this.

The next Saturday was worse, as was the Saturday after that, and the Saturday after that. The longer the Supreme Court took to utter its decision, the more new faces appeared in front of Preterm. Members of the World Workers Party, the Revolutionary Communist Party, and the Socialist Workers Party joined the NOW demonstrators. On the anti-abortion side, a new outfit called the Ethics of Choice Chorus bobbed yellow signs bearing questions such as "DOES GOOD CHOICE NURTURE LIFE, OR DESTROY LIFE?" This group's goal was to engage the opposition in intellectual discussion and stop patients from entering the clinic—not physically like Operation Rescue, but psychologically by posing questions to make the women rethink their decision. Anyone who dealt with abortion patients knew the futility of such an effort, however; women seeking abortions were operating emotionally, not intellectually. Yellow signs blaring questions in bold black letters wouldn't change many minds. As for enlightened discussion between the two factions camped outside Preterm's doorway, Sonia overheard one prochoicer yelling, "You think a woman pregnant by rape should carry the child to term? Why not make the rapist carry the pregnancy?"

After each Saturday, Sonia left the clinic with a headache, sometimes a migraine. The first staffer to greet the patients, she also was the first to behold their faces streaked with tears or scarlet with anger when they, after running the gauntlet outside, arrived at Sonia's desk. When Sonia had transferred from the fourth floor to admitting, she felt that she had witnessed enough raw emotion to last her a lifetime in her nine years as a counselor in the procedure room. During those late spring Saturdays she received yet another unsparing assault. "Who are those people?" one young woman sobbed, clutching her boyfriend around the waist, when they reached Sonia's desk.

"They can't walk in your moccasins," Sonia said gently. "They don't know your circumstances. You only know what's best for you."

Because she worked in the family room where partners and parents waited out their girlfriend or daughter's abortion, Sonia spent much of her day listening to concerns about whether or not abortion was safe, or whether the relationship would change as a result of the experience.

Sometimes the men simply needed to vent their feelings, that they, too, felt the agony of the decision. Sonia would nod and answer their questions, pulling from her desk referrals for professional counseling when she felt her words were not adequate. On demonstration Saturdays, nothing she said seemed adequate.

"This is hard enough without that," said one husband, who sat on the front steps, his fists clenched on his lap. At twenty-one, he worked part-time in road construction, earning barely enough to feed himself, his wife, and their toddler—let alone another child. Last month, he wasn't able to pay the rent. "It wouldn't be fair to the new baby," he told Sonia as they both stood on the steps. But *they*, he said, jerking his head toward the sidewalk, wouldn't understand his dilemma.

"I'd like to see what those people would do if one of their kids got pregnant," sputtered the father of a fifteen-year-old patient as he glared at the singing abortion foes from his perch on the front steps. Demonstrations lured many partners and parents from the family room outside. This father also had once thought abortion was immoral, but when his daughter—his little girl—had announced that she was pregnant, he saw no other options. After slamming his fist through a wall and raging around the house for two days, he calmed down enough to persuade his daughter to call Preterm. How could a baby raise a baby? He and his wife certainly didn't want to go through midnight feedings and toilet training again.

Carolyn knew that she had to do something to calm Saturdays down. Since the antis wouldn't listen to an abortion clinic director, she had tried talking to Ellen Convisser of Boston NOW. A high-school guidance counselor by trade, Ellen was Carolyn's age—thirty-nine—and was known throughout the prochoice community for her quick wit and steadfast dedication to feminist ideals. Ellen had joined Boston NOW in 1983 after a woman was gang raped in a New Bedford, Massachusetts, bar. The rape had sparked a need in Ellen to become active in a movement that would fight for justice for women. In 1985 and 1986, Ellen had lobbied hard and successfully to defeat a proposed amendment to the state constitution to ban abortions, and in 1987, she had been named Boston NOW's president. As the abortion debate heated up, Ellen's thin face and close-cropped brown hair became a familiar sight on Boston TV and in front of the clinics. On Saturdays, she stood among her demonstrators clapping, leading chants, and patrolling the sidewalk like a cop on the beat. When a reporter showed up, Ellen was available to answer questions. Like Bill Cotter, she aimed to blast her message as often as possible.

In a meeting in early June, Carolyn had asked Ellen Convisser to reduce the number of prochoice demonstrators, explaining that their presence inflamed the antichoice protesters and intimidated patients. Ellen held firm. If the prochoice people don't show up, Ellen said, they are surrendering clinic turf to the antis. To allow the antis to frame the abortion debate was debilitating to prochoice activists, and NOW needed to recruit activists to help fight for *all* rights for women, from economic to civil to reproductive. Ellen said that she realized that NOW's agenda was different from that of the clinics, and she was sorry that the clinics didn't view the prochoice demonstrators' presence as support. But NOW was a political action organization which needed to have its voice heard. Besides, she told Carolyn, "we aren't intimidating. Operation Rescue is intimidating." What neither woman said and both knew, however, was that Saturdays in front of the clinics had become a major recruiting tool. Boston NOW's membership had tripled since the demonstrations had begun.

Carolyn gave up. She realized that to many on the prochoice side, abortion was purely a political and ideological debate that somehow had become separated from the women it involved. Ironically, out of the thousands of women who had sought Preterm's abortion services in the five years Carolyn had worked at the clinic, she couldn't think of a single one who had had an abortion for political reasons.

The energies of both sides seemed so misplaced. Instead of chanting in front of the clinics, Carolyn thought, the prochoicers could overwhelm their state legislators, congressional representatives, and senators with their message, using their skills to nudge politicians into implementing a national health-insurance policy similar to that of most developed countries in which contraceptives are available at little or no cost. The most effective forms of birth control—sterilization, the Pill, and the IUD—were expensive in the U.S. The prochoicers could also fight harder to force the federal government to return to family planning clinics the funding that the Reagan administration had cut.

In turn, the abortion foes could devote their energy, time, and money into providing more homes, medical care, and support systems for unhappily pregnant women. Although the antis argued that they did provide the women with shelter, more often they provided only a referral sheet of state and federal programs, many of which had, like the family-planning clinics, suffered severe cutbacks during the Reagan era and would suffer more in the next years as Massachusetts struggled to balance its own billion-dollar deficit. At last count, more than 20,000 Massachusetts families were waiting for food and health care from state services.

Most important, the antis could offer help to the one in five children born into poverty each year, many of whom were born with drug dependencies, AIDS, or birth defects: victims of their mothers' own alcohol or drug addictions. They could fight to improve prenatal care for poor women and thus slice the state's infant mortality rate, which was well above the national average (each year, 7.9 white infants in Massachusetts died per 1,000 live births compared to five out of 1,000 nationwide, and 17.2 black infants died compared to 11.3 nationwide).

The abortion foes could also fight for affordable housing and quality, available child care. They could adopt some of the 8,000 children living in foster homes across the state.

But no, both sides preferred to take their argument to the clinic steps. Carolyn could only hope that the Saturday madness would end when the Supreme Court finally announced abortion's future. But what if it didn't? If the Court trashed *Webster* and *Roe* v. *Wade* remained the law of the land, would the antis continue their vigils? If *Webster* were upheld, would the prochoicers become even more aggressive?

One day at a time, Carolyn would remind herself. One day at a time.

•   •   •

Choosing abortion was not easy for any woman, regardless of how strongly she didn't want to be pregnant. Every woman harbored an element of uncertainty about her decision, of wonderment of what could be. As Kate Horowitz, one of Preterm's doctors, once said, deciding what is best for you doesn't detract from the pain of having to make the choice in the first place. For some women, though, the decision was more complicated than for others. Many women wanted the child, but the circumstances weren't right: either their relationship with their partner was weak or too new to test with a child, or they couldn't afford to start a family, or they wanted to finish college, or high school. Other women harbored religious reservations about choosing abortion, worrying that they would burn in hell as the picketers warned. Some women tormented themselves by believing themselves selfish for choosing their needs over the fetus's.

Every day that they crossed Preterm's threshold, the clinic's abortion staffers were confronted by this ambivalence. It seemed, though, that in the anxious weeks before the *Webster* decision, more women than ever questioned whether they should step onto the examination table.

The no-show rate was high, averaging 20 percent to 25 percent of all appointments on Saturday, Preterm's busiest day, and 15 percent to 20 percent during the week. While no one in the clinic wanted to admit that the increasingly vigorous protests had any effect, the appointment book spoke for itself. No-shows usually called to reschedule, but lately, the missed appointments were permanent. Perhaps the appointments were, as Sonia suspected, fake ones. Perhaps abortion foes were trying to fill up the schedule so that fewer appointments would be available for women who sought the procedure. Or perhaps the no-shows were, as Carolyn thought, women who had reconsidered their decision after spotting outside a photo of a thumb-sucking fetus, or seeing footage of the Saturday protests on the nightly news. Even if Preterm's chaos didn't reach the patients prior to their appointment, other abortion news did. You couldn't flick on the evening news these days without hearing someone arguing that "abortion is murder." It was little wonder to Carolyn that women became overwhelmed with doubts about their decision.

Inside Preterm, nothing that the patients said directly linked their ambivalence with the protests—in truth, patients calmed down by the time they reached the fourth floor, which engulfed them like a sanctuary far removed from the chaos outside. Staffers could only wonder if the demonstrations had triggered doubts and guilt buried deep in the women's subconscious or merely exaggerated the questions at the surface.

One counselor often thought of a patient named Liz, who had roamed Preterm's halls for five hours debating her decision before she felt strong enough to go through with the procedure. Abortion felt wrong to her—it was killing—but at twenty-seven, Liz didn't earn enough as a pipe fitter to afford her own place, let alone her own place plus a baby. Liz's roommates refused to house an infant in their apartment, and her boyfriend said he'd leave her if she had the baby. She had no money for day care, and she refused to go on welfare to stay home with the child. Putting the baby up for adoption, Liz said, would be too painful to endure. She left Preterm with referrals for postabortion counseling.

Then there was Grace, a thirty-nine-year-old opthalmologist, who wished that a sniper would shoot her in the belly so she wouldn't have to decide whether to end her pregnancy. She didn't like children; her boyfriend loved them. He wanted to make her happy, however, so he told her that he would support her decision to abort. She wanted to make *him* happy, so she was considering keeping the child. But she worried that she would hate motherhood and would end up destroying the relationship she had built with this man whom she loved. Grace visited Preterm three times before she finally lay down on the examination table. Even then, she had to get up moments before the procedure started to talk to her boyfriend one more time. He convinced her that he didn't want the baby. Three weeks after her abortion, she regretted having had it.

Kate Horowitz had not performed Grace's abortion. In fact, in her experience as a doctor at Preterm, it was unusual for patients to remain undecided by the time they reached the procedure room. By then, patients either had worked out their ambivalence with a counselor or they had been asked to leave and reschedule after their decision became clearer. Some patients rescheduled four, five, even six times, often leaving the clinic with pamphlets on adoption and referrals for professional counseling given to them by Sonia or by another Preterm counselor.

The few ambivalent women Kate did see were heartbreaking, bursting into tears before Kate had even touched them. They wanted to have the baby but they couldn't, they would say, because they had taken too much medication when they didn't know they were pregnant, or their husband wouldn't support another child, or they had just gotten off welfare and another child would put them back on. Kate would walk to the head of the table, lean toward the patient's face, and softly say, "Most people have mixed feelings about being pregnant when they don't want to be. Considering everything, do you want me to go ahead and do the abortion today?"

In the six years that Kate had performed abortions—five years at Preterm and one at a now defunct women's health center in Cambridge—only two patients had decided to continue the pregnancy.

To Kate, there was a sadness in abortion, a sadness both for the woman and for what might have been. Kate didn't regard abortion as murder, but as an act that caused something not to be. Whenever she felt confused, she reminded herself that the world would not be better if a woman who was not prepared to be a mother became a mother. And, to Kate, carrying a child to term—even if one never saw the child—was a form of mothering.

As an adolescent, Kate, who was now thirty-seven, had listened to her mother, a high-school teacher, fret about teenage girls quitting school because they were pregnant. Inheriting her mother's belief that abortion should be safe and legal so kids wouldn't be saddled with unwanted pregnancies and unwanted children, Kate decided that she would become a doctor and perform illegal abortions. If abortion became legal, she would find another medical crusade, possibly save Woody Guthrie's life by finding the cure for Huntington's disease. But Woody Guthrie died and abortion was legalized, and Kate still performed abortions one or two shifts a week at Preterm. A practicing family doctor, Kate had learned the specialty at a women's community health center in Cambridge, and had moved her expertise to Preterm in 1983 after that center had closed.

Kate was considered something of an earth mother by her Preterm colleagues. She wore sandals to work, wrapped her long brown hair in a bun at the back of her head, and pumped her breast milk by hand into a sandwich bag for her one-year-old son. Preterm's head nurse called Kate the most "centered person" she knew, someone who knew exactly what she wanted. The women who worked as both counselors and medical assistants (they alternated the jobs for variety) loved working with Kate. "She has," said one CMA, Nina Miller, "such respect for patients."

One of those patients was Jolene, a woman who reminded Kate of the difficulty of making the decision to abort.

Kate met Jolene on a Thursday morning in late June, on a day Kate had suspected might be *the* day that the Supreme Court handed down the *Webster* decision. It wasn't, and Kate had gone about her regular duties on the morning shift, spending about twenty minutes with each abortion patient. Her fourth patient was Jolene, a black woman with a wide smile and tortoiseshell glasses. When Kate entered the room, Jolene was already on the table with her feet in the stirrups and covered with a paper sheet.

As Kate flipped through Jolene's medical chart, Jolene chattered to the medical assistant, explaining that she had forgotten everything she was supposed to bring to Preterm this morning—her license, her Medicaid card, her morning's urine. Without pausing, she started talking about her two daughters, ages ten years and five months, and their father, with whom she had lived for years. This was her first abortion.

"My doctor told me I couldn't get pregnant while breast-feeding," Jolene said to the medical assistant. Kate's shoulders tensed. She hated hearing these stories. Had Jolene's doctor actually perpetuated the falsehood, she wondered, or had Jolene misunderstood? It didn't matter. What was done was done.

She's about eleven weeks along, Kate thought as she felt Jolene's uterus with her finger.

"Can the baby feel this?" Jolene asked when Kate injected the Valium and Sublimaze into her arm catheter. "Will the baby feel sleepy?"

"That's doubtful," Kate said.

"Will the baby feel anything?"

"That's doubtful, too," Kate said, walking to the head of the table. Kate had heard enough to know that Jolene needed support. Leaning down, Kate said so softly that the medical assistant almost couldn't hear, "This was a tough decision, huh?"

Jolene bit her lip. "This could be my little boy. But it wouldn't be fair to my daughters." Staring into Kate's eyes, Jolene said that she had worked hard to give her oldest daughter stability and comfort and lots of attention, and that she wanted to do the same for her five-month-old.

She didn't have the energy or the money to give anything to this child inside of her. "I'll just give all the love I have for this," she said resting her hand on her belly, "to my baby girl."

"Only you can make this decision," Kate said softly. "Only you know what is right."

"I know. I know. But it's so hard. I hope I don't hate him."

"Who?" asked the medical assistant.

"The baby's father."

Patients frequently wondered if their feelings for their partner would change after the abortion. They worried that they would blame their man for the pregnancy, or that he would be a painful reminder of the experience. Kate wasn't sure how much of a part Jolene's partner had played in the decision to abort, but she knew that Jolene had not completely worked out her feelings. Before Kate could offer Jolene more time to consider the decision, however, Jolene announced that she wanted to go through with the abortion. Kate didn't feel that it was her position to argue. She proceeded to dilate Jolene's cervix.

"You'll hear some noise," said Kate, as she pressed her foot on the pedal that would begin the evacuation.

Jolene started to sob. The medical assistant held her hand.

"Does it hurt?" asked Kate, glancing up for a second. She wanted to keep her attention on her task—guiding the cannula around Jolene's uterus as the machine's power suctioned out the pregnancy tissue. One false move and she could puncture the uterine lining.

"It *should* hurt," Jolene cried.

"Don't punish yourself."

When it was over, Jolene laid her arm across her eyes and sobbed. "My baby, my baby," she crooned.

After sifting through the fetal parts and ascertaining that the abortion was complete, Kate turned to Jolene, who was crying softly. "It's over," Kate whispered. "You take care."

The ultimate ambivalence, Kate thought. The antiabortionists could rant that women had abortions without hesitation, that women used abortion as a method of birth control. They didn't see these tears. Women like Jolene heightened Kate's respect for the strength required to decide between one's own needs and a child's needs.

Jolene would have to live with her choice, forever remembering that she would have had a newborn, a one-year-old, a twelve-year-old, but that her two existing children needed her more. Who else but the mother could make that decision, Kate thought. The crazies outside?

The Supreme Court? With a last glance at Jolene, who was being tended by the medical assistant, Kate walked out of the room and headed to the nurses lounge for a break. All of a sudden, she felt exhausted.

• • •

It was the final week of June, and still the Supreme Court had yet to hand down the Webster decision. Carolyn worried that the Court would hold off until Monday, July 3, when she and Lorena would be deep in the Pennsylvania woods camping with Carolyn's siblings and their families, away from newspapers, televisions, and telephones. The suspense of not knowing would be unbearable, as would the feeling of helplessness at being so far from Preterm and unable to support her staff. To make matters worse, she wouldn't be able to discuss *Webster* with her siblings, since none of them condoned abortion. Carolyn had long ago accepted their conservative stance and didn't talk much to them about Preterm or about abortion. She wondered if she could maintain that control next week.

Carolyn did not sleep well the night before Thursday, June 29, the last day that the Supreme Court would deliver decisions before the July Fourth weekend. Fran was in Cambridge at a class on teaching advanced sexuality to adolescents, so Carolyn took the boombox into her own office. Weary and nervous, she sat down at her desk and flicked on the radio. If the Court were smart, she thought, it would wait until Monday to hand down the much-anticipated decision. That way, many people would be out of town celebrating the long weekend, and the ensuing demonstrations would be less crowded. Maybe.

The Court must have read her mind. At 10 A.M., the radio station's Washington, D.C., reporter said that according to sources close to the Court, the *Webster* decision wouldn't be announced until Monday. Another letdown, Carolyn sighed. At 10:11 A.M., the reporter said that the Court had handed down two decisions, neither of which was the *Webster* case. Carolyn heard a court clerk in the background yell to reporters, "See you guys Monday." What could she do, she thought, but leave for Pennsylvania and hope that Fran survived the media assault expected at the beginning of next week. "At least people will have the weekend to cool down," she told her secretary.

But on Monday, July 3, the skeletal staff at Preterm was anything but cool. Since Preterm didn't hold an abortion clinic on Mondays and the regular Monday gynecology clinic had been canceled for the holiday, only the downstairs administrative staff and a few phone counselors floated between the boombox in Fran's office and the bagels and doughnuts in the kitchen across the hall.

It was difficult to know what to feel on this overcast summer day. Hopeful? Depressed? Cautious? Fran was anxious. If the Court didn't announce the decision and carried the case until next fall, she would return to Gloucester, the North Shore town where she was spending the holiday weekend with her boyfriend and his family. If the Court ruled, her day would be seriously nuts. Aside from the predicted bombardment of reporters' visits and calls, she would have to attend the press conference held this afternoon by the Coalition for Choice, which was composed of the state's prochoice organizations, including the clinics. With Carolyn on vacation, it was up to Fran to voice the clinic's feelings. She felt nervous, but in control. She wouldn't cry in front of reporters.

At 9:55 A.M., a few staffers clustered in Fran's office. Leaning against the doorway, Lin Sherman from the phone room said, "A news analyst friend of mine in the Midwest predicted they'll put it off for a year."

Fran shrugged. It was impossible to say. Considering all the previous letdowns, the Court could easily prolong the anticipation.

At ten o'clock, Fran shifted restlessly in her chair. Half an onion bagel with cream cheese sat uneaten on her desk and her coffee was cold. The reporter in Washington had no news. Not even a rumor.

At 10:06 A.M. the radio reporter said he believed that the decision had come down. No one in Fran's office moved. It was as if the air had stopped circulating.

"It seems . . ." the radio reporter paused, shuffling through the pages of the decision, "that the Court approved several new restrictions on the abortion law but left the Constitutional rights to abortion. The general principle is expected to be upheld."

Another pause. Lin and Fran exchanged worried looks.

"This is a complicated decision," the reporter said. "The high court overturned . . .

". . . the eighth circuit court of appeals . . .

". . . which struck down the Missouri law."

What did that mean? Fran wondered. Had the Court upheld all of the *Webster* rulings? Would all public hospitals in the nation no longer provide abortions? Had the Court verified that human life began at conception, thereby giving the fetus the same rights as the mother? Or did it mean that the Supreme Court had tossed to the states the freedom to restrict a woman's right to an abortion?

Fran sat frozen, trying to absorb what she had just heard.

CHAPTER SIX

Shades of Gray

Dᴇᴛᴀɪʟs of the Supreme Court's decision on *Webster* v. *Reproductive Health Services* were sketchy for most of the morning of July 3, 1989, as radio and TV commentators grappled with the eighty-five-page ruling. By the time the afternoon news aired, though, they had learned enough to make clear that the foundation of a woman's right to abortion had been rattled.

In a five-to-four vote, the Court had upheld the Missouri statute, which meant that women in Missouri could no longer receive abortions at public hospitals or by public employees, including doctors and nurses. The Court did not rule on the law's preamble, which stated that human life began at conception, calling the statement an opinion that would not affect abortion access. The justices did, however, uphold the requirement that Missouri doctors perform viability tests on women who they suspected were twenty weeks or more pregnant to determine if the fetus could possibly survive on its own.

The decision's deeper significance was that by upholding the Missouri statute, the Court had, in effect, invited all states to impose new restrictions on abortion. The issue was now in the hands of state legislatures, which meant that the abortion battle would be waged in the political arena for years to come.

Although *Roe* v. *Wade* remained the law of the land, the 1973 ruling's unraveling had begun, and would most likely continue. In the fall, the Court announced, it would hear three more abortion cases, two of which pertained to parental notification by minors seeking abortion, and one that involved requiring clinics to meet the same medical standards required of small hospitals, which would put most of the nation's abortion providers out of business, including Preterm. As Justice Harry Blackmun wrote in his dissent of *Webster*, "a chill wind blows."

Doris Merrill, a Preterm nurse, was lounging on Long Beach, a popular spot on Massachusetts' North Shore, with a group of friends when she heard the news blast from a radio on the blanket in front of her. This can't be, she thought. Immersed in her struggle to cope with the memories of this coastal area where she and her husband Shelley had spent so many summers with their two sons, Doris had forgotten about *Webster* over the weekend. She hadn't ventured back here since Shelley had died the year before, but she knew her husband wouldn't have wanted her to shut out these friends, many of whom had vacationed with them, or forgo such a happy part of their family life. So, with trepidation, she had accepted the July Fourth invitation. She didn't regret her decision, but her renowned quick wit and cackle that could penetrate walls had only occasionally cracked through the loneliness and deep sense of loss that had overwhelmed her since arriving here on Saturday.

And now on this sunny July day, as the catamarans cut through the ocean and holiday revelers sipped beer from cans wrapped in brown paper bags, the Supreme Court had delivered another loss. Doris, frozen in her beach chair, began to cry.

Would she lose her job? That's selfish, she scolded herself. She could always find another job. But what would happen to the patients if legal abortion no longer existed? Barely five feet tall, with a large round chest and short brown hair streaked with blond, Doris had a special touch with patients, a gentleness, and a motherly concern. She was especially good with young women. Sitting on the beach, she thought of the thirteen-year-old black girl she had once tended who said that she had gotten pregnant because her boyfriend "forgot to take his pill." Would that child, so ignorant of her own body and of contraception, now be forced to have a child? She thought about the woman who carried the AIDS virus, compliments of a relationship with a man who hadn't told her that he was infected. Would she be forced to bear a baby doomed to a miserable life and an early death? Or would she fall prey to a back-alley abortionist?

At sixty, Doris remembered hospital emergency rooms as chambers of horror during the years of illegal abortion. She had been a nursing student at Boston's Beth Israel Hospital in the 1950s, a witness to women with rubber catheters dangling from their vaginas, women who had douched with Lysol, women who had tried to jab the pregnancy with anything they could find that was long and sharp. The prochoice signs of a coat hanger slashed with a red line roused all-too-vivid memories for Doris. To return to those days was unfathomable.

As she listened to experts on the radio discussing *Webster*'s implications, it seemed to Doris that she could no longer count on anything, that everything she believed in and depended on would evaporate. Shelley, her marriage, their life together—gone. And now perhaps safe abortions would also disappear. When she had joined Preterm's nursing staff ten years ago, she had thought that only retirement would stop her from providing quality medical care and supporting women through their trauma. She had never imagined that the Supreme Court would one day recant its 1973 decision to legalize the procedure.

Doris had planned to watch the July Fourth fireworks on the North Shore that evening and return to her home in Newton, a Boston suburb, the next day. Now she knew that she had to leave immediately. Boston NOW had planned a demonstration at Boston's federal court-house this evening and Mass Choice had organized a "Day After" rally at the State House tomorrow, but Doris yearned to be home by herself to think about what the Court's ruling meant to her, to Preterm, and to the women she served.

To Doris—and to the rest of her Preterm colleagues, for that matter—no sign or slogan or demonstration could capture abortion's impossible complexity. Despite what activists on both sides of the debate would have liked the public to believe, those inside the clinic walls recognized all too well that there were no absolutes. Abortion wasn't a black-and-white issue, but one of varying shades of gray.

•   •   •

In the hot July days that followed the Court's decision, as abortion rights advocates charged that they would crush all antichoice legislation and the antiabortion forces promised more victories, one battle cry was heard again and again: fetal rights versus women's rights.

The Supreme Court had attempted to find middle ground in 1973 by declaring in *Roe* v. *Wade* that in the first trimester of pregnancy the abortion decision was a matter between a woman and her doctor, and that during the second trimester, the state could intervene only to protect the woman's health. The Court ruled, however, that the state had enough interest in a fetus twenty-six or more weeks old to forbid abortion in the third trimester unless the woman's life or health were endangered.

To the antis, *Roe*'s structure was preposterous: The fetus was a human being from the moment of conception, with a constitutional right to live. To many abortion rights supporters, *Roe* didn't sit well either: The mother's wishes always superseded those of the fetus, at any stage in the pregnancy. To those who worked on Preterm's fourth floor, however, *Roe* embraced abortion's complexity. To provide abortions meant a daily struggle to balance the stories of contraceptive failure and desperate life situations against what abortion destroyed.

And what abortion destroyed was unnerving.

It was easy to shrug off an aborted pregnancy as nothing more than a sack of blood and globs of tissue—as many prochoice activists did—if one never saw fetal remains, or products of conception (POC), as they were known in medical circles. But the nurses, medical assistants, and doctors who worked inside procedure rooms knew that while an eight-week POC was indeed a sack of blood and globs of tissue, an eleven-week POC harbored tiny arms and legs and feet with toes. At twelve weeks, those tiny hands had tiny nails. Although the fetal head was too small at that stage to withstand the evacuation machine's suction, pieces of face—a nose and mouth, or a black eye (all fetal eyes are black in the first trimester) the size of a pea—were sometimes found in the aftermath.

Later abortions spawned even more gruesome fetal remains. Between the twelfth and sixteenth week, early in the second trimester, the fetus almost doubled in length as its body caught up to its large head, and it filled out to the point where it looked like a human baby for the first time. Since the fetal skull was still soft, the head did not come out whole during the evacuation, but the legs and arms and rib cage made it through intact. The hand of a second trimester fetus, as a Preterm doctor described it, seemed big enough to shake.

Most of Preterm's abortion staff didn't volunteer to work "seconds." Late first trimester POCs were hard enough. The counselor/medical assistants (CMAs) met regularly to discuss their feelings about their work, and often the discussion focused on the POC. Inside a procedure room, facing the contents of the uterus, there was no denying what abortion was. One CMA, Nina Miller, felt that she should explore the contents of the cheesecloth sack to prepare her for dealing with human tissue in medical school, which she planned to attend the next year. As a biology major, she was fascinated by the veins and villi, the tiny threads waving from the tiny placenta, of eight- and nine-week POCs. On the human level, though, she was horrified by the little arms and legs lying in blood. Each time she asked herself, "What are we doing here?" And each time she went home to reconsider her commitment to helping women end pregnancies they didn't want. Only the woman knew her situation, Nina would remind herself. Only the woman could decide whether she was ready to be a mother. Nina always returned to work recommitted, but that commitment didn't carry her into second-trimester procedure rooms. That, she thought, was more than she wanted to see.

Even many of Preterm's nurses, women with more medical experience than the CMAs, preferred to limit their services to first-trimester abortions. For Deb Andrews, a nurse, an eight-week fetus wasn't a baby, and an abortion at that stage was no more disturbing to her than having teeth cleaned at the dentist. But a fifteen-week fetus had a nose and lips and ears, and Deb preferred to avoid the rooms where that fetus was being evacuated from its mother's womb. Although intellectually she knew that there were justifiable reasons for delayed abortions—she herself would have terminated her third pregnancy in the second trimester, had she contracted German measles as her doctor had feared (at twenty weeks' gestation, the fetus tested clean of rubella and four months later Deb delivered a healthy daughter)—Deb found the sight of fetal parts that looked like baby parts too upsetting to offer her assistance during later procedures. "Reality hits," she admitted.

For doctors, the operation was the most taxing. In the early days of legalized abortion, second-trimester procedures had been performed by injecting a saline solution into the woman's abdomen, which would cause the woman to go into labor and expel the fetus. Although this procedure was easy for the doctor, it was painful for the woman, forcing her into what could be several days of labor only to deliver a dead baby, or worse, a live baby, which occasionally happened. Often, in addition, the women were prey to hospital nurses who didn't believe in abortion, who whispered in the women's ears at night, "God will punish you."

When the dilation and evacuation, or D&E, method became perfected enough to master later pregnancies, women were saved the horror of labor, delivery, and hostile nurses. The doctor, though, assumed the disturbing task of having to crush the fetal skull and bones with forceps, suction out the remains, and then arrange the limbs, backbone, and skull to make sure that the abortion was complete.

Preterm's Kate Horowitz didn't want to learn the skills necessary to perform second-trimester abortions. Occasionally, she became embroiled in evacuating a fourteen-week fetus in what she thought was a first-trimester abortion because the woman's first day of her last menstrual period (LMP) was earlier than remembered or she had missized the woman's uterus slightly during the pelvic exam. Each time, Kate hoped that she would never have to do another. The later the pregnancy, the softer the uterus, the greater chance of perforating the uterine wall with a dilator or cannula, a mistake Kate feared even during first-trimester procedures. Using the larger cannula, dilators, and hose needed to accommodate the larger pregnancy made Kate feel clumsy, more likely to puncture the uterus. She always made it through the surgery safely, but then she faced the grisly chore of sifting through the fetal parts, a job which frequently got to her even in late first-trimester abortions.

Staff reluctance to perform "seconds" wasn't much of a problem for Preterm since less than 6 percent of its 10,000 abortions each year were for pregnancies between thirteen and seventeen weeks, Preterm's cutoff point. Although Repro Associates offered abortions up to twenty-two weeks, Dr. Waldo Fielding, Preterm's medical director, felt that late second-trimester abortions should be performed in a hospital in case the woman needed a blood transfusion or emergency care: The later the pregnancy, the greater the risk of complications.

Although early second-trimester abortions were not significantly more risky than first trimesters, they were more painful, more expensive ($550 compared to $320), and more time-consuming. Second-trimester abortions at Preterm were a two-day affair. On Tuesdays, patients went through the preliminaries—admitting, medical screening, group and individual counseling—plus a final stop in a procedure room for laminaria insertion. In the early days of abortion, doctors had dilated a second-trimester patient's cervix with stainless steel rods, each one larger than the next, just as in a first-trimester abortion. But in a second trimester, the cervix must be opened significantly wider to accommodate the larger cannula. The wider the cervix opened, the more the uterus would contract, and the more pain the patient would feel. That agony ended with the advent of laminaria, slivers of seaweed which, after being inserted into the woman's cervix, expanded as they absorbed moisture, gently opening the cervical entrance to the point where the woman didn't need to be dilated the next day, just evacuated.

Waldo performed the clinic's four to six "second tris" scheduled each week on Wednesdays. At sixty-eight, he had performed so many later abortions that, to his own dismay, he had become immune to the sound of fetal limbs thumping against the glass jar into which they emptied from the evacuation machine's hose, and to arranging the fetal parts afterwards. "I don't sugarcoat it," he would say. "There is no question what I'm doing in a second trimester. I'm destroying potential life. But I feel the same way about a woman having a second as I do about a woman having a first-trimester abortion. She's the one who is important—the life that is, not the life that would be."

Doris Merrill and Waldo had worked together in Beth Israel's delivery room when she was a young nurse and he was a young obstetrician-gynecologist. The nurses loved him, Doris remembered, the tall doctor with the wavy hair who arrived in the delivery room on weekends wearing Bermuda shorts, reciting lines from movies, shuffling across the hospital floor as if he were on stage. In those days, doctors were God, the unquestionable authority, and Waldo enjoyed the adulation. Thirty years later, his days of private practice over and his medical skills used only at Preterm several mornings a week, Waldo still enjoyed professional respect, but was equally subject to teasing. "Did you just get your period?" Carolyn Wardell joked the time that she spotted blood, which had splattered on him during a procedure, on the crotch of his surgical scrubs. He crossed his legs in mock embarrassment.

Waldo had been startled in the summer of 1971 when Harry Levin approached him about serving as medical director of a womens' health-care clinic in Brookline that Levin said would offer abortions as soon as abortion became legal nationwide, which Levin felt would be soon. Although Waldo had performed therapeutic abortions at Boston hospitals, which required a psychiatrist's note claiming that the woman's mental and emotional health would be seriously threatened if she carried the pregnancy to term, he hardly thought of himself as an abortionist. He had just finished his book, *Pregnancy: The Best State of the Union*, a guide for women on what to expect from conception through delivery, and was enjoying a busy ob-gyn practice in Brookline.

His credentials were strong. A graduate of Dartmouth College and of the Dartmouth and University of Michigan medical schools, he was on the faculties of Harvard, Tufts, and Boston University medical schools, and was a senior visiting surgeon at Boston City Hospital. Waldo didn't need another job, but he was intrigued. Like Harry Levin, he believed that change in the abortion law was inevitable, and he wanted to be part of helping women get abortions under conditions that wouldn't relegate them to second-class citizens or endanger their lives. If Waldo Fielding had learned anything from twenty years in hospital emergency rooms, it was that there were no limits to what women would do to terminate an unwanted pregnancy.

The path that Doris Merrill, who was one of the four nurses who assisted Waldo with seconds on Wednesdays, took to Preterm was not as direct. After leaving Beth Israel's delivery room in 1960, she had worked as a civilian nurse at a U.S. Navy base in Bermuda, where her husband, Shelley, who was a musician, had a gig. When they returned to Massachusetts, Doris had worked as a nurse at Mount Ida Junior College in her hometown of Newton. After three years of dealing with college women's menstrual cramps and strep throats, though, she planted herself at home in 1973 to tend to her two young sons, not returning to work for another six years. Like Waldo, Doris hadn't thought about doing abortion work, but when a friend from nursing school said, "You must come to Preterm," she applied at the clinic and was hired. Doris liked the idea of working with people committed to providing medically safe abortions in a positive atmosphere. She also liked the idea of not having to work nights or weekends, as she would have had to do if she worked in a hospital. The hours were good— 7:15 A.M. till midafternoon—and she would learn new skills, such as how to perform a pelvic exam.

Preterm had been very good to Doris. During the last two years of Shelley's battle with brain cancer, when Doris was at home caring for her husband more often than she was at Preterm caring for patients, she never missed a paycheck. After his death, her work had become a haven from her empty home, a place where she felt useful and wanted.

Screening patients for their medical histories was both the most pleasant and the most difficult of Doris's nursing duties. When she helped patients in the recovery room, they were either too weepy, too crampy, or too much in a hurry to leave to converse at length, but in screening, they talked. With the procedure before them, many of the women wanted to air their feelings, to explain their situation, as if to justify why they were there. After providing their medical history, they talked about their ten-month-old daughter who still didn't sleep through the night, their lover's hair-trigger temper, their husband's alcoholism. They talked about drug addiction and abuse and forced sex. Those stories made Doris feel as if the abortion issue were divided into "them"—the protesters on the outside—and "us"—the patients and providers on the inside. "They" had never seen a patient with so many track marks from wrist to shoulder that there wasn't a clear spot to insert an IV. How dare "they" decide that that woman should be a mother?

Although Doris was as uncomfortable as her colleagues with second-trimester fetal remains, she felt that she was a professional with skills that she could offer to patients. She wouldn't end her own pregnancy after twelve weeks, if at all, but that was her choice, not the choice of other women. Only they knew their situation. Besides, in a "second," she had little contact with the POC. Her responsibility in "second tris" was to the woman, not to Waldo, who had a medical assistant to hand him utensils and face the abortion's aftermath. Doris inserted the IV catheter, started the IV fluids, and, if she had time before Waldo arrived, tried to calm the patient by pressing her thumb on the patient's forehead, asking the patient to put all of her feelings on the pressure point, to imagine that she was numb from the waist down. Usually the technique worked; the patient relaxed. During the procedure, Doris would offer her hand for the patient to squeeze, or if the abortion were particularly painful, a notepad for the patient to bite. Even with sedation, the cramps of a second-trimester procedure could be acute. Doris knew what Waldo was doing at the end of the examination table as he pored over the legs and ribs and hands, but she chose not to look.

It wasn't that Doris ignored the truth, but rather that her commitment was to the woman, not to the fetus. And a woman who delayed ending a pregnancy until the second trimester, she knew, had her own unique and very compelling reasons.

· · ·

Jenny Sampson twisted a piece of her frosted hair around one finger and stared out the window of Preterm's fourth-floor waiting room, wondering how everything had gotten so out of control. It was Wednesday, July 26, a perfect day for tanning at the beach or sipping margaritas at an outdoor café, not sitting in an abortion clinic with cramps that felt like her insides were being pulled out. Yesterday, the nurse who had inserted the laminaria had mentioned that Jenny might feel some discomfort as the tiny sticks of seaweed slowly expanded her cervical opening to make today's procedure easier, but the "discomfort" was so intense that Jenny had gone to bed at seven o'clock last night to try to sleep away the pain. The picketer outside Preterm yesterday morning had been right, Jenny thought, when he warned her that "they'll hurt you in there."

In her heart, though, Jenny knew that she couldn't blame the nurse, or Preterm, only herself. Jenny, who was twenty-two, rarely hesitated to make decisions. Headstrong, her mother called her. But the spring had been so hard, between getting laid off from her job at the hair salon and breaking up with her boyfriend Jim, that sometimes she felt too depressed to get out of bed.

Jenny hadn't realized that she was pregnant right away. Her period in April had been weird—sort of spotty—but it was still a period and she hadn't even considered that she might be pregnant. She and Jim had practiced withdrawal. Then May slipped by without a menses, then June. She had thought she was safe, though, because she didn't suffer from nausea, tender breasts, or any other pregnancy symptom. Jenny figured that the stress of the spring had jolted her menstrual cycle out of whack. So she continued to enjoy Alabama Slammers and Mudslides and didn't mention her fear to Jim, who was her ex-boyfriend by then.

Jim had been good to her when they'd first started dating a year ago. He had called her daily, taking her to dinner and clubs and parties. But once he had her affection, he became loud and abusive, yelling at her if she wasn't home when he called, accusing her of cheating on him. Easygoing by nature, Jenny had shrugged it off, reasoning that he was jealous and insecure. He simply needed love. And cash. An unemployed carpenter, Jim was always asking Jenny for money for beer, for drugs, for bail when he was arrested for disorderly conduct. And she gave it to him, thinking that this time he'd learn. If she gave him enough love and security, he'd change. He didn't, and in time she realized that she should walk away. Jenny was attractive in her own way, with deep blue eyes and a friendly smile set in an oval face. But feeling fat from chowing down too many potato chips in front of the TV during her unemployed days that spring, she worried that if she lost Jim, no one else would go out with her. Then Jim broke up with her in May, announcing that he already had another girlfriend.

Jenny's mother and friends were pleased; no one liked Jim. They thought he took advantage of Jenny. For a few weeks, Jenny hung out in her room at home, depressed and lonely, but then she landed the job at a hair salon in her hometown of Revere, just north of Boston, and she began to feel better, almost happy. Her pants had begun to feel a little snug, but she credited the potato chips, not pregnancy. Not until the end of June, when her jeans would barely zip, did she accept that something was wrong.

Please don't make me be pregnant, she had prayed as she dropped the home pregnancy test's dipstick into her urine.

Now, Jenny looked around the waiting room, focusing on the woman with the dark circles under her eyes who was crying quietly.

This woman had cried yesterday, too, as they both had waited for the laminaria insertion. Jenny hadn't cried yet today. She had her mother, who was a nurse, here to help her through. She glanced at her mother, who sat beside her absorbed in a *Good Housekeeping* magazine. Her mother had been so great about all of this, so understanding and supportive. If only Jenny had gone to her sooner.

Even after the home pregnancy test revealed what she had so long denied, Jenny couldn't decide what to do. She didn't tell anyone, not even her mother, who had dealt with an unwanted pregnancy of her own. When Jenny was a kid with three younger siblings, all of whom were still in diapers, her mother had become pregnant with a fifth child. Jenny's stepfather was dead set against abortion, but her mother knew that caring for the kids was her responsibility, not his, and that she couldn't handle a fifth child, physically or emotionally. The other children would suffer. After the abortion, Jenny's stepfather hadn't spoken to her mother for weeks.

In the days following the pregnancy test, Jenny felt all warm inside when she envisioned a little baby—something soft and snuggly that would love her and need her. But how would she afford a child? Her new hairstyling job was fun, but it paid only six dollars an hour, not nearly enough to pay for her own apartment, let alone a baby's medical bills and food. Jenny refused to go on welfare, which she thought of as "sponging off of the state." And who would care for the baby while Jenny worked? She couldn't pay for day care and her mother was consumed with her own job. What if the baby were deformed from all the drinking she had done in the past few months? She had read about fetal alcohol syndrome and the brain damage that too much drinking caused.

Even though she and Jim had split up, she still felt compelled to tell him she was pregnant. To her surprise, he wanted her to have the baby. "A baby will calm me down," he had told her. "It will show me responsibility." Sure, she said. If he wasn't responsible enough to hold down a job, how could he be responsible for a child? He hadn't mentioned getting back together, let alone getting married. Even if he had, she would have told him to take a hike. Since their breakup, she had gained enough distance from Jim to realize that he promised a lot but never followed through.

Adoption was out of the question. After spending nine months with this child growing inside her, she knew she would be too attached to it to give it up. If she did, she would spend the rest of her life wondering who was raising her child, what her child was like, if her child was happy, or if her child resented her for abandoning him or her. Jim was adopted and had said that the cruelest thing a woman could do was to give her child to someone else and that he had always felt unwanted and rejected.

Hoping that she'd miscarry or that she'd wake up and the pregnancy would be magically gone, Jenny let days pass, then weeks. When the Supreme Court issued its *Webster* ruling, Jenny became acutely aware of the news for the first time. Everywhere she turned abortion headlines screamed at her, one side trying to guilt-trip her into keeping the pregnancy, the other side shouting that she had a choice. It's now or never, she told herself one morning, and dialed Preterm's number, which she had discovered in the phone book.

Now, a young woman in green surgical scrubs called, "Jenny S.?" Introducing herself as the medical assistant, the young woman led Jenny into a small room with an examination table, an old-fashioned medical cabinet, and a sink. Jenny undressed from the waist down and climbed onto the examination table, biting her lip as she lay with her feet in the stirrups, her legs spread in the most vulnerable of positions. Worn out by the cramps, Jenny wondered if she had the energy to make it through this procedure. She wouldn't mind if she passed out in the middle; that way she'd avoid the wrenching pain she envisioned she would soon feel. Staring at the ceiling, Jenny lay as still as a stone, trying to concentrate on anything but her fear of what would happen to her in the next half hour.

Doris, who usually assisted the doctor in second-trimester abortions, was off that Wednesday, replaced by June, a tiny dark-skinned nurse with a wide smile and a no-nonsense bustle to her walk. "Hi," June greeted Jenny, and quickly set to work. Normally chatty, Jenny couldn't muster more than a "hi" in response. She flinched as June inserted into her left arm the IV catheter into which the medications and sedation would feed. The first injection would be sugar and water, "extra lunch," June explained. The next would be a combination of Valium and Sublimaze, which would relax her.

Jenny nodded, even though her muscles were so tight that it felt as if they would never relax again. A paper sheet lay between Jenny and the table, but still she felt the cold of its yellow vinyl cover. She listened to June's footsteps as the nurse padded around the room preparing the equipment for the procedure. As tense as a soldier expecting the first shot of enemy fire, Jenny waited for the doctor to open the door. Hang on, Jenny told herself. This will be over in fifteen minutes.

Funny, she had thought the same thing on her first visit here two

weeks ago. During medical screening, when the nurse had said "your uterus feels a little big" as her finger probed inside Jenny's vagina while her other hand pushed down on Jenny's belly, Jenny had known she was sunk. A doctor concurred with the nurse's suspicion of an advanced pregnancy and suggested that Jenny have an ultrasound, the test in which sound waves were bounced off the fetus to form its picture on a monitor. The ultrasound would tell them more exactly how pregnant Jenny was. Although Preterm had an ultrasound machine, it was an old model and none of the doctors working that day knew how to use it. Jenny was referred to another doctor in Brookline who performed ultrasounds regularly.

But just as Jenny had delayed calling Preterm, so she delayed calling the ultrasound doctor. She had, however, finally told her mother. She had had to. Jim had promised to give her the $320 fee for the abortion, but on the morning of her appointment he was nowhere to be found. Jenny had driven home from Jim's house in tears, collapsing in the arms of her mother, who hugged her and gave her the money. When she put off calling the ultrasound doctor, her mother had sat her down and asked if she were ready to be responsible for a child. Jenny had said no; she wanted to be married when she had kids, with enough money that she wouldn't have to worry about affording their Cheerios. Gathering her resolve, she had called the ultrasound doctor, but he had been booked and couldn't see her for yet another week.

Add up all those weeks and Jenny knew that she shouldn't have been surprised when she spied a head and legs and arms that moved on the ultrasound monitor. But she was stunned. She couldn't believe it looked like that, like a real baby. She asked her mother if the doctor tore the baby apart before he turned on the machine during an abortion. Her mother told her no, although she knew that dismemberment was standard procedure in later abortions. Why upset her daughter even more? "You have plenty of time to have children," her mother had said.

"Hello, Jenny, I'm Dr. Fielding," Waldo said as he marched in the door, glancing at her chart. "Any questions?" Jenny shook her head no. She looked quickly at the tall man with the white hair and white jacket, then returned her gaze to the ceiling. If she didn't look, maybe it wouldn't hurt.

The IV medication helped. Jenny felt so lightheaded that she barely felt Waldo remove the gauze which the nurse yesterday had placed over her cervix to ward off bacteria. The speculum felt cold inside her vagina, and she couldn't help but jump a little when Waldo tugged out the laminaria, which had swollen into a clump. June had told Jenny that her cramps were good; they indicated that the laminaria were doing their job and dilating her cervix, which meant that Jenny would be spared the painful process of Waldo dilating her with stainless steel rods. Jenny tried to smile, but couldn't. Her head buzzed from the medication, making it easy to ignore the activity at the end of the table.

"Now, you'll feel a little pinch as the doctor injects the anesthesia into your cervix," June said. Even the IV medication couldn't take the bite out of the lidocaine shot. Jenny winced. "Ouch," she cried when Waldo inserted the cannula. The uterine contractions made her gasp. It felt as if someone were twisting her insides tighter and tighter. God, the cramps. If they were this bad with sedation, what would they be like without it? She was trying to be a trouper, but the cramps, the cramps. Jenny pressed her hands against her stomach.

"It is easier if you keep your hands by your side," advised June. "Here, hold my hand."

Jenny gripped her hand so hard that June flinched.

"You'll hear the machine," Waldo warned, as he stepped on a pedal which turned on the suction. The machine's whir sounded just like a vacuum cleaner.

"Breathe," June instructed gently. "Deeply."

Jenny tried, but the pain ripped from her abdomen down through her vagina. Waldo continued probing her uterus with the cannula, ensuring that he was emptying it of all its contents. Immersed in her pain, trying to breathe, Jenny couldn't hear the thump of fetal parts passing from the hose into the glass jar. "Oh God, Oh God, Oh God," she said, turning her head from side to side.

"You're doing great," said June. "Count to five. One . . ."

"Twooo . . ." Jenny muttered.

"Three . . ." June coached.

"Four . . ." Jenny whispered, breathing heavily.

"Five."

Silence. Waldo removed from the glass jar the cheesecloth sack which caught the fetal parts, dumping the parts into a basin at the end of the table, between Jenny's feet. Two legs, two arms, two fists, a skull, a backbone, a placenta.

"We've got it," he announced.

Jenny, holding her stomach with both hands, whimpered. Waldo placed the fetal parts in a container to be sent to the laboratory for inspection as a medical assistant cleaned up. If the abortion were incomplete—if parts were missing—or the pregnancy harbored a disease such as cancer, the laboratory would contact Preterm, which, in turn, would contact the patient. Jenny rested, breathing deeply, trying not to cry. She felt woozy from the medication and slightly nauseous. She hoped she wouldn't throw up.

She had been nearly sixteen weeks pregnant, and now it was gone. Her insides felt hollow. She'd walked into this room full; now she was empty. She was relieved. She was sad. Her baby would never be. Jenny could have more children, as many as she wanted, Waldo had told her. The abortion had gone perfectly. After resting for a day or two and resisting baths and sex and anything that might risk infection for two weeks, she would be fine.

But she didn't feel fine. The cramps were still intense as her uterus contracted, shrinking to its prepregnancy size. June told her to breathe deeply and relax, that the pain would subside in a few minutes. Jenny closed her eyes and concentrated on filling her lungs with air. The cramps gradually faded.

"Are you ready to get dressed and go into the recovery room?" June asked.

Jenny wanted a few more minutes to rest. She closed her eyes again, her legs stretched out straight on the table beneath the white paper sheet that covered her, her hands folded across her belly. Waldo looked at June. "That," he said softly so that Jenny couldn't hear, "was an easy one."

•   •   •

Easy is a relative term. For Waldo, Jenny Sampson's abortion was easier than most because she had lain still, not thrashed in pain on the table as many patients did, which allowed Waldo to evacuate her pregnancy efficiently. For Jenny, the abortion wasn't easy at all. Instead, it was painful enough that she swore she would never relive the experience. She would take the Pill faithfully, and if, God forbid, contraception failed her, she would never, ever wait beyond eight weeks to end a pregnancy. She had learned her lesson about the power of denial, as did most women who had later abortions. In all of Waldo's professional years, he couldn't remember any woman who had had more than one second-trimester abortion.

The challenge, of course, was to prevent all abortions after the twelfth week, which Waldo, and Doris, and June, and anyone who worked in women's health care knew was an impossible goal. As long as there were women and men on this planet, there would be second-trimester abortions.

Women delay ending a pregnancy for a variety of reasons, but the vast majority—more than 70 percent, according to a study conducted by the Alan Guttmacher Institute—fail to realize that they are pregnant in the early stages. Some women with irregular menstrual cycles may not notice an absent period. Others, such as Jenny Sampson, have a false menses. They can easily ignore their suspicions if they don't suffer any other pregnancy symptoms, as many women don't. In a study Waldo conducted in 1978 for the American Journal of Obstetrics and Gynecology, one-fifth of the women interviewed said that they had denied their worst fear until the reality became too evident to ignore.

In no one is that power of denial as strong as it is in a teenager. One of the blessings of youth is feeling invulnerable, and teenagers, who compose nearly half of all women seeking second-trimester abortions, are likely to spend several weeks wishing that the pregnancy would mysteriously dissolve. By the time their bellies bulge—the point of no denial, or at least the point where others will notice—they are well into their second trimester.

Often, moreover, teenagers don't know their bodies well enough to read the pregnancy signals. Teens are likely to believe the myths, such as "you can't get pregnant the first time," or "you are safe if the boy doesn't penetrate." One Preterm patient, stunned to learn that she was fifteen weeks pregnant, had never had intercourse; she and her boyfriend had lain together naked without penetration but close enough to enable a determined sperm to reach its goal. In another scenario, a young woman whose pregnancy resulted from rape or incest may deny the possibility that she's pregnant. She may keep the condition a secret out of shame or fear of her perpetrator, who may be a relative.

Many pregnant teenagers, though, don't notice any symptoms to ignore. A missed menses or two, or even three, means little; teen periods may be irregular or haven't yet begun. The delay can be lengthened if the teenager has difficulty figuring out the logistics of how to get an abortion. Should she call a doctor, a hospital, or a clinic? If she can't tell her parents, where will she get the money for the abortion? If she can't drive, how will she get to the place where she'll have the abortion? Making the appointment is even more difficult for teenagers who live in one of the thirty-three states, including Massachusetts, that require pregnant minors seeking abortions to notify one or both of their parents or seek court consent. If she can't or won't tell her parents, the young woman must either maneuver her way through the court system to convince a judge that she is mature enough to make the decision, or she must find a way to get to a state where minors don't need a parent's approval for abortion.

Weeks pass as teenagers postpone telling their parents and as older women postpone telling their husbands or partners, fearing reprisal, scorn, or rejection. Weeks pass as rural women, or poor women from states where Medicaid doesn't subsidize abortions, make arrangements to travel to a city where abortions are available. As the number of abortion providers dwindled—the Alan Guttmacher Institute found that between 1985 and 1988 the number of providers in rural areas in the U.S. dropped by 19 percent—it seemed logical to assume that even more women would be delayed in seeking help.

Some of the most difficult second-trimester cases Preterm counselors faced involved women who wanted the pregnancy, but whose plans were changed by tragedy. One woman's husband had just died. Grief-stricken and with five children at home, she didn't have the energy or the income to care for a sixth. Another woman's much-wanted fetus was found to have its organs on the outside of its body. For other women, the pregnancy worsened existing medical conditions such as cancer or heart disease. Pregnancy had caused migraine headaches so severe for one Preterm patient that she spent her first three months in her bedroom with the curtains drawn, paralyzed by pain. Hoping the agony would end soon, she continued the pregnancy until her doctor told her that the migraines would accompany her through the entire nine months. Crying uncontrollably, she entered Preterm, sixteen weeks pregnant.

Ironically, at Preterm, the medical staffers who saw the result of a woman's delay didn't know the reasons for it. The women explained their decision to Preterm counselors in private sessions, not to the medical assistants, nurses, and doctors. To Doris Merrill, the reason didn't matter. One week slipped quickly into the next, and whether the pregnant woman was a thirteen-year-old who didn't know she was pregnant or a thirty-three-year-old who had spent weeks asking friends for money for the procedure, Doris's attitude was the same: This woman knows her circumstance better than anyone else. Only she can determine if she is ready to be a mother.

•   •   •

The Supreme Court's *Webster* decision helped rivet the nation's attention on late-term abortions by its support of the Missouri law's requirement that doctors must perform fetal viability tests on women whom they suspected were twenty weeks or more pregnant. Although medical science claimed that twenty-four weeks was the earliest a fetus could possibly survive outside of the womb, the Missouri law allowed for a wide margin of error. Had Jenny Sampson been living in Missouri that summer and had delayed her decision for another three or four weeks, she would have been subject to an expensive and sometimes risky procedure called amniocentesis, the only test capable of determining fetal lung maturity. Had she been unable to raise the money for the test—which involves fluid being withdrawn from the woman's amniotic sac—she would have been forced to carry the pregnancy to term. Even if she had the test and it had proved that she carried an unviable fetus, by the time the results arrived, she would be in her twenty-fifth or twenty-sixth week of pregnancy and carrying a potentially viable fetus. Under *Roe* v. *Wade*, she would be unable to receive an abortion that late in her pregnancy unless her health or life were in jeopardy.

The irony of the late-trimester debate was that so few abortions were performed after the twelfth week; only 9 percent of all abortions nationwide were performed between thirteen and nineteen weeks of pregnancy, and fewer than 1 percent were performed after twenty weeks, of which the overwhelming majority were requested because of grave fetal deformity or because the fetus carried a fatal disease such as Tay-Sachs.

Nevertheless, *Webster* presented a very real threat to those women who did need an abortion after the first trimester, and prochoice groups across the country began drafting legislation to combat the possibility of a Missouri-like law being passed in their own state. In Massachusetts, a committee of the Coalition for Choice consulted with doctors, lawyers, clergy, health-care providers, and women's groups to determine the most appropriate wording for an amendment to the state's constitution which would protect the right to abortion in case the Supreme Court eventually overturned *Roe* v. *Wade*. The thinking was that if the fundamental right to reproductive freedom were written into the constitution, the right to choose abortion and birth control would be safe in future elections, and money and energy could be directed to other problems, such as preventing unwanted pregnancy and reducing infant mortality.

After weeks of meetings, however, the coalition's committee was still wrangling about the amendment's specific language. In order to meet the midsummer deadline for filing amendments intended for the 1992 ballot (the next year the public would vote on constitutional amendments), the committee filed seven proposals, each containing a different combination of rights. One protected a woman's right to choose and refuse birth control (a *Webster*-like statute could outlaw certain birth-control pills and the IUD) and public funding of abortion, but it didn't protect a minor's access to abortion. Another protected minors but not unrestricted choice of birth control. The biggest controversy, though, centered on whether the right to abortion should be protected through the entire pregnancy. Three proposals set the gestational limit at twenty-four weeks, one set it at viability, and three set no gestational limit. Four said that abortion should be allowed in the third trimester to save the life and health of the mother; three allowed third-trimester abortions in cases of rape and incest. To narrow down the amendment's focus, the coalition called a meeting of all of its members.

The meeting was held in a windowless conference room on the fourth floor of One Lincoln Plaza, an office building in downtown Boston. The evening was muggy, a fitting end to the hot and hazy summer day that preceded it. Outside, the air was so still you could smell the fumes from cars shooting down the nearby Southeast Expressway. Inside, the air conditioner struggled without success to blow a cool breeze through the conference room. The forty-eight women and three men who surrounded the conference table fanned themselves with copies of the seven proposed amendments. Not all of the seventy prochoice organizations which comprised the coalition had sent representatives, but Fran, Preterm's delegate, was impressed with the turn-out. She wondered if the oppressive air would defuse the debate.

Unlike the antiabortionists who shared one goal—abolishing abortion—those who called themselves prochoice held differing views on the definition of abortion rights. All of those views were represented in this stuffy conference room. On one end of the spectrum were those who believed that abortion was a woman's perogative throughout all nine months: that she was not a walking incubator; that there were always situations in which late abortions were morally justified. On the other end were those who were disturbed by the idea of abortion after the twelfth week and sought restrictions. Members of the League of Women Voters, dressed in plaid skirts and cotton blouses, sat at the end of the conference table across from members of the Gay and Lesbian Alliance with their T-shirts and sandals. Women from political groups such as Mass Choice and the American Civil Liberties Union arrived in their business suits and Nikes. Fran opted to sit in the middle of the table next to Leslie Loveless, a Planned Parenthood spokeswoman.

Fran wasn't sure if she were in favor of proposing any amendment at

all. She was doubtful that any language could encompass such a difficult issue. Carolyn had said earlier that day that she thought the
amendment was a waste of time, that the prochoice forces should
concentrate on electing politicians who support abortion rights. Carolyn had considered attending the meeting, but, believing that her
responsibilities to her daughter preempted her responsibilities to Preterm after 5 P.M., she had decided to stay at home that night and let
Fran do the talking.

The discussion began calmly. Nicki Nichols Gamble, director of the
Planned Parenthood League of Massachusetts (PPLM) and chairman of
the Coalition for Choice, introduced the seven amendments. Susan
Newsom, Planned Parenthood's public relations director, reported that
72 percent to 74 percent of the people polled in a recent PPLM survey
were in favor of an amendment protecting a woman's right to reproductive freedom. The question, of course, was the amendment's language.
Should it satisfy the prochoice element or the voting public?

"You won't pass an unrestricted abortion law in western Massachusetts," said a member of the League of Women Voters from Spring-
field, a western Massachusetts city. "Think of the campaign the
antiabortionists will run against us. They'll show those fetus pictures
with arms and legs . . ."

"The antis always show those fetal soup pictures," interrupted a
woman from Boston NOW, who regularly stood guard against Operation Rescue in front of Preterm on Saturdays. The "fetal soup" pictures
were posters of piles of fully formed fetuses in garbage bags.

"We have to fight for what we want. You should always go in with the
strongest position, not the weakest," chimed another Boston NOW
representative.

But the strongest position will offend the "mushy middle," the vast
majority of voters who are uncomfortable with late-trimester abortions, protested the woman from League of Women Voters. If you lose
the mushy middle, you lose the vote.

"It is better to do nothing than lose," echoed Jamie Sabino, a Boston
lawyer. A large woman with waist-length brown hair, Jamie was considered brilliant among the prochoice brigade, a true leader, and a voice
of reason. She had been primarily responsible for battling the judges
and legislators in complicated cases involving minors and parental
consent, and she had always won. But her conciliatory presence didn't
calm the debate. The coalition couldn't risk proposing a watered-down
amendment just to please the voters, said a member of the Reproductive Rights Network. The amendment will shape the prochoice move-

ment; therefore it must stand for protecting all women throughout the entire pregnancy.

"We're talking *lives!*" a voice boomed from the back.

Fran felt as if she were watching a tennis match as she turned her head from side to side, from speaker to speaker. Sometimes the debate sounded like a competition of who was the best feminist, the strongest advocate of a woman's right to choose. In a time of war the troops should unite, not splinter, Fran thought. The prochoice forces needed to unify against the antis, not separate. But Fran sensed that there would be no agreement tonight. Each member and organization had its own agenda. Compromise seemed as impossible between the prochoice factions as it was with the antis.

The president of the statewide chapter of NOW said that her organization's philosophy was based on a woman's right to choose, which meant that the amendment should protect women, not fetuses, at all stages of pregnancy. The president of the Religious Coalition for Abortion Rights (RCAR) said that her organization would hesitate to approve an amendment for unrestricted abortions; RCAR believed in a woman's right to choose but that the more mature the fetus, the more valuable it became. The president of Mass Choice, the only statewide organization focused on abortion alone, posed the option of no amendment at all.

Fran sat silent. She didn't know what to say. In theory, she believed in a woman's unrestricted right to end a pregnancy. In reality, she knew what a sixteen-week aborted fetus looked like and was horrified at the thought of aborting a twenty-six, twenty-seven, or thirty-week fetus. Fetuses that mature had a good chance of surviving on their own. Preterm's secretary knew of a healthy and happy two-year-old in her church who had been born at twenty-four weeks. That morning, Carolyn had wondered aloud why women pregnant from rape and incest should be allowed to have an abortion at thirty-three weeks if other women couldn't. The women may have been so traumatized that they didn't have the emotional strength to have an abortion early in the pregnancy, or they may have been too ashamed, angry, or victimized to admit the violation. But, Carolyn said, at some point—after viability—the fetus did have rights. Fran agreed, but she—who had left newspaper reporting after two years because as the objective observer she wasn't free to voice her opinions—didn't share her thoughts with the others at this conference table. She saw no perfect combination of requirements in the proposed amendments. Most of all, she saw no understanding of abortion's complexities.

"Who frames this argument: us or the opposition?" snapped Ellen Convisser of Boston NOW, stepping into the debate. "It is divisive to make a cutoff at twenty-four weeks. Boston NOW won't support anything that is not unrestrictive."

These people are political activists, Fran thought. Their work was critical to protecting abortion rights, but how many of them knew the reality of abortion, had seen the reality of what it destroyed? Fran felt like standing up and saying to those arguing for unrestricted abortions, "You haven't seen the little feet. They look just like the little feet push-pins the antis wear." As a provider at Repro once said, if half the prochoice people saw the fetal remains of a second-trimester abortion, they would jump the fence into the antis' arms. But none, it seemed, had seen a later procedure. To them, a six-week zygote was the same as a twenty-two week, twelve-inch, thumb-sucking fetus with hair and eyebrows and fingernails and fat deposits.

Fran's head began to ache and her legs were so hot they stuck to the chair. The Coke she sipped didn't cool her off. Fanning herself with the pages of amendment proposals, she wished that the meeting would come to a close.

The debate might have raged until the next morning if not for the fact that the building closed at 10 P.M. At 9:30 P.M., two hours after the discussion had begun, the only thing that the members had been able to agree on was that they needed to show a united front to the public. With their list of amendments before them, they decided to vote on which proposal, or proposals, they found acceptable. Fran placed her hands in her lap.

An amendment without any restrictions? No, she thought. I can't approve that in good conscience, and neither would the voting public. Twenty-six coalition members, though, could. No amendment at all? The meeting had convinced Fran that an amendment was a good idea, not as the be-all and end-all of prochoice efforts, but as insurance: one step in the war to preserve reproductive rights. Fourteen others around the conference table disagreed. An amendment with a twenty-four-week restriction? Reluctantly, Fran raised her hand, and was joined by ten other hands. In a sense, she felt as if she were contradicting her belief in a woman's right to choose, but she knew too well what late abortions destroyed to be able to sanction them.

Although the majority of the room had voted against restrictions in the amendment, the debate had been too divided and too spirited for the coalition members to feel that they had reached a consensus. The next step was for the coalition's steering committee to meet and, taking the evening's discussion into consideration, try to arrive at one amendment, if any.

The meeting over, the activists collected their empty Diet Sprite and Diet Coke cans and filed out into the night. It was 9:45 P.M. and the air was still choked with car exhaust fumes. Fran drove home confused.

"How dare they?" seethed Carolyn the next day when Fran told her about the arguments for unrestricted abortion. "They blast the antis for their all-or-nothing attitude, but they share the same trait."

Several weeks later, the coalition announced that it had settled on a specific amendment, one which would protect a woman's right to abortion in the first twenty-four weeks of pregnancy or at any time to safeguard her life or health or in case of rape or incest. Members of NOW were disappointed in restricting the right to the first two trimesters. Carolyn could only shake her head at the reaction.

"The problem with radical political activists," said Carolyn, "is that they don't feel. They don't see the shades of gray."

CHAPTER SEVEN

In *Webster's* Wake

S ERGEANT Bill McDermott smirked as one of Bill Cotter's sidewalk counselors raced up to a tall black woman—over six feet, McDermott guessed—strutting toward the side streets behind Gynecare in downtown Boston. Her frizzy black wig and bright red lips didn't fool the detective; he'd spotted the Adam's apple and hands the size of catcher's mitts. McDermott knew a drag queen when he saw one. The sidewalk counselor, apparently, did not.

"Please don't kill your baby," pleaded the counselor, a blond-haired woman in pink pants, her hands clutching rosary beads and dozens of pamphlets.

"Whaatttt???" bellowed a deep voice from under the wig.

"Abortion isn't the only option," the counselor continued breathlessly, holding out a pamphlet. "We have money, and shelter, and . . ."

"Git away from me!!!" the hooker snapped, recoiling from the pamphlet the woman gripped. The counselor retreated, letting her subject continue to sashay past the mob at Gynecare and down an alley, disappearing into the bowels of Boston's tenderloin.

The detective chuckled. It was a little after seven o'clock on this cloudy Saturday morning in late July, an hour when Tremont Street usually belonged to the hookers from the nearby Combat Zone, Boston's fading red-light district, looking for one last trick of the night. But the crowd of abortion foes clustered in front of the building that housed

Gynecare had usurped their turf, and the working girls in their Spandex miniskirts, tube tops, and high heels were forced to cross the street. In twos and threes, they migrated over to Boston Common, the city's center green, and stood not far from where Bill McDermott had stationed himself to watch Operation Rescue at work.

McDermott figured that about 300 people had filed into St. James Church in Stoughton, a suburb about twenty minutes south of Boston, earlier this morning. But he estimated that only 200, if that, were planted in front of 177 Tremont Street now. Where were the others? Still riding the subway? Traveling by car? Were they headed here for a second wave, or to another clinic for a surprise attack?

So far, this rescue was typical: Half the abortion foes clogged the building's doorway while the other half stood on the sidewalk singing, ignoring the growing ranks of prochoice counterdemonstrators arranging their "KEEP ABORTION LEGAL" signs only feet away. Hardly the unique maneuver McDermott had anticipated Operation Rescue would attempt for its first blockade since the *Webster* ruling three weeks before. The detective had thought that Darroline and Cotter, heady with the boost from the Supreme Court, would storm the clinic and smash equipment, drop a slab of concrete in front of the entrance, or do something similarly dramatic. McDermott had wondered if they would emulate the rescue in West Hartford, Connecticut, in June, at which 800 abortion foes from around New England and New York had descended on the Summit Women's Center. Two hundred protesters had charged inside, jamming elevators, pouring maple syrup on equipment, and smashing raw eggs on surgical utensils. Outside, one group of demonstrators had blocked the building's entrance while another group stood in the parking lot singing and praying. Two hundred and sixty-one had been arrested, including Cotter, who had blocked a stairwell. Prepared to stay in jail indefinitely, Cotter, along with almost 100 others, had refused to give his name. Only when he learned that his mother was in the hospital suffering from complications after heart surgery did he volunteer his identification, which allowed him to go free.

Since the Court handed down its *Webster* decision, McDermott had found Cotter rejuvenated, almost perky. One morning in front of Preterm, he had greeted McDermott with a "Hi ya, Sergeant," and a spring in his step. He's a new man, McDermott thought, immediately suspicious of the agenda lurking behind Cotter's good humor. After all, at a press conference hours after the *Webster* decision was handed down, Cotter had warned that Operation Rescue demonstrations would escalate.

Darroline, too, had seemed extra ebullient. Although Rescue's leaders expected police presence at Rescue events, they rarely did more than nod at the detectives. At the pre-rescue rally at St. James Church two nights ago, however, Darroline had chatted amiably with McDermott in the parking lot about her plans to adopt a three-year-old black child. She had even given the detective a copy of the latest Operation Rescue video produced by Rescue's leader Randall Terry. Sandwiched in between shots of bloody fetal limbs and interviews with antiabortion leaders such as Bishop Austin Vaughan of New York and the Reverend Jerry Falwell of the Moral Majority, was a frame of Darroline, nodding her head and saying that saving babies "is what it's all about." McDermott wondered if Darroline thought that she could woo him into supporting her movement, or at least into allowing her people to close down a Brookline clinic for an hour or so. Whatever, it seemed to McDermott that the Supreme Court's decision had added an extra gleam in Darroline's eyes.

In contrast, some of McDermott's antiabortion sources had seemed complacent in *Webster*'s aftermath, claiming that since the Court had responded to their message, they could now swing golf clubs on Saturday mornings instead of kneeling in front of an abortion clinic. But those people were the soft cores, the ones who didn't like to get arrested but who felt a religious obligation to stop what they considered murder. They were good people who paid their taxes and made sure their kids finished their homework. They weren't the Darrolines and Cotters. They weren't the ones to watch.

Fearing the worst, McDermott had geared up for a 500-person rescue today, recommending full protection for Brookline clinics. A tall order, he knew, since much of the police force either was on vacation or had other summer weekend plans. Fortunately, Repro had announced that it would close for the day to avoid the hassle of a rescue, and the state police had agreed to guard Planned Parenthood. That meant that the Brookline cops could concentrate on Preterm. By 6:30 that Saturday morning, twenty officers stood in front of 1842 Beacon Street inside the square corral they had built of metal barricades. Sipping coffee, the cops waited for McDermott, who trailed the abortion foes, to call them with orders to prepare for an attack or to go home—preferably the latter.

McDermott was as weary of Operation Rescue as the rest of the force, probably more so; he had assumed all Rescue responsibility since his partner, George Driscoll, had traded his detective's badge for a briefcase last month when he became Brookline's assistant town coun-

sel. Now McDermott was the one the clinics called when Bill Cotter
looked particularly suspicious, as if he were ready to invade, during his
early morning pickets, or if picketers wandered too near the clinic
entrance. McDermott was the one who spent his mornings cruising
Beacon Street to check on clinic activity and his evenings chatting with
his antiabortion sources at local coffee shops. The beat might have been
more interesting if he could have developed some kind of relationship
with Cotter, but every time he tried to nudge Cotter into spilling his
plans, Cotter repeated laconically, "I can't tell you that, Sergeant."

Without any clue to Cotter's interests or hobbies outside of Rescue,
McDermott had a lot of fun imagining Cotter's secret life. One morning
driving down Beacon Street with George Driscoll several months back,
the two detectives had painted a scenario of Cotter as a closet drag
queen, a guy who traveled to Times Square on weekends to prance
around in garters and hose, slathered in hot mustard. As they pulled up
in front of Preterm, Cotter, his rosary beads dangling from his coat
pocket, waved to them. They laughed so hard they rocked the cruiser.

But Cotter wasn't waving to McDermott this morning. In fact, he
and Darroline had begun to peel people away from the rescue, sending
them down Avery Street to the left of Gynecare. Dressed in their battle
gear—worn blue jeans and faded shirts—the two Rescue leaders
looked grim as they stood on the sidelines barking orders. Constance
Smith, Rescue's third leader, was absent. McDermott had heard that
the former nun had left the country to live in England as a nanny. He
wondered if she feared the consequences of Brookline's federal lawsuit
against Rescue. Constance was one of the people charged with racketeering in the RICO suit. If she were found guilty, she would be
required to help pay Brookline the $75,000 the town demanded in
restitution for the costs of the early rescues. Bill Cotter and Darroline
Firlit were also named in the suit, but both had claimed that the
litigation wouldn't dampen their crusade. Darroline had ripped up
the documents naming her in the suit within seconds after receiving the
papers in the Brookline police station on the afternoon of April 29—as
she began her jail time for participating in that morning's rescue at
Preterm. Cotter had said that his activities wouldn't change, that if he
and his movement buckled under the lawsuit, Rescue would die.

McDermott's eyes narrowed now as he watched Darroline and Bill
talking intensely, their heads close together. Something was up. Perhaps he hadn't been too cautious in preparing for a huge rescue today.
Perhaps the 200 people in front of Gynecare were a decoy and Cotter
had 400 more stashed away elsewhere. McDermott didn't think so, but

you never knew. The detective crossed Tremont Street and ambled over to the two leaders. "What's going on?" McDermott asked innocently.

"Don't say anything," McDermott heard Cotter whisper to Darroline. Then, nodding to McDermott, Cotter said loudly, "Let's go for coffee."

Sure, McDermott thought. Go for coffee and leave this rescue? Not these two.

Without so much as a look at McDermott, Darroline nodded and followed Bill down Avery Street. McDermott gave them a few feet before he began shadowing them. Walking briskly, they turned, saw the detective, and broke into a gallop. Jogging left on Washington Street, which ran parallel to Tremont, and up another side street, they disappeared into a subway station, not far behind the pack of rescuers that they had herded away from Gynecare.

They're headed for Brookline, McDermott decided. He returned to his unmarked cruiser and radioed Frank Hayes, the captain of the Brookline detectives, to prepare Planned Parenthood and Preterm for an assault. The early morning clouds had given way to hazy sunshine and the temperature and humidity had crept up to shirt-soaking levels. Driving down Beacon Street toward the clinics, McDermott hoped that the Brookline cops had remembered to bring a lot of water and towels to the clinics; this would be a hot one.

McDermott had driven almost to Coolidge Corner when a Brookline lieutenant radioed that he had spotted a Budget Rent-A-Truck parked suspiciously alone on a side street one block up from Planned Parenthood. Would that truck transport rescuers to another clinic? the detective wondered as he pulled a U-turn and screamed back down Beacon Street. McDermott arrived at the truck just in time to see Darroline and Cotter load fifty people into the enclosed back, like generals ordering paratroopers into a plane. They yanked down the rear door, leaving it open a crack for ventilation, and then bolted to the front cab where the driver, a heavy-set man with a bushy black beard, switched on the ignition.

Great, McDermott thought, as he watched the truck pull away from the curb. The back door will fly open, everyone will fall out, and we'll have a human tragedy on Beacon Street.

He thought of pulling the truck over and charging Darroline and Bill with endangering lives. But if he stopped the truck, some of the people could hop out and form a line crossing the street, as other rescuers had done around the country: While the police struggled to get the people out of the street, the truck roared away, taking with it enough protesters to attack a clinic. McDermott decided to follow instead.

Down Beacon Street to Kenmore Square. A U-turn onto Commonwealth Avenue, which led either to Brookline or the Allston-Brighton section of Boston, home of the Crittendon Hastings House. Crittendon—which offered abortions along with a multitude of other services, including a residential program for homeless pregnant women—was a strong candidate for a rescue. It hadn't been hit since February when nine rescuers, including Darroline, had sneaked inside and locked themselves together by the neck in one of Crittendon's procedure rooms. For six hours they lay there in their winter coats in eighty-degree heat—Crittendon staffers had turned up the thermostat and shut the door—before they finally relinquished the keys to the locks.

But the truck passed the Allston-Brighton turnoff. When it turned left on Chiswick Road, which led to Cleveland Circle, three blocks from Preterm, McDermott knew where they were headed.

The plan, McDermott pieced together later, was to launch a surprise attack on either Preterm or Planned Parenthood. The state troopers in front of Planned Parenthood were too intimidating, but Cotter and Darroline had learned from one of their scouts cruising Beacon Street that the cops in front of Preterm were sitting on the steps, flipping through *The Boston Herald*. While the police lounged in front, the rescuers planned to race inside Preterm from the back.

But by the time the truck bumped into place behind Preterm, McDermott had already ordered the police to lock the doors and stand alert. The charging abortion foes stood on the back stairs, lost, with nothing to do but sing and wait for their leaders to issue further directions. Their leaders, though, were busy.

"You stupid bastards," McDermott yelled at Darroline and Cotter, shaking his finger in their faces. "If anyone had gotten hurt, or died from falling out of that truck, I'd hold you two responsible. No seatbelts, no safety precautions. The back door wasn't even locked . . ."

Cotter and Darroline looked at the ground, stunned by the verbal assault. As soon as Captain Hayes arrived to calm McDermott down, they fled.

"I thought he was our friend," McDermott overheard Cotter say to Darroline.

Friend? McDermott thought.

"To the front!" Darroline ordered the handful of rescuers standing on the back stairs.

No sooner had Cotter started to sit down among the pool of bodies jammed in front of the barricade, than he was handcuffed and hauled off. Darroline was next. The first row of the thirty or forty people sitting on the sidewalk tried to crawl under the cops' legs. The cops pushed them back. More protesters crept forward. And the cops pushed them back. The dance had begun. Police patience, though, was short. Within minutes, the crawling protesters were dragged off to the side, handcuffs slapped on their wrists.

More than 100 prochoice demonstrators had gathered at Preterm by six o'clock this morning, just as prochoice demonstrators had gathered at the other area clinics. The plan was that most of them would race to the targeted clinic once Operation Rescue landed, while a skeletal force would remain at the other clinics just in case Rescue tried a "double-header." When Darroline and Bill arrived at Preterm, only fifty or so prochoice activists remained. Within minutes, though, several pro-choice demonstrators had raced to nearby pay phones to call more recruits. Fifteen minutes later, their numbers had doubled. Thirty minutes later, the number had tripled. By that time, Gynecare's block-ade was over and all of the prochoice support had moved to Preterm. By eleven o'clock, less than forty-five minutes after the Budget Rent-A-Truck had pulled into Preterm, more than 300 abortion rights activists massed on the sidewalk in front of 1842 Beacon Street.

"Hey, hey, ho, ho, Operation Rescue's got to go!" they chanted.

"All we are saying, is give life a chance," the handful of prayer supporters sang, altering the words to John Lennon's "Give Peace a Chance."

"Hey!" a woman with gray curly hair shouted from the prochoice crowd. "That's *our* song!"

In retaliation, the prochoicers began to sing their version of "Row, Row, Row Your Boat":

"*Roe, Roe, Roe* v. *Wade*, we will never quit . . . Operation Rescue, you don't scare us a bit."

"I love you Lord!" the prayer supporters sang in response.

The cacophony was deafening, rising with each minute as each side tried to outchant the other.

"Blah, blah, blah," the clinic escorts crowed, trying to drown out the opposition's singing.

"They'll make Hamburger Helper out of your insides in there!!" yelled one of Rescue's sidewalk counselors to a patient.

The barricades already being in place combined with the quick arrests had allowed the police to create a safe corridor through the crowd for patients. Easy access, though, seemed of little comfort to the women seeking Preterm's abortion services this morning. Clutching their partners or their parents, encircled by clinic escorts, patients bowed their heads, hiding tears and identity, visibly cringing at the cheer that roared from the prochoice faction as they crossed the threshold into the clinic. McDermott feared that an angry boyfriend would punch one of the sidewalk counselors in the mouth. Violence was only a heartbeat away at these demonstrations; it was just a matter of time before someone would get hurt.

But both sides were stunned into momentary silence when the Massachusetts state troopers goose-stepped off their bus. Backs ruler-straight, faces grim, the troopers surrounded the barricade, replacing the snake of prochoicers who had linked arms around the steel barriers to create their own human fortress. In their pressed uniforms and broad-brimmed hats, the state policemen stood rooted in place, arms crossed, eyes staring straight ahead. It was as if the cavalry had arrived. The Brookline police were now free to clear out the last of the blockaders.

The state troopers' effect was immediate. Less than an hour after it had begun, this rescue was, as far as McDermott was concerned, over. By 11:15 A.M., the blockaders were en route to the police station, the handful of remaining prayer supporters were cordoned off in a pen of barricades, and the prochoice roar had settled down to a hum. The only matter left to attend to was Scout.

Scout was the code name of a round fellow with red hair who had secured himself by the neck with two Kryptonite locks to the driveshaft of the state police bus. Lying face-up on the ground, he stared at the undercarriage, praying along with a woman who sat cross-legged on the ground next to the bus. "And though I wander through the valley of death . . ." they mumbled.

"I'm down here to save babies," Scout told reporters and photographers who knelt next to the bus, notebooks and cameras in hand. "I will stay here until I'm told to leave by my leaders." He said he hadn't eaten since yesterday morning and had drunk very little to prepare for this venture. He would not hesitate, he added, to relieve himself there underneath the bus if he had to.

"I hate to tell you this," said Captain Hayes, leaning down under the bus to face the protester. "But we're not even going to try and get you out. The state police don't need this bus until Monday, so you can stay here all weekend."

Two state troopers, standing guard by the bus, suppressed smiles.

"Charlie has the key," Scout said quickly. "Tell her."

"Charlie" was Darroline's code name, which she had assumed while sitting in the Atlanta jails for blockading clinics during the Democratic National Convention the summer before. Anonymity was critical if the abortion foes were to prolong their jail sentences and achieve their mission of congesting the courts and prisons.

"I guess you'll have to stay there," said Captain Hayes after returning from a chat with Darroline, who had been bused to the police station. Darroline would not give up the key.

Scout returned to his prayers. A Brookline policeman crawled underneath the bus to remove the driveshaft, which he succeeded in doing an hour later, dragging Scout and his two locks out with the piece of undercarriage. Scout waved to reporters as he was led to the waiting police car.

So this is it, McDermott thought. The wave of the future. Surprise tactics. Psychological warfare. Cause a commotion at one clinic long enough to catch the police off-guard at another. Had Rescue's plan worked, Brookline police would have been unlocking protesters from Preterm's radiators and evacuation machines until Sunday night. But it hadn't, and McDermott relished the satisfaction of foiling their plans, once again. Shortly before noon, the detective hopped in his car and headed to the police station. So, he thought en route down Beacon Street, the Supreme Court's decision hadn't done much for Rescue after all. Darroline and Bill hadn't recruited enough people for a 300-person blockade, let alone the 500-person one McDermott had anticipated. McDermott guessed that the minions felt that the Supreme Court had done their work for them and weekends were once again for barbecues and naps.

Minutes later, after the last patient had entered Preterm, the state troopers had left, and the prochoice supporters had begun to pack their signs into their vans, the remaining twenty-five antis formed a circle to conduct their final prayer, a tradition at the end of every Saturday demonstration. But instead of congregating to the side of the clinic as they usually did, the group stood smack in front of the clinic stairs. One by one the police inched forward, forming a circle of their own around the protesters.

"How great thou art . . ." the antis sang—and then lunged toward Preterm's front door.

Half ran, half dropped on their knees and crawled. In the chaos, one rescuer punched Jeffrey Allen, the chairman of the Brookline Board of Selectmen, who had been chatting with police at the bottom of the stairs. Another grabbed the ankles of a staffer who had been standing on the steps. Carolyn Wardell, who was perched on the stairs to watch the end-of-the-day prayer, shrieked and bolted inside, clutching her chest.

The police grabbed shoulders, arms—anything of the protesters they could hold onto. Within seconds, the aggressors were corralled. Those who put up the stiffest fight were arrested. The others were pushed back to Beacon Street, where they knelt at the curb. Dusting himself off, Jeffrey Allen, an athletic man in his late thirties with a face so round that McDermott had accused him of having had his cheeks plumped up by surgery so that all the Jewish mothers in Brookline would pat his face, assured the police he was fine.

"Let's go," Captain Hayes, whose tooth had been chipped in the scuffle, instructed his men. "If we leave, they'll leave."

The twenty cops walked down the sidewalk and out of sight around the building. The handful of remaining rescuers trotted over to the stairs and sat down. Since an invasion was impossible because the front door was locked, they began to sing. "We exalt thee . . ." Seven minutes later, they stood up and returned to the sidewalk, where they chatted and laughed and sipped soda that someone had brought in a cooler.

"We believe the clinic is closed," hollered a red-haired pregnant woman, the assigned leader after Cotter and Darroline were arrested. "Although women are still in there having their children killed, block-ading is no longer useful. What would be more useful is to go to the Brookline police station to sing and pray for our brothers and sisters in jail."

They left, and Captain Hayes and his men emerged from around the side of the building. The plan had worked. All of the police, except for the two detail men who would stay on duty until 2 P.M., left.

A total of thirty-one rescuers were arrested in Brookline and thirty-six in Boston that day. Back at the police station, McDermott watched the arresting process, identifying the rescuers who refused to give their names, a refusal which meant that they would stay in the downstairs cell block for the weekend. Cotter encouraged the sacrifice. Those who gave their names and paid fifteen dollars were released, which Cotter discouraged.

The group was desperate, McDermott thought, when he heard about the antis' last-minute attack. Desperate and frustrated. And well they should be. The Brookline police had thwarted Rescue's most elaborate plan so far. Cotter and Darroline had spent money for the truck and probably hours, even days, plotting the rescue's intricacies.

Rescue's two leaders would be bonkers, McDermott thought. Darroline and Billy C. needed a win to attract more people to their cause, yet all they had earned was another defeat.

But Cotter was cunning, Darroline was bold, and there would always be the "Scouts" to lock themselves to driveshafts. The police may have won this battle, but the war was far from over. Exhausted, McDermott grabbed his car keys and headed home to his deck to read the Saturday paper and sleep.

•   •   •

For the next several weeks, it looked to Carolyn Wardell as if the clinics were winning the battle, at least as far as the courts were concerned. Two days after the July 22 rescue, Middlesex County Judge Catherine White had finally issued an injunction sought by Planned Parenthood and the other abortion providers against Operation Rescue, claiming that obstructing access to abortion clinics violated the civil rights of women seeking the clinics' services. Punishment could range from heavy fines to years in jail. Operation Rescue had appealed, contending that the court order was too broad, too vague, and violated Rescue's First Amendment right to free expression. A state Appeals Court judge thought otherwise and upheld the lower court's decision. Operation Rescue appealed again, this time to one justice on the three-panel Supreme Judicial Court. The justice, Joseph Nolan, was reportedly an ardent antiabortionist.

On August 16, less than a month after the initial court order, Judge Nolan lifted the injunction permanently—without explanation.

Carolyn nearly exploded when Fran broke the news to her the next morning. "Good thing I didn't hear this on the radio while driving to work this morning," Carolyn ranted. "I would have driven off the road." As always when she was angry, she stormed through the first floor, stopping to rant to Osa the treasurer, Sarah the bookkeeper, Sonia, Fran, Lin, whomever was around. "We get no support," she fumed. "Not even from the courts. Here we are, trying to provide a service that is legal, within women's constitutional rights, and a judge says it's OK for those rights to be violated."

Back in her office, Carolyn tried to think of how best to react. Nolan's move would give Operation Rescue just the kick it needed to get its numbers back up. Without facing penalties of heavy fines and years in jail, those zealots would stop at nothing to make Preterm inaccessible to women. Carolyn had grown so paranoid that for a moment last week she had wondered if the cockroach head she discovered in the fettucine Alfredo she had brought back to Preterm from a local restaurant had been placed there on purpose. "And for the director of Preterm, a pinch of cockroach," Fran had teased.

"I'm not hungry anymore," Carolyn said, tossing her meal into the garbage.

Now, as she sat in her blue swivel chair staring out her office window at the beige brick building across the street, she wondered if she would ever gain control of what felt like an uncontrollable situation. From the moment she had returned to Brookline from her July Fourth holiday in Pennsylvania, the antiabortion forces had been relentless. Life before the *Webster* decision seemed peaceful compared to what had followed in its wake.

Carolyn had been deeply saddened but not surprised by the Supreme Court decision, which she had heard through the static of her car radio while driving from the campsite to a shopping mall on July 3. Pretending not to hear her teenage niece beg for a music station, Carolyn had leaned closer to the radio, as if that would help her grasp the details. When they reached the mall, Carolyn ran to a phone booth and called Fran. She knew that she wouldn't be able to discuss the decision with her family. Good Catholics all, her sisters and their spouses never even mentioned sex, let alone the politics of abortion. Once, Carolyn's brother-in-law had asked her if Preterm performed abortions, and when she said yes, he'd dropped the subject. But that was OK with Carolyn. Years ago, she had learned to become comfortable with their different perspectives. Their bond was based on more than politics. And, in a way, she had enjoyed being alone with her thoughts that week in the Pennsylvania woods; she was able to think about *Webster's* possible repercussions without being inundated with other peoples' opinions.

Carolyn returned to Preterm the next Monday refreshed. But no sooner had she tossed her briefcase in her office than she discovered in her mailbox a postcard addressed to "Baby Basher and Abortionist Carolyn Wardell at Preterm Murder Incorp." On the front of the postcard, the mailer had pasted a photo of a decapitated fetal head, dripping tissue, held by forceps over a petri dish, with the words "Freedom of Choice??" and the caption: "This baby was murdered at Preterm Clinic then tossed in a trash can and buried by Operation Rescue."

The author wrote: "Before Rescue Operation [*sic*] finishes with Preterm, you'll be spending $180,000 per year on security. But what is that compared to 18 million Preterm makes per year on bloody abortions. A drop in the bloody bucket of murder. I'd like to see your head on the end of a bloody pike."

Dangling the postcard in front of her, Carolyn said to Fran, "Look at this." Fran nodded. She, too, had received one. Hers, which was addressed to "Fran Basche, Jew Abortionist," boasted a drawing of an unconscious naked woman, complete with pubic hair, on a table draped with a banner that read "TEENAGE VICTIM OF ABORTION."

Both Carolyn and Fran, the two most publicly visible members of Preterm, were accustomed to receiving odd, if not nasty mail. Last month, Carolyn had received a pair of tiny baby booties with a note asking her to find a new job. Postcards bearing Biblical quotes, such as ". . . do not kill the innocent or the righteous, for I will not acquit the guilty . . . Exodus 23:7" were not uncommon. But these two cards, received three days after the *Webster* decision, marked a new era of hate mail. Carolyn was terrified that the author, who was clearly crazy, would try something crazy. She had never received a personal threat before and wondered if the author would hurt her, or Lorena. When she remembered that her phone number was unlisted and her address difficult to find, she felt a little safer—for herself, but not for the clinic. Would a letter bomb follow? In July, an arsonist had torched an abortion clinic in Concord, New Hampshire, destroying only medical records, thanks to a sophisticated alarm system. Was Preterm next?

It felt as if the *Webster* decision had granted the antiabortionists a license to try anything. Emboldened by Washington's support, Operation Rescue protesters were no longer content to sit on the front steps and sing "Jesus Loves the Little Children" until the cops hauled them away. They wanted to do damage. Carolyn had been terrified on July 22 when the rescuers had charged the doors at the last minute, desperation etched on their faces. She feared for her safety, the safety of her staff, and the safety of their patients. As clinic director, Carolyn was responsible for protecting them.

The question was how. Preterm didn't have the money to renovate the fourth floor with a security door and system or to add extra police detail at $22.50 an hour. Screening patients at the front door for possible impostors was unfair to customers of the building's other businesses.

Carolyn felt worn down, as did her staff. Saturdays drained her CMAs, nurses, and doctors, who never knew what to expect when they arrived at 1842 Beacon Street. If it wasn't members of the Ethics of Choice Chorus waving their yellow signs bearing questions—"HOW

DOES HUMAN ABORTION ADD TO YOUR DIGNITY?"—it was clusters of prochoicers cheering patients as they neared the clinic. Even more grating were some of the activists' new tactics. On one Saturday, a fellow—no one was sure to which political group he belonged—stood in the middle of Preterm's sidewalk and demonstrated on a rubber penis how to use a condom. On another Saturday, some women began singing, "If you know where your clitoris is clap your hands . . ."

Occasionally, TV crews in search of a story filmed the demonstrations, which meant hours of staff time devoted to soothing women upset by the glare of public attention on the intimate decision they were about to make. Many women feared that family members, coworkers, or neighbors would spot them on the evening news. "It's *nobody's* business," shouted one patient once she was safely inside the building. Because of the lengthy counseling sessions, patient flow was sluggish; it wasn't unusual for the staff to finish work at 6 P.M., two to three hours later than usual.

Meetings between the Brookline abortion providers on how to handle the demonstrations—especially the increasingly vocal prochoice contingent—and meetings with the prochoice contingent itself didn't achieve much. Both sides repeated their same argument. The providers argued that if fewer prochoice advocates were present, there might be fewer antichoice advocates; therefore, the patients—the reason why the prochoicers stood in front of the clinic in the first place—would suffer less. The prochoice leaders responded that the clinics didn't own the abortion issue; that political activists had a right to demonstrate. By the end of one heated meeting, the activists had made only a few concessions: They wouldn't cheer as patients crossed the clinic's threshold, and, for a few Saturdays, they would limit their presence to fifteen. They vowed, though, to call in the troops if the antis outnumbered them.

In effect, Saturdays would remain the same. Carolyn could hardly blame the tenant who returned Fran's memo to all businesses of 1842 Beacon Street warning of the July 22 rescue with the note: "We tenants are sick and tired of this. Buy your own building and let us business people attend to our customers and patients. Move out!"

Since the July 22 rescue, Carolyn had considered closing the clinic on Saturdays. She loathed the idea; it felt as if the antis had broken her. She worried about the women, especially teenagers still in high school, who couldn't schedule weekday appointments. She also worried about the effects of a Saturday closing on Preterm's shaky finances. Saturday was the clinic's busiest day, averaging fifty to sixty patients—five to fifteen more than weekdays. As crass as it sounded, Preterm needed the income from the added abortions.

But how much more could her staff—and patients—tolerate? Her administrators were tired of alternating Saturday duty. Some of them were unnerved by dealing with annoyed cops and aggressive protesters. Lin Sherman of the phone room had shaken for days after the Saturday when she had been in charge of the outside chaos. And only 100 demonstrators had showed up. What would she have done if there had been a rescue of 500 or 1,000? Or if there were an invasion?

Most importantly, Carolyn needed to focus on other issues. The clinic had run at a deficit for the past two years; now Carolyn wanted to concentrate on promoting services other than abortion, such as mammograms and tubal ligations, which could potentially generate more income than the abortion clinic. Fran's hours should be spent fundraising and promoting Preterm to the community, not calling the Brookline police and organizing volunteer escorts. For the past seven months, Carolyn's energy had been sapped by fighting the negative, by reacting instead of acting. Now *she* wanted to set the agenda. It was the opposition's turn to react.

Judge Nolan's dissolution of the injunction was the catalyst Carolyn had needed in order to act. On the August afternoon of Judge Nolan's ruling, Carolyn and Fran ate lunch at the Eagles Deli a few blocks from Preterm and discussed closing the clinic on Saturdays. Picking at her tuna fish sandwich, Fran agreed that the effort was worth a try. Carolyn returned to her office feeling stronger for having Fran's endorsement. She closed her door and dialed Jeffrey Allen at his law office in downtown Boston. He wasn't in, his secretary said, but she would have him return the call.

Last winter, Jeffrey Allen had rejected Carolyn's idea of closing on threatened rescue days. In his view, the town would be outraged if the clinics closed, feeling as if the $75,000 already spent on police protection had been a waste. Carolyn didn't think that he'd be pleased with this plan to close on Saturdays. What she didn't anticipate was that he'd be furious.

"Carolyn, you can't," he blasted when he called back an hour later. "That's giving them just what they want. You can't give up the fight now. Preterm is the leader. If you quit, they'll all quit."

Closing on Saturdays won't stop the antiabortionists, he argued. They'll blockade during the week. Sure, he admitted, the fight wasn't pleasant—he, too, was tired of receiving hate mail and threats—but they couldn't give in. "When the going gets tough," he said, "keep going."

Carolyn hung up feeling totally defeated, overwhelmed by the irony that last year at this time she had sat in Jeff's office demanding police support, that women's rights to abortion deserved protection. Although Carolyn felt that Jeffrey Allen was motivated politically—he didn't want to lose face in front of the community by conceding to the antis—she was impressed with his commitment to women. He had mentioned that one woman in his office couldn't make an appointment on a weekday; she needed Saturday services, as did many others.

But didn't Jeff Allen understand that dealing with the Saturday circus of antiabortionists and prochoicers was like having a migraine that wouldn't go away? Closing on Saturdays was a way to end that migraine. The activists wouldn't show up en masse during the week; most of them had jobs, didn't they? Preterm could handle small numbers of weekday demonstrators. If Preterm closed on Saturdays, Carolyn could stop shuttling Lorena to friends' homes on Friday nights. She could start planning new programs, such as the educational seminars on women's health care that she had intended to offer this fall. But that evening, working out to her Jane Fonda tape as Lorena looked on shouting, "You're doing it wrong, Mom," Carolyn felt like a failure. We are here for a cause, she told herself.

That night, as she tossed and turned in bed, Carolyn came up with a compromise: Reduce the number of Saturday patients and make the last scheduled appointment at ten o'clock instead of noon. That way, Preterm would avoid the most intense hours of the Saturday demonstrations. In the past few months, protesters—both prochoice and antichoice—who had stood at Planned Parenthood all morning had migrated to Preterm once Planned Parenthood had admitted its last patient, which was usually any time after 9:30 A.M. If Preterm's last patient arrived at ten o'clock, those protesters would have no reason to travel to 1842 Beacon Street. The crowd in front of Preterm would be smaller, more manageable, and Carolyn could cut down on costly police detail hours.

The next day, Carolyn scheduled an all-clinic meeting for the following Friday. She was nervous about the meeting; she didn't like speaking in front of large groups to begin with, let alone to propose plans that she knew would spark heated debate. Would her staff think she was weak if she proposed closing on Saturdays? Or would they be thrilled to have two weekend days off? Would they want to reduce patient numbers? Or would they consider that it meant admitting defeat?

The night before the meeting, Carolyn dreamed that so many people showed up for the all-clinic gathering that she was forced to wander through the crowd with a microphone. When people raised their hands to talk, she thrust the mike in their faces like a talk show host. Awaking the next morning, her brain still fuzzy from sleep, Carolyn thought for a minute or two that the meeting was over. She was depressed to realize that it wasn't.

Pale and puffy-eyed, Carolyn greeted her staffers that Friday afternoon as they filtered into the family room and settled down on the chairs and couches she had arranged in a semicircle. First the phone counselors arrived (people calling in would receive a recorded message during the meeting), then the CMAs. Fresh out of college for the most part, dressed in their stretch pants and oversize shirts or in jeans and boots, they looked so young to Carolyn. The nurses and doctors followed, appearing more worn, more frazzled—from added years or responsibilities, Carolyn couldn't be sure.

Sitting underneath the TV and in front of the bookcase, Carolyn faced the family room full of expectant faces. She crossed her ankles and held her hands in her lap. Controlled. Calm. All-clinic meetings were rare and harbored the intensity of the unknown. Carolyn had to do her best to defuse the tension as all eyes focused on her.

Carolyn began by presenting the option of closing on Saturdays. As she spoke, her voice felt small, almost weak. Maybe she *should* have used a microphone. But, as it turned out, her voice didn't matter. The staff wanted to talk. Opinions blasted as soon as she paused for breath.

"I'm proud that we're still open on Saturdays when other clinics have backed down," said Kaylah, a CMA, from her perch on a couch next to Carolyn. "It's empowering to know we won't fall apart."

"Yeah, and if the antis are so extreme, who is to say they won't attack in the middle of the week?" a phone counselor piped up from across the room.

Jackie, one of the admitting officers downstairs, raised her hand. "Patients are freaked out," she said firmly. "You have to ask yourself is it worth it?" Carolyn nodded, not surprised at Jackie's vehemence. The downstairs staff, especially those in admitting, faced the teary patients who had forged their way through the weekend hubbub outside. They saw firsthand the anxiety, sometimes terror. By the time the upstairs staff saw the patients, many of the women had calmed down.

"Patients are forewarned by the phone room about Saturdays when

they make their appointments," said Dawn, who directed patient flow upstairs. "It's their choice to come, and it's worth it to have the choice."

And so the arguing went. Predictably, many on the first floor thought that closing was a stellar idea. The fourth-floor medical staff felt that closing meant defeat. If you're committed, you're committed, thought Doris Merrill, who had worked many a Saturday nursing shift. She had felt proud that throughout the miserable circumstances the staff continued to provide patients with the help they sought. There was no quick solution to the dilemma, she knew. But if you can't take the heat, get out of the kitchen. She was glad she wasn't Carolyn, that she didn't have to please this staff.

"There used to be ten to fifteen protesters on Saturday," said Lin Sherman of the phone room. "Now 100 is not a lot of people. How bad will it get?"

"We are one step away from a Saturday brawl," chimed in Fran.

"I won't let *them* make the decision for us," shouted a CMA.

"Let's explore other options," suggested Carolyn, and launched into her idea of scheduling the last Saturday appointment at ten o'clock. The room was silent for a minute as the staff digested the concept. Then, one by one, voices burst around the room like gunfire. Great idea. Not so great an idea. Marian Wolfsun, the director of counseling who worked every Saturday, loved the thought of avoiding the last two hours of Saturday, the "grand finale," she called it. But what about the patients? interrupted a CMA. Many women, especially minors who go to school during the week, can only make an appointment on Saturday.

Carolyn sat back and listened as the staffers thrashed out the idea, arriving at a compromise of their own: Schedule the last appointment at ten o'clock but don't reduce the number of patients. Yes, they knew, the family room would be more congested since fifty-plus patients would arrive in three hours instead of five. Yes, many women would wait longer downstairs since the flow would clog in admitting. But the phone counselors could warn women making appointments on Saturdays about the wait. Better yet, they could offer the women the option of making appointments during the week. If the women decided to go to another clinic, fine, but at least Preterm wasn't reneging on its duties.

Carolyn was uncomfortable with asking patients to wait for so long to have their procedures. Already, abortion patients' key complaint was that they had to spend three, four, or five hours at Preterm. Even on weekdays, when the sidewalk was quiet, patient flow upstairs often slowed because of a doctor or counselor shortage. But staffers claimed that they were willing to assuage the Saturday patients if they grew restless in the various waiting rooms.

"OK," Carolyn said. "Let's try making the last appointment at 10 A.M."

Adding that she would look further into securing the fourth floor, Carolyn thanked her staff. They left in groups, just as they had arrived, chattering among themselves. Carolyn knew that this afternoon's discussion would be the subject of many a phone call tonight.

Cutting back Saturday hours certainly wasn't ideal, Carolyn knew. Nor was it a long-term solution. For the short run, though, it might make the hardest day of the week a little less hard and cause the antis and the pros outside of Preterm's door to be a little less troublesome. Still, Carolyn was a long way off from feeling in control. The antis, once again, had put her on the defensive, forcing her and her staff to devote energy to reacting to their tactics, wasting time that could be better spent improving patient care. Even though the prochoice crowd was a factor in creating the disturbance the antis were the crux of the chaos: If they disappeared, so would their prochoice opposition.

But they wouldn't—at least not in the immediate afterglow of the *Webster* decision. Of that Carolyn was sure.

CHAPTER EIGHT

Abortion
for Birth Control

AUTUMN that year wasn't a particularly pleasant time at Preterm. Patient numbers had begun to dip by five or six appointments a day, averaging forty-five to forty-seven abortions on weekdays, maybe fifty on Saturdays—too few to balance the abortion clinic's income with its costs. A smaller patient load meant smaller staff needs and there were rumblings of layoffs.

Carolyn Wardell didn't think that fewer women sought abortions because fewer women were becoming pregnant. Rather, she believed that women who once would have chosen abortion might be carrying their pregnancy to term, possibly because they had been bullied out of abortion by seeing protesters, either in person or on television, shouting about babykilling. If the outcome of fewer abortions were wanted children reared in happy homes, no one would complain. But Carolyn and the rest of her staff could only wonder about the quality of life for babies born out of desperation.

The staff hardly blamed patients for bolting from the clinic on Saturdays. One look at the family room was enough to turn even the most resolute woman around. Although fewer protesters clogged Preterm's sidewalk now that the last patient was admitted at ten o'clock—fifty demonstrators didn't seem like a lot that fall compared to the hundreds during the summer—the chaos had moved inside. To accommodate the same number of patients in fewer hours, the number of appointments per hour had nearly doubled. Patients, their friends, and parents packed themselves into the admitting area, a space no bigger than a tennis court's serving square, so tightly that they couldn't twitch without bumping into one another. Those who couldn't squeeze in spilled into the hallway and sometimes outside onto the front steps.

At the front desk, Sonia was frantic. She felt as if she were a clerk at Bloomingdale's during the Christmas rush, signaling one woman at a time to sit at her desk to receive a medical chart while a crush of other patients and their partners stood seven deep before her. Once a patient was sent upstairs, her escort was left to find a seat in the family room— no easy task. On Saturdays, it wasn't unusual to find young men sprawled on the floor, perched on chair arms, or lounging on the family-room coffee tables.

Upstairs, no one was much happier. The bottleneck in admitting created a bottleneck on the fourth floor. Despite piles of *The New Yorker* and *Time* and *Vogue* and a television blaring old movies and cartoons, the patients moaned with boredom and hunger as their wait stretched from five, to six, to seven hours. Crabby patients made for a crabby staff, and by late afternoon compassion had turned to clock-watching.

Solutions were few. Cutting back the number of Saturday appointments was one way to relieve the congestion, but the staff refused to deny any woman an abortion. One nurse suggested letting patients spend more time downstairs with their partners to soften the wait. No, Sonia vetoed. When the patient tells her boyfriend that they'll be stuck at Preterm till late afternoon he'll explode—just what the already crowded family room didn't need. Sonia knew that many patients never told their partners about the wait in the first place, fearing that the men wouldn't accompany them if they knew that they would be stuck at Preterm for four, never mind eight hours. Another staffer suggested returning to the old system of offering appointments until noon, but Marian, the director of counseling and the administrator in charge on Saturdays, killed the idea. We'll have protesters eating lunch on our steps like they did last summer, she said.

And so the Saturday craziness continued.

Even during the week, the mood upstairs was tense. Perhaps if the abortion news on the outside had been promising, the staff might have felt less anxious. But as politicians around the country launched into the first round of elections and legislative battles since the *Webster* decision, Preterm's staffers felt anything but secure. Although their jobs and abortion access were safe in Massachusetts for the time

being—Michael Dukakis was still governor and was still promising to veto any bill restricting abortion that landed on his desk—the election was merely a year away and only one gubernatorial hopeful, Lieutenant Governor Evelyn Murphy, was unequivocally and historically pro-choice. Anything could happen. If the Bay State politicians took their cue from other politicians across the country, local women could, once again, find their reproductive options limited.

It seemed that the *Webster* decision had unleashed all the antiabortion legislation that had been brewing for the past sixteen years. Around the country, lawmakers were preparing an onslaught of bills restricting the procedure. Some legislators hoped to abolish abortion in all circumstances and treat doctors who performed the operation as criminals, sentencing them to ten years in prison. Others sought more of a compromise, requiring women to obtain spousal consent and minors to obtain parental consent. Some bills stipulated waiting periods between counseling and the procedure, or required that doctors explain fetal development in detail to women seeking abortions. Still others curtailed all abortions except in cases of rape, incest, and if the pregnancy endangered the mother's health. Abolishing "abortion for birth control" is what they called it.

Abortion for birth control. Abortion for birth control. Over and over again, this sound bite resounded from politicians and antiabortion activists. It was a phrase that was intended to categorize abortions into justified and unjustified: into abortions for women who acted responsibly—those who were pregnant as a result of situations out of their control, such as rape or incest; and abortions for women who didn't act responsibly—those who were pregnant because they hadn't practiced contraception, or hadn't practiced it correctly.

Preterm staffers cringed at the phrase. Did those politicians sitting far away in their leather chairs behind mahogany desks think that women embraced their lovers envisioning a $320 operation that began with their legs spread apart, their feet in stirrups, and culminated in wrenching cramps? Did they think women liked sitting in a clinic's waiting room for hours, feeling guilty and sad and nauseous? Didn't those politicians educate themselves enough to understand that if abortion were a woman's only means of birth control, she might have as many as two or three abortions per year, or up to thirty in her reproductive lifetime?

That was not to say there were no repeat patients at Preterm. Indeed, over a third of the clinic's patients had had a previous abortion, a reflection of the national statistic, which (according to the Alan Gutt-macher Institute) hovered at 39 percent. The majority of those patients, both at Preterm and around the country, had had only one previous abortion. Considering the odds of conceiving unintentionally during the thirty or more years a woman may be sexually active and fertile, two abortions raised no eyebrows at Preterm. Mistakes happen. Who hadn't left their diaphragm in the drawer at least twice? Many patients had gone on the Pill after their first abortion, but, on the recommenda-tion of a doctor, had later taken a break from ingesting the hormones. If they failed to use a backup method, or if they used a backup method with a high failure rate such as the sponge, they found themselves back on Preterm's fourth floor. Sometimes, women missed just one pill and forgot to double up the next day, which left them unprotected for over a week. Others had never missed a day, but hadn't been told that the antibiotic they were prescribed for strep throat or a yeast infection had negated the Pill's effectiveness.

The women who scheduled an abortion appointment in June, and again in October, and again in January, were a different story. These women weren't, for the most part, conscientious contraceptors who occasionally slipped up; these women were often mired in a pattern of destructive behavior.

Usually the younger staffers, the idealistic counselor/medical assis-tants who joined Preterm believing that they could empower women to take control of their fertility and their lives, soured first when their efforts went unrewarded. Martha Laker, who was twenty-five, had counseled women about birth control and had volunteered at a rape crisis center during her college years. She had felt that the women she had talked to had walked away feeling a little less victimized, a little more in command. At first, she had felt the same as a CMA at Preterm. After a year and a half, though, it seemed that every day she saw a patient whom she had seen before. One day in July she counseled a patient whom she had counseled in April. The next day, she assisted a pa-tient whom she had assisted through an abortion in February. She counseled another woman four times. "It feels as if nothing I say sinks in," she told her coworkers when she announced that she was quit-ting Preterm to work as a medical assistant in a family health-care clinic.

At Preterm, Martha and her colleagues were not considered thera-pists, but peer counselors. Abortion counseling involved one session (unless the counselor spoke to a patient on a repeat visit)—not long-term treatment. Consequently, the clinic didn't seek women with master's degrees in social work or psychology, but thoughtful, sensitive women who were good listeners. The kind of women everyone turned to in a crisis, women who intuitively knew the right thing to say, who would not interrupt a narrative with their own interpretation or stories. The clinic felt that women contemplating abortion didn't need a professional psychiatrist, but rather someone to ask them the questions that would make them recognize whether or not terminating the pregnancy was the best decision for them. Preterm spent months training its counselors through seminars, role playing, observing, and being observed to tailor their innate skills to abortion counseling.

The counselor's responsibility was to determine that the patient was making her decision on her own and that she wasn't being coerced to abort by her parents, boyfriend, or husband. The counselor asked if the woman had support—people she could talk to about her experience—and how the woman felt about abortion. A counselor's goal was to offer the woman enough information about contraception and encouragement to use it that the woman would leave Preterm committed to using birth control religiously. When that goal failed—and counselors saw the same patients again and again—they, like Martha, often burned out.

Then there were counselors such as Joan Holland, who after nine years at Preterm was still going strong. Unlike many of her younger colleagues who craved variety and worked as both medical assistants and counselors, Joan only counseled. Also unlike her younger colleagues, Joan wasn't frustrated by patients whose medical charts were as thick as magazines, filled with pages of notes from previous abortions. Instead, she was challenged. It wasn't that Joan was immune to the redundancy, but rather that, at forty-five, she had gained enough perspective to see past the obvious—the fact that the patient was back again, despite previous lectures on contraception—and analyze the reasons behind the frequent pregnancies. After talking to hundreds of women, Joan Holland understood that not all repeat patients were lazy about slipping in their diaphragms, nor were they all victims of failed contraception or forced sex. Joan knew that the truth fell somewhere in the middle.

Her quest was to help these women figure out how to gain a sense of control over their bodies, their lives, and their futures. In some cases, the job was as easy as finding a birth-control method that the women would like, or at least feel comfortable using. In others where the issues ran much, much deeper, the job was more complicated, and for Joan, far more interesting.

. . .

It was late morning on a Tuesday in mid-October and Joan was hungry. She was always hungry just before her lunch break, but in the old days before Preterm's financial crunch, she could openly snack on the hard candies that the clinic offered in bowls—supposedly for patients— scattered around the fourth floor. In an effort to cut costs, however, Carolyn had asked the staff not to indulge in the goodies, so Joan had to slip the "contraband candies," as she and nurse Doris called them, surreptitiously into her pockets or her bra, whichever was easiest. On this sunny fall day when the leaves outside had just begun to turn yellow and orange, Joan sneaked into the nurses' lounge to stick her hand under her sweater for the lemon hardball she had swiped from the recovery room.

"This is women-involved-with-deadbeats day," she told Doris Merrill, who sat on the beige couch in the lounge, relishing the last minutes of her break from the recovery room. Joan and Doris had been friends for years, ever since Joan began working at Preterm, and they loved nothing better than to share gossip about their mutual friends, all of whom had once worked at the clinic. This morning, however, Doris listened as Joan regaled her with stories of the patient whose boyfriend had coldly told her to "get unpregnant," and the twenty-year-old day-care provider living on $15,000 a year whose unemployed boyfriend, father of three and not yet divorced from his first wife, wanted her to keep the baby. "No way," she had told Joan. "I want to be married and financially stable when I have a family." Still, she had no plans to split with the man, and seek someone who could promise her that future.

Doris nodded. She, too, had heard her share of stories from the mangled relationship front when she screened patients for their medical histories. She was no psychologist, and neither was Joan, but both women had been in the abortion business long enough to connect weak or abusive relationships with low self-esteem, which, in turn, was connected with women feeling a lack of control over their lives. Often, what these women felt they couldn't control was their fertility. "No matter what I do, I'm always pregnant," one of Doris's patients had lamented.

Feeling that nothing they did would prevent the inevitable pregnancies, these women often found it easier to go through yet another

abortion than to try and take charge of their destiny. Neither Joan nor Doris was surprised to see them back in Preterm's waiting room several times in a year. Although counselors had informed the patients that any intrusive surgery harbors some risks, they also said that abortions, even repeat abortions, had a less than 1-percent complication rate. Some women tested that statistic. Fearing that the procedure had left them sterile, they refused to use birth control to see if their body still worked. When it did, they simply made another appointment.

Joan finished crunching her lemon candy and returned to the front desk on the fourth floor to pick up another chart. Scanning the front page, her back to the women in the waiting room, Joan read about Chloe, her next patient. Chloe was twenty-three, an unemployed waitress with a high-school diploma who received Medicaid benefits. She had had one child and three abortions. This was her fourth. Joan turned around and called, "Chloe R.?" A wiry woman with long, straight brown hair and a thin, pinched face stood up from her chair. She looked hard at first, her mouth drawn in a tight line, but when she smiled at Joan, her face softened and she seemed vulnerable, almost childlike.

"Hiiii," Joan said, grinning warmly. Joan was a striking woman with dark hair cut into a pageboy and a slim shape that reflected her afternoons working out to aerobics tapes. When Joan laughed, which was often, her eyes crinkled and her mouth opened so wide that her jaw almost touched her chest. When she spoke, she drew out the last word of each sentence, as if she couldn't decide whether or not to end her thought. Patients wrote on their evaluation sheets that they found Joan warm and helpful, that Joan really listened to them. And she did. Joan was fascinated by her patients' lives, which was one of the reasons she had gotten into the business in the first place.

While her two children were young in the mid-1970s, Joan, a speech therapist by training, had become inspired by the women's movement and began working part-time at a women's health-care referral service in her hometown of Framingham, a suburb west of Boston. Listening to the stories of beatings and failed birth control, Joan discovered that she liked working with women in crisis. Not only did she feel that she was helping these women find some relief, but she also felt that she was learning firsthand about a world of crack and prostitution and sexual abuse that she otherwise would only have read about. When she heard that Preterm was hiring abortion counselors, she jumped at the chance. Although she complained about patients who lied—drug addicts were notorious for claiming that they hadn't shot up in a week when, in fact, they had shot up just hours before their scheduled abortion, which meant that they shouldn't have any IV medication (the combination of drugs could prove lethal)—Joan enjoyed her patients and the feeling that maybe she had helped soften their trauma that day, or even had helped them reflect on other issues that plagued them.

Now, she introduced herself to Chloe and held up the medical chart for Chloe to read. "Is this you?" she asked. Chloe nodded and followed Joan to a room no bigger than a walk-in closet. Chloe sat in the chair next to the window, and Joan sat across from her, the table between them covered with birth-control devices and a package of tissues.

Joan was less concerned that this was Chloe's fourth abortion in six years than she was curious about Chloe's background and the possible reasons why Chloe kept finding herself pregnant. Perhaps Chloe, like many of the repeat patients Joan had talked to, had been unable to find a contraceptive method that worked for her. Many of Joan's patients couldn't use the Pill because of a medical condition such as diabetes or high blood pressure, and they feared the IUD's possible dangers— uterus perforation, excessive bleeding, pelvic inflammatory disease, sterility. That left them with barrier methods. Prescribed a diaphragm after an abortion, some of the women discovered that they were uncomfortable touching themselves and refused to use the device, or only used it occasionally. Some of the women Joan talked to had said that by inserting the diaphragm they felt that they were initiating sex, and they didn't like being the aggressor. Others said that they didn't have the willpower to stop lovemaking long enough to slip in the rubber barrier. Still others had the willpower to stop the act to squirt their cervix with spermicidal foam, only to find moments later that their partner had whipped off his condom before he penetrated. One patient said that her boyfriend had removed her contraceptive sponge during sex. He complained that he could feel it.

What, Joan wondered, was Chloe's story?

"Sooo," said Joan, crossing her legs Indian-style on the chair, daintily spreading her jeans skirt over her knees. "How are you doing?"

Chloe smiled weakly. "OK," she said.

"We're going to talk about your choice of birth control and your decision," said Joan. "Where would you like to start?"

"I'm going back on the Pill," Chloe said firmly.

"You were on it before?" Joan asked.

"I was on the Pill since the last time I was here," Chloe said. Joan glanced at the chart. Chloe was last at Preterm in February, eight months ago. If Chloe had been on the Pill and had liked it enough to plan to return to it, then it seemed to Joan that the issue wasn't so much the method of birth control, but the consistent use of birth control. Perhaps if she got Chloe to talk more about her life, Joan could figure out why Chloe didn't take better care of herself by doing what she could to prevent the pregnancies.

In her years at Preterm, Joan had talked to many women who had given up trying to contracept, women the politicians would accuse of using abortion for birth control. Joan found that some of these women were functional in every other aspect of their lives—their jobs, their relationships—but couldn't master contraception. Others were so beaten down by problems—drug addiction, poverty, violent mates—that remembering to take a pill was a last priority. One of Joan's counseling colleagues was fond of saying, "I know the hazards of overeating, yet I still overeat. Other people know the hazards of smoking and they still smoke. Some women know the hazards of unprotected intercourse and they still have unprotected intercourse. No one is perfect. Who are we to judge?"

If you say you won't judge a woman on her first abortion, then you shouldn't pass judgment on her eighth abortion, Joan felt. What were the options? Punish these women by making them mothers? What kind of life would their children have? Moreover, if the woman wasn't taking responsibility for her own fertility, how could she be responsible for a child? In a sense, Joan believed that these women were being responsible by admitting that they weren't fit to be parents and acting on it.

Now, Joan listened intently, her eyes never veering from Chloe's face, as Chloe began to explain the events that led her to Preterm again.

When the Pill-pack Preterm had given her had almost run out, Chloe told Joan that she had ordered a refill, but had left the new pack in her car overnight. The car was stolen—by her boyfriend, who was angry at her. She called the police, who nabbed him, but her boyfriend claimed that the car was his. An auto mechanic, he occasionally worked on police cars, and the cops had believed him. A few days later, Chloe and her boyfriend made up and she got her car back, but the pills were gone. Weeks later, after another fight, her apartment caught fire. She thought her boyfriend was responsible, although he denied it. But that didn't matter; a week after the fire, her boyfriend was arrested for selling crack and was tossed in jail, where he still sat. They had made love three times after her pills ran out.

Whether or not the tale was true didn't matter to Joan as much as the fact that Chloe was involved with a loser. "How long have you known your boyfriend?" Joan asked.

"Years," Chloe said. "Since high school. He's the father of my son." She looked down and began studying her fingernails.

Yes, Chloe sighed, this was abortion number four. As a teenager, she hadn't used birth control, and of course she had gotten pregnant. That was abortion number one. She had tried asking her partner to use condoms, but sometimes she forgot and sometimes he refused. Abortion number two. Then, at age twenty, she'd given birth to her son. For almost three years after that she had stayed on the Pill, but then she had stopped, just to take a break, and hadn't bothered to use another method. She had thought that the Pill still worked for a couple of months after the last one was swallowed. Within a month, she was pregnant and scheduled her third abortion at Preterm in February.

Joan asked Chloe if her boyfriend helped her financially.

"He's given a total of eighty-five dollars in support since my son was born," Chloe said, nearly spitting at the dollar figure.

The relationship hadn't always been this bad, Chloe added in defense. Her boyfriend drank heavily, always had, but he didn't begin yelling at her until he started freebasing cocaine. When the seizures struck, he stopped the coke for awhile, but the habit was too ingrained and the freebasing continued, as did the screaming.

Chloe was another woman-involved-with-deadbeat, Joan concluded, and Chloe knew it. Why didn't she leave him? If he had given her only eighty-five dollars in three years for her son, she wasn't dependent on him for money. Although Chloe had said that he had never hit her, perhaps she feared for her safety. After all, the guy had stolen her car following a fight. No telling what he would do if she broke up with him. Joan felt, though, that fear didn't keep Chloe in that relationship. Rather, Joan sensed that Chloe was one of those women who lacked confidence and self-esteem and believed that she didn't deserve any better than this schmuck. Joan asked how Chloe felt about her boyfriend.

"I don't want anything to do with him," Chloe said.

Good, Joan thought, moving on to her next question. "What about the guy who brought you here?"

Chloe paused. "He's nice," she said, "but he's uh . . . uh . . ."

"Too nice," Joan filled in.

"Yeah."

What Chloe meant was that he was too nice for her, Joan suspected. Women who sought no-goods usually found nice guys boring. The women didn't feel good enough about themselves to accept a better relationship with a nice man so they sought the company of a guy who'd be rotten to them. Joan could stop the counseling now; many counselors would. Chloe was clear in her decision to terminate, she had emotional support from friends and from this guy in the waiting room, and she promised to swallow the Pill every day for the rest of her reproductive lifetime. But Joan wasn't satisfied.

One reason Joan had become a counselor was because she knew she was good with people and that she was intuitive, and with that combination she might be able to help them see something in themselves that they might not see alone. Joan had a good feeling about Chloe. Chloe said that she wanted to get off welfare, wanted to raise her son in a secure environment. She recognized that her boyfriend was bad for her, but she was still attracted to him. Maybe if Chloe understood that attraction a little more, Joan thought, she might not repeat the mistake.

"Did you come from a dysfunctional home?" Joan asked. She often used psychology terms with her patients. Sometimes she had to rephrase the question or put it in simpler language if the patient didn't understand the lingo. But Chloe knew just what Joan was talking about.

"Yeah," she said, nodding. "Real dysfunctional."

Chloe revealed that her mother was a pediatric nurse who had lived on Demerol and vodka. Her father had started drinking the minute he got home from work, even before he said hello. The drinking sparked fights, and Chloe had grown up with a lot of screaming and not many hugs. Her grandparents, too, had been alcoholics and abusive. From listening to patients and through study, Joan had arrived at her own theory that low self-esteem was often linked with a history of substance abuse. Given her unstable family background, how could Chloe be anything but confused? She had grown up without knowing what nurturing really was. How could she have a high self-image that demanded a supportive, loving home life? Her ex-boyfriend also hailed from a family of alcoholics.

"Has anyone ever discussed with you why you would be attracted to guys with a lot of problems?" Joan said. "That's why I asked about your background. There's no way I thought you had come from a happy home. Of course you'd seek these kinds of men."

Chloe cocked her head to one side and stared at Joan.

"You're used to it. You have low self-esteem. You don't think you deserve any better."

Chloe nodded slowly, almost painfully. "You bet," she said.

Joan's purpose wasn't to tear Chloe down, but rather to alert her to the self-destructive pattern that she may not have recognized. It was up to Chloe to do the rest. Joan finished their session by trying to build up Chloe's confidence, applauding her accomplishments, noting that she had ended an ugly relationship and had tried to use birth control responsibly. Women having their umpteenth abortion didn't need to feel any more guilty than they already did.

"Thank you," Chloe said, as she stood to leave.

"Take good care," Joan said. "If you need to talk any more, we have lots of professional counseling referrals."

Chloe nodded in a way that made it clear that she wasn't ready to explore her past to change her present. If, however, after this counseling session, Chloe returned to Preterm in three months, Joan wouldn't feel defeated. Joan did her best to help her patients practice contraception and control, but she knew that these women were ultimately responsible for their own lives.

Later, in the nurses' lounge, Joan replayed the session with another counselor, a young woman in her early twenties named Anna Biagio. Anna was sensitive to the plight of repeat patients; she had had three abortions herself. She had used birth control faithfully from the moment she became sexually active at age fourteen, but she had stopped two years later when she broke up with her steady boyfriend. At a party, one thing led to another with a new guy and two months later, Anna, then a junior at Brookline High School, had had an abortion at Preterm. For the next few years she'd used a diaphragm and then switched to a cervical cap, a thimble-sized rubber or plastic cap that fits snugly over the cervix. Even though the cap claims a 98 percent success rate, Anna became pregnant twice while using the device, which she had received from a doctor in New York. After her third abortion, she was examined by a physician's assistant at Preterm who said that her cervix was an irregular shape and therefore not a good host for a cervical cap, that Anna should never have been prescribed one.

Anna returned to the Pill, but developed a rash as a side effect. She got a bladder infection from the diaphragm, and the last time she had used condoms and foam the foam squirted everywhere but where it should have. Now she didn't know what birth-control method to use next, but if she understood anything, it was that repeat abortions were understandable, forgivable, and not always preventable.

"You were giving her therapy," Anna accused Joan of her session with Chloe, believing that Joan had overstepped her duties as a counselor.

No, Joan said. All she did was try to show Chloe that she was stuck in a bad pattern that many women of alcoholic families find themselves in, and that she could break the cycle. Whether Chloe broke the cycle or not was up to her. Joan could only hope that she would.

"Joan H.," a voice called through the intercom, indicating that Joan's services were needed. Joan stood up, straightened her skirt, took a deep breath, and walked toward the front desk to meet yet another patient.

• • •

The daily picketers had never perturbed Joan much. Dismissing them as obsessives incapable of understanding—or of trying to understand—the complicated lives her patients led, Joan sailed past them every morning, her cup of coffee and bran muffin in hand. Sometimes she'd snap and tell them that they all should be "committed," but that was only if they were especially annoying in their pleading with her to find another job. To Bill Cotter, she was polite, since he occasionally reminded her that she left her car window open.

That fall, though, the picketers seemed more energetic, more aggressive, and it became harder and harder for Joan and her colleagues to ignore their spiel. Taking a cue from politicians across the country, the abortion foes sprayed patients, staff, and even pedestrians wandering toward the trolley stop, with their abortion catchphrases. Women used "abortion for convenience," they said. "Selfishness is the reason babies die," one man preached. "Money is the reason babies die." They borrowed another slogan, "adoption, not abortion," from President Bush, and yet another, "postabortion syndrome," from psychology experts.

Ignorance, Joan thought. Pure ignorance.

One morning, not long after her session with Chloe, Joan sauntered past Alice, the picketer who wore pink sneakers and whom the cops called "Frog Mouth" because of how wide she opened her mouth when she hollered at patients ascending the stairs toward the clinic entrance. The clinic staff called her "Earmuffs" for her winter headgear. A stocky woman in her mid-forties, Alice trailed patients holding up a poster of an eleven-week fetus and chanting, "Your baby has a heartbeat. Your baby has brain waves." On this fall morning, rainy but warm, with her brown hair matted against her head and her pink sneakers soaking wet, she handed to patients a pamphlet entitled "Olivia's Story," a first-person account of a woman who had suffered an emotional breakdown after her abortion. Alice didn't bother passing a copy to Joan—the picketers recognized the staffers as easily as the staffers recognized the picketers—but Joan had seen enough of the pamphlets scattered around the clinic to know what they said.

Adoption was an unselfish, loving option, Joan felt, but few of the women she had counseled were willing to endure nine months of heartburn and swollen ankles, nine months in which they would bond to the life growing and kicking inside of them, only to spend hours in labor to deliver the child into unknown hands. Although certain adoption arrangements would let the birth mother stay in contact with the adoptive families, most women whom Joan encountered felt that that would be too traumatic, both for them and the child. Women who had given a baby up for adoption rarely, if ever, endured that anguish again.

Christina, one of Joan's counseling patients, was one of those women. The picketers had had their effect on Christina six years ago when she was sixteen, pregnant from the first time she had made love with her high-school sweetheart, and scared. A lovely girl with long, curly black hair and round blue eyes fringed with dark lashes, she had walked toward the clinic steps, her father and boyfriend trailing behind her. "You don't want to do this," an old man had shouted. "You're killing your baby." Raised Catholic, Christina was already unsure of her decision to abort. She froze in place on the sidewalk, sobbing.

Urged on by her father, Christina edged inside the clinic, proceeding as far as the counseling session before she was sent home to reconsider her decision. Her counselor thought that Christina's reasons for choosing abortion—she wanted to go to her junior prom and play field hockey—lacked substance. Walking down Preterm's steps, Christina thought, "I'll never return." She couldn't keep the baby, however; she had nowhere to live. Her mother, with whom she had lived since her parents' divorce twelve years before, had kicked her out of the house when Christina had told her that she was pregnant. And her father said that his new wife thought that Christina and a baby would be intrusive.

Christina moved in with her grandmother and attended a new high school during the months before she gave birth to a baby boy. Ryan, she called him. Suffering from an infection, she stayed in the hospital for nine days, feeding her boy, holding her boy. Rationally, she knew that without a home, a high-school diploma, or job prospects, she had nothing to offer a child. A life on welfare wasn't fair to either of them. But when she left the hospital without him, she felt as if she would never be whole again. Since then, she couldn't pass an infant, a toddler, or any young child without staring, trying to envision what he'd look like now at age five. She wondered if he were a good boy or a terror, if he had black curly hair like hers or blond hair like his father. She and her boyfriend had broken up long ago; the relationship hadn't withstood the pressure of the pregnancy.

Five years later, having finished high school and enrolled at Boston University only to drop out to waitress because she felt she had no direction, Christina stood in front of Gynecare, demonstrating for abortion rights. One of her opponents, an elderly woman, asked her if she'd ever had an abortion.

"No," Christina retorted. "But I had a child I surrendered to adoption, and it's the worst pain I've ever known. It's criminal to ask women to do that." The elderly woman walked away. A week later Christina was raped. Two months later, she was back at Preterm.

"I could never give up another baby," Christina told Joan. Nor could she raise a child conceived in violence. He was a waiter at the tony restaurant in Boston's Back Bay where Christina waitressed. After work one night, a group from the restaurant had headed over to Christina's apartment to drink a few beers and relax after an evening of waiting on tables. Sometime after 2 A.M., the guests disappeared, all except for him. Drunk and tired, Christina had offered to call him a cab. When he returned from the bathroom, he knocked the phone out of her hand. With his forearm pressing against her neck, he forced her to walk backward and fall on the bed. She kicked and struggled, trying to squeeze her legs together, but he overpowered her. When it was over, she curled into a ball and hissed, "Get out." He left, to go home to his wife.

Christina had heard the abortion foes' arguments for continuing a pregnancy resulting from rape. Rape is violent enough without having two victims instead of one, they said. The mother begins to heal from the attack with the child's birth. But Christina knew that as long as she was pregnant, she would feel vulnerable. And as guilty as she felt to be ridding herself of the life that grew within her, she came first. She wouldn't let the abortion foes get to her again. Losing a seven-week fetus which weighed less than an aspirin tablet didn't compare to losing a seven-pound wailing baby with hair and fingernails who looked just like her.

Christina could argue with the abortion foes until she was hoarse and her words wouldn't penetrate, Joan knew. On this rainy fall morning, Alice stood in front of Preterm passing out "Olivia's Story" as if the deep depression described in the pamphlet that followed Olivia's abortion would follow every woman's abortion.

Never mind that the American Psychological Association reported scientific data suggesting that abortion had few, if any, negative psychological consequences, or that the U.S. Surgeon General, C. Everett

Koop, an avowed antiabortionist, wrote a letter to President Reagan stating that after talking with twenty-seven different groups and examining 250 studies on the psychological effects of abortion, he could not conclude that abortion had significant or lasting health effects on women. Women who had had an abortion, Koop found in his study, were no more likely to suffer miscarriages or premature birth in future pregnancies than other women. Although some psychological experts interviewed by Koop found that abortion was stressful enough to throw a woman into "posttraumatic stress disorder," a breakdown similar to that suffered by Vietnam veterans, others found abortion to be no more stressful than other major life events or losses.

To be sure, there were patients who regretted their decision, or who felt profoundly guilty or depressed after the procedure. For some women, the grieving sprang from religious conflicts: They had grown up agreeing with their church that abortion was wrong—until they themselves faced a crisis pregnancy. Other women suffered because they felt that they had been forced into ending the pregnancy, either for economic reasons or because their partner didn't want the child. For others, such as a Preterm patient named Julia Nichols, the profound despair she had felt for weeks after her abortion resulted from repressed emotions.

Regardless of how certain a woman is of her decision to end a pregnancy, abortion is still a loss. For the two weeks between discovering that she was pregnant and her abortion appointment, Julia's conviction to abort had never wavered. Blond and athletic with piercing blue eyes, Julia was twenty-four, en route to graduate school in health administration, in love with her boyfriend of four years, but not ready to get married or forgo her dreams to become a mother. After the procedure, she had wept with relief. Even the next day, she was elated. Two days after that, while driving home from work, she burst into tears. The tears flowed for over a month before Julia called Preterm for a counseling reference. Through her therapy at a community-based agency called COPE (Coping with the Overall Pregnancy/Parenting Experience), Julia discovered that her reaction to the abortion wasn't the source of her troubles, but a symptom.

Since her parents' divorce when she was a teenager, Julia had avoided hurt by dealing with life intellectually, not emotionally. Instead of letting the confusion about ending the life inside of her surface, she suppressed it, nearly exploding with sadness afterwards. Although she absolutely didn't want the pregnancy, she recognized on a deeper level that it was a part of her and the man she loved. After the abortion, she felt that she had lost something. To arrive at accepting her decision, her counselor helped her work through the stages of grief, similar to those experienced when we suffer the death of a loved one: denial, anger, bargaining, depression, acceptance. Julia wrote down the reasons why she had had the abortion so that she had something tangible to refer to whenever she felt unsure or guilty about her decision. She knew that she had made peace with the decision one afternoon when, as her mother ranted about the evils of abortion, stopping only long enough to ask Julia what she thought about the girlfriend of a neighbor's son who had decided to end her pregnancy, Julia shot back:

"You have no business discussing that woman's situation. Only she knows what is best for her."

It was difficult, if not impossible, for an abortion counselor to predict how a patient would react days, or weeks, or even months after the procedure. Joan had counseled long enough to sense when she was working with a woman who might be troubled after the procedure. She would offer that woman references for postabortion counseling. Catholic women, for instance, were referred to Boston's Paulist Center to discuss their fears and guilt with a priest who was not an abortion rights advocate but who acted as a pastoral counselor to help the women work through their pain. Preterm's counselors were not therapists and therefore were not trained to cope with the complex issues that these women needed to resolve. Often, patients would call the phone room for help and a counselor would offer them a list of referrals, from private psychologists to community health agencies such as COPE, which offered sliding pay scales.

The bottom line, as Joan and her counseling colleagues knew, was that the healthier a woman was emotionally and mentally when she had her abortion, and the more certain she was of her decision, the less grief she suffered afterwards.

But to Alice, the picketer, "Olivia's Story" said it all. All the patients were the same. Alice didn't care about the woman who drank a quart of vodka a day and was responsible enough not to want her baby to suffer mental retardation from fetal alcohol syndrome. Nor did she care about the drug addict who had just kicked the crack habit and needed all her strength to stay straight. She didn't care about the forty-two-year-old woman with twelve children who had suffered a stroke while on the Pill, an infection from the IUD, and discomfort from the diaphragm, and whose husband refused to use condoms.

These were the people behind the sound bites on the evening news; the women who "used abortion for birth control" and who were "too selfish" to choose "adoption, not abortion." These were the women the picketers and politicians never saw. Upstairs, a roomful of them waited for Joan. With a last look at Alice, Joan walked inside.

CHAPTER NINE

An Evening
with Randall Terry

R ANDALL Terry had been two hours late the last time he'd pounded a pulpit in Boston, but the crowd hadn't seemed concerned as it sang and prayed joyfully. On that evening last April, 800 people had jammed into the Basilica of Our Lady of Perpetual Help in Roxbury, a predominantly black section of Boston plagued by poverty, murders, and drugs—a section many of those attending the service had never visited.

Now, on this autumn evening seven months later, Randall Terry would speak to his Boston fans in Randolph, a middle-class suburb south of Boston. The host church was St. Bernadette's, a large square structure of tan brick which stood proudly on a busy thoroughfare lined with neon signs advertising mufflers and take-out Chinese food, an avenue clogged with teenagers driving their parents' station wagons as they cruised for fun on a Saturday night. Yet even St. Bernadette's benign environment hadn't been enough to lure the mobs of disciples that Randall Terry usually attracted. When the charismatic Randall Terry couldn't draw more than 300 people—and when even those 300 were impatient for the show to begin instead of alert with expectation—the message was clear:

Operation Rescue was in trouble.

It was almost eight o'clock, and once again the founder of Operation Rescue was late. The rally was scheduled to begin at 7:30 P.M. The local rescuers had begun filing past the mosaic windows and into the hard wooden pews of this simple church over an hour ago, many dressed as if they were headed to Pier Four for dinner: the women's black leather pumps gleaming and the men in jackets and ties. Children, with a few exceptions, were left at home. This wasn't an ordinary rally in which the abortion foes received instructions on how to crawl under barriers, a rally in which they felt comfortable in jeans and T-shirts, holding squirming toddlers. This was an event. They were here to drink inspiration from Randall Terry, their spiritual leader, the man who had recognized and acted upon what he called their sin of inertia, of letting the unborn be killed for the past sixteen years without interfering. This was the man who had begun orchestrating their journey toward repentance for allowing this evil. But as the minutes passed and they saw no sign of their leader, Terry's Boston admirers grew fidgety.

Filling nearly two-thirds of the church, the crowd—ranging from teenagers to young marrieds to gray-haired women and their balding husbands—had already sung "I've Been Redeemed" and "What a Mighty God We Serve," standing and swaying with the words, their arms reaching toward heaven, mouths open, eyes closed. They had already prayed silently, the Catholics kneeling, the Protestants sitting, and in unison as they recited the Lord's Prayer. They had listened to a Protestant man explain how he had found a soulmate in a priest as they knelt together before "an abortion mill," how he had learned that the devil must not divide the two religions. They had listened to the small, lithe woman with the pageboy cut who shot photographs at every rescue describe the D.C. Project, three days of seminars and rescues in the nation's capital in November, and inform them that round-trip Amtrak tickets were available from Boston for $110. But attention was scattered. One by one, every few seconds, a head would twist toward the entrance at the back of the church, as if looking at the entrance might make the man appear.

Would he show? Was he in trouble? Had he been tossed in jail again?

"Randall Terry is stuck in traffic in the Sumner Tunnel," a bearded man announced from the altar, his back to the large wooden cross hanging on a mauve backdrop. The audience released a collective groan. The Sumner Tunnel led from Logan Airport to the expressways surrounding Boston. Its congested traffic had been known to delay cars for hours. Heads bowed, members of the audience whispered to one another, filling the sanctuary with a buzz of concern. Sensing the anxiety, the man at the altar cleared his throat and smiled. "Although our special guest has not arrived," he said, his hands gripping the lectern, "there is another special guest in the room."

He paused. The whispering stopped. All eyes were on the man with the beard.

"Jesus is with us."

Grins crossed faces. "Amen," the crowd murmured.

"Amen," the man replied.

The guitarist in front strummed a few chords and the crowd stood. "Greater is He that is in me," they sang, swaying and clapping. "Greater is He that is in me . . ." For the moment, the audience was placated.

Although Darroline Firlit maintained to the press that her people were just as enthusiastic, just as ready as ever to lay their lives on the line to "save children," Bill Cotter had admitted to reporters that numbers were slipping. Rescue needed Randall Terry to work his magic, inspire the locals once again to pit themselves against the clinics and police. Of late, neither Cotter nor Darroline had had much success.

Contrary to Cotter's prediction to the media last July, Operation Rescue demonstrations had not "escalated" with the momentum of the Supreme Court's *Webster* decision. Since July—in fact, since the April 29 rescue at Preterm—Cotter had not been able to persuade even 100 of his soldiers to blockade clinic entrances and face arrest. Most of those who showed up at rescues preferred to stand on the sidelines and pray.

Even the crowds at the rallies held two nights before a rescue were dwindling in size and energy. Few new faces dotted the rallies' crowds, a sharp contrast to the hundreds of hands that raised at rallies last spring when Cotter asked "How many of you are new to Rescue?" Rows of pews remained empty at the outfit's events in the fall of 1989, and the singing that had rocked St. Agatha's the March before with its force had faded in subsequent gatherings to that of a Sunday church chorus.

Perhaps the protesters' interest had dimmed along with the novelty of spending Saturday mornings in front of clinics and Saturday nights on cold jail floors. Perhaps they were tired of having little success to savor. Although rescuers believed, or said they believed, that they had saved babies at every blockade and that they had seen patients flee from the demonstrations, they had no way of knowing whether the women had rescheduled their appointments or simply had returned to the clinic later that morning. The hard truth was that with the exception of the invasion of WomanCare in Hyannis in August, Operation Rescue: Boston had not met victory.

The abortion foes hadn't closed Gynecare or Preterm on July 22 despite that day's blockade. They hadn't closed Planned Parenthood on the Thursday morning in late September when twelve rescuers had attempted an invasion. The protesters had huddled on the steps outside the locked clinic's door for less than an hour before the Brookline police swept them into the wagon and off to jail. The abortion foes hadn't even closed Gynecare two days later when 100 protesters descended on the Boston clinic and forty-eight were arrested for unlawful assembly and breach of the peace as they tried to crawl under the barricades and block the entrance. Only in Hyannis, on Cape Cod, had Operation Rescue been able to stop abortions.

In the late afternoon of August 31, 200 rescuers from Greater Boston, Rhode Island, and New Hampshire had gathered on the lawn in front of the office building that housed WomanCare in Hyannis. Within the hour, a young woman accompanied by a young man entered the second floor office and asked for a pregnancy test. As she talked to the receptionist, her companion opened the door for fifty-seven demonstrators. The throng rushed into the waiting room, where four joined their necks with bicycle locks.

Patients inside the clinic fled out a side door. Patients outside were told to reschedule. The clinic was closed; the police told the rescuers that they could occupy the waiting room, which sat twenty-four, until they were ready to walk out voluntarily. That way, the police told the press, neither rescuers nor police would get hurt in the scuffle of carrying the protesters down a flight of stairs. Early the next morning, when the protesters still refused to budge despite the sweltering heat (the staff had shut off the air conditioning) and full bladders (they were denied bathroom use), the police began toting them down the stairs and into waiting wagons. At 3:30 A.M., eleven hours after the siege began, the last demonstrator was out.

But Hyannis had been, more or less, an expected win. Ever since WomanCare had opened three months before, the clinic staff had complained about lack of police response to its calls when picketers trespassed on the clinic lawn, followed staffers home, or when one staffer found a dead squirrel outside her house with a note saying "Murderers will be murdered." The police claimed that they did monitor the clinic, but unobtrusively, often by plainclothes officers. The police, though, had not leapt to action in early August when someone stuck small crosses on WomanCare's lawn and spelled out "Murderer" in wood chips on the ground and in wax on the door. So it was little wonder to anyone that Operation Rescue had been able to close the clinic.

"Bill Cotter and Darroline send their apologies that they can't be with you tonight," the man with a beard told those in St. Bernadette's sanctuary. "They are in Chicago at a strategy meeting. They are missing tonight's rally for *your* benefit," he said, pointing at the crowd, as if the crowd were responsible.

Obedience was an Operation Rescue creed, and since Bill Cotter and Darroline were the bosses, questioning their absence—regardless of how suspicious it seemed that the two leaders would miss a night with Randall Terry—was out of line. Yet chatter erupted. To distract the audience, the photographer returned to the microphone to applaud the sidewalk counselors, who, as she said, stood in front of the clinics "morning after morning," risking cold, rain, and rejection. "Fred Pulsifer," she called. Fred stood up, his gray wiffle cut looking freshly clipped. He smiled quickly at the applause and sat down.

"And Marie Henden," the photographer called. Marie, a short woman in her mid-thirties with long brown hair and very round, very blue eyes, stood up and waved frantically to the crowd, grinning. Marie was known as "Speed Bump" among the prochoice crowd for the way she planted herself in front of patients as they tried to enter the clinic. The Brookline police called Marie annoying for her cries of "assault" on Saturday mornings, claiming that the clinic escorts had shoved her as she tried to tell patients that she knew of adoption programs and financial help for pregnant women. She had carried one plea to court— instigating the lawsuit four months after the alleged incident. In the suit, Marie Henden charged that at a rescue in December 1988 in front of Repro Associates, Susan Newsom, Planned Parenthood's spokesperson, had demanded that Marie stop talking to a patient, alleging that when she hadn't, Susan had punched her in the chest with her fist. Susan Newsom, who was astounded by the accusation, said that she had stood at the sidelines of the rescue and had never seen Marie Henden until the case's first court hearing.

At the trial, Marie and her witness, another woman involved in Operation Rescue, could not agree on the place of the incident or on how many people surrounded Susan, only that they had identified Susan as the culprit after seeing her interviewed on television. They said that they had recognized Susan's short haircut and clothing (turtleneck and jeans). The judge declared Susan not guilty, saying that there was no evidence that she had hit Marie Henden. Marie told the press that she had brought the suit to court only to prove that "this kind of behavior is unacceptable."

After Marie's introduction, a silence hung momentarily over St. Bernadette's. And then old Bill Clarke spoke up.

"Four babies were saved this week!" he shouted from his seat near the altar.

"Praise God," said the photographer, who still held the pulpit.

"Praise God," murmured the audience, clapping lightly.

The guitar player began to strum another song, but the zeal had waned. The crowd sang, but few swayed, and even fewer lifted their arms toward heaven. One woman rested her head on her husband's shoulder. He yawned.

It was 8:10 P.M., and still no sign of Randall Terry.

•   •   •

Outside St. Bernadette's, Bill McDermott sat in the Brookline Police Department's blue unmarked cruiser, puffing on a stogie, tired and cranky from another early morning patrolling demonstrations up and down Beacon Street. These people, he thought as he watched the antis file into the church, were like a boil on the ass. Every time you sit down, you know they're there.

Fortunately for the sergeant, the past few Saturdays had been quiet. The Rescue folks had stood in front of Brookline's three clinics in small clusters of ten or fifteen, praying and singing, or clamoring about adoption and financial assistance for patients. Even the New England Christian Action Council, the group that stood in front of Preterm with their yellow signs full of philosophical questions, had not lured more than forty people for its "fall kick-off" in early September. The only trouble the cops had faced lately was separating the prochoice escorts from the antis as both competed to usher the patients from their cars to the clinic steps. McDermott felt sorry for the patients, especially the young ones, who were probably frightened enough by the prospect of abortion. He worried that one day the parent of a minor would haul off and smack anyone, prochoice or antichoice, who blocked the path.

This morning had been calm, except for the prochoice demonstrators teasing the elderly woman with the limp. As usual, she had stood in front of Preterm's steps, clasping wads of pamphlets, many of which fluttered to the ground. "Grandma," as the prochoicers called her, always wore a yellow coat and hung a purse over her wrist, as if she were going to church. "Repent," she would call, her stare unblinking, as the patients ascended the steps. "This could be the day you find Jesus."

The prochoicers loved to engage "Grandma" in debate. "A man and a woman don't make babies," Grandma, whose real name was Georgia Nagle, told them as they questioned her beliefs. "God makes babies. You have no right to destroy God's work." And then the argument would begin as the prochoicers shouted, "How can you say that?!!" But on this Saturday morning, they had simply swiped some of the pamphlets that had fallen from the elderly woman's hands onto the ground.

"They're interfering with my freedom of speech," Georgia Nagle had complained to McDermott. "The law says we can demonstrate unhampered on the sidewalk."

McDermott nodded politely and told the prochoicers to return the material. Under his breath, he muttered, "You've been unhampered all your life."

Now, eight hours later, parked in a dark alley across the street from St. Bernadette's, McDermott was hidden from the rescuers, but they weren't hidden from him. Although he couldn't see inside the doors very well, he had a clear view of the lighted entrance to the sanctuary. Fred Pulsifer, Marie Henden, Bill Clarke—all of the regulars had stepped inside. All except Bill Cotter and Darroline.

McDermott couldn't imagine that those two would miss a chance to rub elbows with Randall Terry. What were they up to? Were they escorting Terry from the airport? Or had they been told by their lawyers to steer clear of Rescue's national leader, that to be seen with him would cement their roles as local leaders and provide more evidence for Brookline's RICO lawsuit against them in federal court? They hadn't been as friendly to McDermott since the July 22 rescue at Preterm, when he had blasted them for carting their people around in the back of a closed truck. Darroline no longer chatted with McDermott when she saw him observing her and her people. Now she glared at the sergeant whenever they met either in court or in front of a clinic, her eyes narrowing and her mouth setting into a straight line. Were Darroline and Cotter plotting something big? McDermott wondered. Rescue had to do something big, or else it would die.

Was that "something" Randall Terry? Perhaps, and that's why McDermott was here instead of at home reading a book. Reading was his hobby, he would say. From Charles Dickens's *A Tale of Two Cities* to Norman Mailer's *The Executioner's Song*, any book was fair game. He wasn't, however, especially fond of detective novels. He had enough of that in real life. Tonight, that detective work meant counting heads and cars and checking the pulse of his "muffins" to try to determine if Randall Terry could reignite the passion that had fizzled in the past few months under Cotter and Darroline. Tomorrow, that detective work meant scouting out his Rescue sources for reviews of this evening's rally.

One of McDermott's sources was an ex-convict named Sam who had found Jesus while serving time in prison for armed robbery of a liquor store. He had found Rescue when he was released. Recently, Sam had told McDermott that people in Rescue were tired of spending sunny fall days in front of abortion clinics when they could be watching a football game or traveling up north for a foliage tour. "I ain't no snitch," Sam would say to McDermott when the sergeant "bumped" into him in the local coffee shop—and then he'd continue to talk. People were especially tired of attacking Gynecare, Sam said. They wanted to return to Brookline because Brookline clinics "killed most of the babies in New England" and they wanted to show the town that they weren't afraid of the RICO lawsuit that Brookline had filed against Rescue's leaders. Besides, Sam said, a lot of rescuers were tired of Bill Cotter and his lousy strategies that never worked.

McDermott had watched enough of Randall Terry on Operation Rescue videos and television to recognize that the thirty-year-old leader oozed a charisma about which Bill Cotter could only dream. Tall and gangly, with a head of wavy hair and a flair for pounding walls and doors and pulpits for emphasis, Randall Terry epitomized the fire-and-brimstone preacher. "Beloved," he would tell his audiences, "The killing must stop!" On television talk shows and debates, he played the annoying kid in class who talked incessantly, forever interrupting his opponents with his verbiage, his snickers, sometimes open laughter. And he was clever, coining such terms as "aboratorium" and "death-scorts," terms that stuck in his audience's memory.

Cloaked in the Bible, Randall Terry demanded the return to a society in which fornication meant procreation, children prayed in schools, and the traditional family unit returned. Terry's enemies were feminism ("Radical feminism hates motherhood, hates children for the most part, and promotes lesbian activity," he often said), Planned Parenthood (for encouraging the young to indulge in sex by providing them with contraception and sexual education), and the American Civil Liberties Union (for supporting a woman's right to "kill her own children"), to name a few. Whether you considered Terry a prophet or a nut, you listened when he had the stage. He was, above all, a scene-stealer.

McDermott hadn't known what to expect for numbers at St. Bernadette's tonight, but he had expected that those who did show would stand outside the church waving signs of "WELCOME RANDY," or scattering rose petals on the ground, or something to hail their messiah. Instead, the abortion foes had streamed quietly into the sanctuary, nodding solemnly to each other in greeting as if they were attending mass. Only a small cluster of men stood outside the church, too deep in conversation to notice whether any of the cars pulling into the lot harbored their leader. The only thing out of the ordinary that the sergeant had noticed was that one of the men outside, Bruce Henden, Marie Henden's husband, wore a suit jacket and tie. McDermott had never seen "Big Bruce," as he called him, dressed in anything but dirty dungarees and faded T-shirts. Everything about Bruce was big, from his height—well over six feet—to his bushy black beard to his girth, and McDermott didn't hesitate to tease him at Saturday demonstrations. "You've got to lose some weight," McDermott would say, pointing to Bruce's belly, which hung over his belt.

"I'm trying, Sarge," Bruce would say, sucking in his gut. "I'm trying."

At least McDermott could joke with some of these people. Once when he had run into "Scout," the little redheaded guy who had locked himself underneath the state police bus at the July 22 rescue, in Brookline Municipal Court as Scout had waited for a pretrial hearing for some blockade—it was hard to remember which one—McDermott had asked, "Can I talk to you a minute?"

"Only on God's terms," Scout had replied.

"OK," McDermott said. "Your fly is open."

Scout looked down at his gaping zipper and blushed.

Bill Cotter was not so good-humored about McDermott's barbs. When McDermott pointed to Cotter's sneakers, torn and grimy, and asked what happened to the new shoes he had seen Cotter sport, Cotter replied stonily, "That's not funny." McDermott felt that he made Cotter uncomfortable. Every time Billy C. saw the cop, he'd roll back on his heels, stare straight ahead, and utter, "Hi, Sarge," when McDermott's eyes met his. McDermott didn't bother trying to engage Cotter in a philosophical argument about abortion as he did with some of the others. "What would you do if your daughter were raped and became pregnant?" he once asked some of his Rescue pals he "ran into" at the coffee shop.

"God's will . . ." one fellow began to say.

"You're full of shit," McDermott interrupted. I know these people, he thought. They're white Irish Catholics, blue-collar workers, who would take their little Becky out of state and figure out some way to justify the abortion rather than suffer the humiliation of an illegitimate pregnancy. He loved nothing more than to tell Bob Delery, a longtime sidewalk counselor in front of Planned Parenthood, that half of Preterm's patients were students from Boston College, a Jesuit school. "No," Bob Delery said, refusing to believe it.

It was almost 8:15 P.M. and McDermott wondered if Randall Terry would show. Settling back in the seat, he stared at the church, an innocuous brick building set back from the street, a church he had entered less than two months before for the funeral of his cousin, Michael, who in his early fifties had died of a massive coronary. The thought was enough to make McDermott shudder. Michael wasn't more than ten years older than McDermott, who had enough of his own health problems to worry about.

Two years before, the sergeant had been hospitalized with acute pancreatitis. He didn't think that his beer drinking had caused the illness—he drank, but he didn't drink *that* much—but he wasn't about to risk that agonizing pain again. He'd sworn off beer and Scotch and prime rib and fried clams, anything the doctor warned might spark another attack. He didn't miss the fried food or the beef, and he shrugged when asked if he missed the drinking. At police parties, he volunteered to drive home those who had imbibed a few too many brews.

If the pancreatitis didn't get him, he sometimes mused, maybe the Agent Orange that he had probably inhaled in Vietnam would. He had enlisted in the army at age eighteen in 1967 after his football career at Northeastern University had been cut short in his freshman year by a shoulder injury. Required to spend only one year in Southeast Asia, he had volunteered for another. "I was alive and thought why not continue?" he explained later. "Youth is a dangerous thing." He lasted another six months, brought home by injuries to his back and shoulder. He didn't talk about Vietnam much, but when he did, it was often in reference to the shrapnel he had collected in his foot, which had caused the amputation of a baby toe. He hadn't earned any awards for his military service, but Uncle Sam had paid for his education.

An admitted slack-off during his first round of college, McDermott had returned home to Brookline on a Thursday and registered for classes at Lowell State College the next Monday. He feared that if he didn't go to school right away he might never do it. The next year, 1970, he married a woman from his native Brookline and transferred to the now-defunct Boston State College to continue his liberal arts studies. He had wanted to be a history teacher, but sometime that year a friend of his suggested that they take the police exam. McDermott joined the Brookline police force and his friend became a teacher. As a young cop, he worked the usual details at hotels and stores and construction sites, finished his bachelor's degree with a double major in criminal justice and English, had four kids, now ages eight to eighteen, and became a detective. He loved being a detective, walking the streets, knowing the junkies and their informants. He liked going undercover, dressing in a black leather jacket, growing a Fu Manchu mustache, and hanging out with drug dealers. "Hey," one of his Brookline High School classmates had called to him once at his drug hangout. "What are you doing here? Aren't you a cop?" The place had emptied out.

McDermott kept his family life private, sometimes telling friends and fellow cops stories about his kids, but not often. He had met his wife in high school, and no, he would say, they weren't childhood sweethearts. What got them together when he returned from Vietnam? "She must have been lonely," he responded. But the marriage was going on twenty years, withstanding his avoidance of holiday gatherings ("Something from my childhood," he said) and his endless late nights and early mornings scoping out criminals, or in this case, abortion foes.

On nights like this, he felt like a character in a bad detective novel. McDermott certainly didn't feel he was taxing his investigative powers sitting in his cruiser waiting for Randall Terry to arrive, nor patrolling Beacon Street every morning, nor processing forms that the abortion foes had filled out complaining of police brutality. "Jesus Christ," he would swear to himself whenever he saw another of his "muffins" enter the police station with a complaint. Through gritted teeth, he would politely offer his assistance.

The old lady with the limp, Georgia Nagle, had visited him in the police station after Marie Henden had been arrested for stepping on Preterm's steps despite warnings from the police to stay behind the clinic's private-property line. "She is a saint," Georgia Nagle had told McDermott, her eyes filling with tears. The eyes of the arresting policeman were those of "the devil," she said, and the women in the blue bibs (the clinic escorts) "weren't human."

"They're devils," she said. "And they steal my pamphlets."

"With all due respect, ma'am," McDermott said. "I've seen you out there and I admire your dedication, but I've seen you drop those pamphlets."

"Oh no," she replied. "The devil takes them."

She's fucking nuts, McDermott thought.

But he was stuck with Georgia and the rest of them as long as Rescue kept up its tricks and as long as the court injunction remained lifted. Planned Parenthood had appealed Judge Nolan's decision in August to allow clinic blockades, and the full Supreme Judicial Court bench had agreed to hear the case. So far, the court had not issued a verdict, which meant that McDermott's antiabortion friends could blockade till they were blue without worrying about the $500 fine (or the $2,500 fine, if they were organizers) that could have been levied on offenders had the injunction stayed in force.

Sometimes McDermott feared that he'd work the Operation Rescue beat forever. With George Driscoll gone, McDermott was the only cop in Brookline who had studied Rescue locally and nationally and had cultivated sources. McDermott knew where to find "the wino," the rescuer with the red face and bulbous nose who ran around blockades with a video camera, and Sam, the ex-convict, as well as the fellow whose wife and daughter were active in Rescue. And he knew the questions to ask to make them talk. They trusted him. He didn't know why; maybe because he was Irish Catholic as many of them were. They couldn't tell him what clinic was targeted because they themselves didn't know—the leaders still kept details within Rescue's hierarchy— but they offered him the dates of meetings and rumors of future rescues.

Through them, McDermott gathered enough information to prepare the police force and to convince the chief of his Rescue expertise. McDermott sighed. Operation Rescue needed to attempt something unique, perhaps a massive invasion of Preterm or Planned Parenthood, to kindle his interest again. It wasn't that he wanted the movement to succeed; he only wanted the challenge of foiling Cotter and Darroline.

At 8:20 P.M. a van and a couple of cars pulled into the church parking lot. The car doors opened and McDermott recognized the lanky silhouette, bushy hair, and wire-rimmed glasses of Randall Terry. He didn't look like a messiah or even like a cult hero as he and several men walked briskly in the darkness toward the church.

Inside the sanctuary waited 300—or so McDermott estimated— malleable minds. If the abortion foes hadn't been falling over themselves with enthusiasm for Terry when they had entered the church, maybe they would be when they exited, brimming with their leader's encouragement. From his vantage point across the street, McDermott couldn't see into the church to watch the crowd's reaction to Terry, but he heard ripples of clapping.

After a few minutes, when it was clear that all who intended to hear

Randall Terry were inside and there were no more heads to count, McDermott switched on the ignition and turned the cruiser toward Brookline. Had Boston's Soldiers of God spent too many nights in jail, seen too many failed rescues, to succumb to Terry's pressure? Or would they, once again, try to put his theory that "if you say it is murder why don't you act like it's murder" into practice? Was a surprise invasion in store? A big rescue? Or nothing?

Of one thing McDermott was sure. He needed a long vacation from these people, and he wasn't likely to get one any time soon.

· · ·

Randall Terry bounded to the altar like a game-show host jogging to his position behind the microphone. Wearing a short-sleeved plaid shirt, light green pants, and white sneakers, he apologized for being inappropriately dressed. He hadn't had time to change.

"We got off the plane, grabbed a bite to eat, and got stuck in traffic," he said breathlessly, his voice both loud and a little high pitched. "Someone had an accident on the bridge, or the bridge had an accident on the bridge, or the . . ." he paused to let his audience laugh. "Then we drove down a one-way street and two angels died protecting us. It was awesome."

Unlike some public figures, Randall Terry appeared the same way in person as he did in magazine photographs and on television. He had the same coarse, wavy hair that puffed on top of his head, the same lively—some might say hyperactive—presence. So far, his reception at St. Bernadette's had been warm—lots of smiles and clapping—but not effusive. There had been no rose petals tossed at his feet, as Sergeant McDermott had expected, nor was there a standing ovation. The 300 pairs of eyes in the audience stared at the man behind the pulpit, the man who had inspired more than 20,000 arrests across the country for his cause. But no sooner had this man ascended to the altar than he descended, offering the microphone to one of his associates, Pat Mahoney of Florida, who had flown to Boston on the plane with Terry.

"I have my suit on," Mahoney, a dark Irishman, said to the audience as he smoothed down his lapels for effect. "The truth is, Randall Terry doesn't even own a jacket."

Boston's rescue folk laughed politely, a good sign for Terry, not because the audience recognized the joke—Terry's tailored suits and impeccable grooming were well documented by the press and in his own Operation Rescue videos—but because laughter meant that the crowd was loosening up. Like any effective speaker, Randall Terry knew enough to relax his audience with humor before socking it with his message—and his pleas for donations. He came by this gift both naturally and by practice. Terry wasn't an ordained minister, but he was a graduate of the Elim Bible Institute, near Rochester, New York, where he had grown up.

Randall Terry came from a family of feminists, which many believed to be a major force in what his opponents called his crusade to squash women's freedom, to push them back into a position of subservience. His mother's three sisters all had been activists in civil rights and women's equality in the 1960s. During the next decade, they had spoken publicly for legalized and safe abortion. One aunt became a spokeswoman for Planned Parenthood in Rochester, New York. Each of the four sisters had had an unplanned pregnancy in her youth; Randall Terry was the product of one. He frequently told reporters that he was glad abortion hadn't been legal back then.

But Terry's route to Operation Rescue wasn't as simple as rebellion against strong-minded aunts. A talented musician with an occasional marijuana habit and hair so full it could almost graze both sides of a doorway, the teenage Randy Terry quit high school four months shy of graduation to hitchhike cross-country to become a rock-and-roll star in California. He returned home several months later after his backpack was stolen while he slept on a beach in Galveston, Texas.

Where he found Jesus was a subject of speculation even in his family. Some relatives claimed that Randy had been "saved" during his travels; others said it had happened when he returned to his parents' home outside of Rochester. One of his aunts told a reporter for *Mother Jones* magazine that shortly after his return to New York, Randy locked himself in his room claiming he was Jesus Christ, emerging two days later saying that he had misinterpreted the message, that he was Jesus Christ's messenger. Terry himself told the *Mother Jones* reporter that he had begun preaching three months after his return to New York when a lay preacher from the nearby Elim Bible Institute bought an ice-cream cone from Randy, who was working at a local ice-cream stand. Noticing Randy's Bible on the counter, the man began talking theology and later that night, as the two were driving on the highway, they picked up a homeless elderly woman who received Terry's first sermon.

After that, in between flipping hamburgers, pumping gas, and selling used cars, whatever he could do to earn a dollar, Terry preached—to his family, to hitchhikers, to victims of accidents he happened to be near. In 1986 in Vestal, New York, near Binghamton, the site of Operation

Rescue's national headquarters, he bolted past medics in the kitchen of a local restaurant to pray over a cook who had severed his hand in a meat grinder. He was charged with obstructing the administration of medical aid. Terry went on to earn his high-school equivalency and attend classes at Elim Bible Institute, where he met his wife, Cindy.

In truth, it was Cindy who began picketing the Southern Tier Women's Center in downtown Binghamton in 1984, pleading with women not to abort their babies, telling them that she couldn't have one and would take theirs if they didn't want it. The Terrys were, in fact, having difficulty conceiving. (Several years later, Cindy gave birth to a daughter. A few years after that, the Terrys became foster parents of three biracial children.) Once her husband—who had been inspired by a bumper sticker that said, "ABORTION: PICK ON SOMEONE YOUR OWN SIZE"—got into the act, though, Cindy faded. Instead of pleading, Terry used force, slamming his body against the patients' car doors, and, once, barging into the clinic screaming the name of a patient whose identity he had uncovered. He said that the concept of Operation Rescue—stopping abortions by preventing women from entering clinics—had come to him in a "vision." His "vision" came after Joe Scheidler, founder of Pro-Life Action Network, otherwise known as PLAN, wrote his book, *Closed: 99 Ways to Stop Abortion*, which included the idea of blockading clinic entrances. Scheidler later said that he didn't begrudge Randy's rescue movement, that he was glad someone was acting "to save babies."

Pat Mahoney stood tall at the altar, exuberantly praising the efforts of his Florida followers, telling how their prayers had shut down a Miami abortion clinic. After an article about the clinic appeared in the *Miami Herald*'s Sunday magazine, the state of Florida had closed the clinic's doors, citing a litany of unsanitary and dangerous conditions, from unsanitary equipment to a failure to "determine" if women were pregnant before they were given abortions to a staff doctor who was a convicted sex offender.

"It's a miracle," Mahoney said.

Since Mahoney was organizing the "Veterans Campaign for Life" and the D.C. Project in November, it was only fitting that he pitch these upcoming events to the Boston audience. He described how war veterans from around the country would congregate on Sunday, November 11, to rescue the unborn at "a local D.C. abortuary."

"The veterans in Florida are losing weight right now to fit into their uniforms," Mahoney said. His audience laughed.

Three days after the veterans' rescue, the D.C. Project would begin with a prayer rally, followed by a day of seminars and training in activism and two days of local rescues. The red, white, and blue pamphlet circulating in the audience called for church leadership and "each Christian to repent for their failure to act in response to the abortion holocaust."

"Our goal is to make our nation's capital abortion free!" Mahoney said. "We will end with an evening of praise and celebration."

The question, of course, was where the celebration would be held if all those attending the three-day project were tossed in jail for blocking D.C. abortion clinics. But no one in the audience asked. Some nodded their heads, but most sat silently, their faces blank, reflecting neither disinterest nor enthusiasm for Randall Terry's latest plan to attract national attention. The crowd clapped courteously as Mahoney stepped down from the altar.

"He's made them all happy, and now I'm going to make them all depressed," said Randall Terry, taking his place at the microphone as if he were talking to himself. Then he looked up and stared directly at the people in the congregation, a searching look as if he would find the answer to life's questions in their faces. With the D.C. Project pitch out of the way, Randall Terry could concentrate on regenerating enthusiasm for his work.

Operation Rescue's leader needed some strong public relations pull with his followers on that fall evening. Several weeks before, a federal appeals court in New York had upheld an injunction barring protesters from blockading abortion clinics, ruling that fining the organization— $25,000 for each violation of the injunction—was within the law. Even more recently, in Atlanta, Terry had been convicted of trespassing and unlawful assembly during the Democratic National Convention in July 1988. There was a good chance that the judge would slam him with the full sentence: two years in jail and a $2,000 fine. Strong leadership was critical to the Rescue movement, and Terry needed to assure his people that Rescue would still be stable even if he were in jail. He needed to encourage them to continue their work, his work.

"I'll probably go to jail," Terry said softly into the microphone. "Pray for my dear wife. May God's will be done."

The crowd mumbled. Several women clicked their tongues in disgust at the thought of their spiritual leader behind bars.

His head bowed, Randall Terry stood at the altar, taking a breath before he launched into his sermon. "Beloved," he said quietly, "I've been reading the Book of Jeremiah, and I have been troubled by it."

Beware, he said, the Lord's vengeance will descend as it did in the

Book of Jeremiah on the people who did not worship the Lord, who prayed to false idols and practiced child-sacrifice. Jeremiah had warned those people that they would be ravaged by drought and famine so severe that they would revert to cannibalism. And, Terry boomed, a man ate the flesh of his son, only to lose his wife to plague six months later. His voice dropping, Terry said, "We are in so much trouble before God.

"The day is coming when we may find ourselves hiding in the hills to protect our families, or locked up in huge holding facilities," Terry shouted, his hands clutching the sides of the lectern. "We may find our churches seized, closed, or burnt to the ground. Some of us will lose our children. Some of our wives will be ripped open. You may have to spend your life's savings for a loaf of bread."

The audience belonged to Randall Terry. No one so much as twitched.

"It's coming, beloved," he said, pausing, "because of the blood!"

The blood, his audience knew, was the blood of abortion. All eyes were focused on Terry's face, which was lined with streaks of sweat. Some of the women looked frightened.

"Pretend this is 1959," Terry said, his voice softening once again. "Who would believe that there would be the brutal murder of 25 million children, that we'd begin to starve our newborn infants, that we'd have public school systems where it is illegal to pray in school, that we'd have a school system that teaches third graders how to use a condom and practice safe sex, that one day mayors will announce gay pride week, that people will abduct children, photograph them nude, sell them to pornographic magazines, and that people will buy them? Should I continue??!!"

Without waiting for a response, he did.

"That TV sitcoms will mock Christianity. Do you want me to continue?"

This time he didn't. He paused, then asked, "Where will we be thirty years from now? And what are *you* doing to stop America's slide into hell?" His audience looked ashen. He had reached them. Several men in one aisle nodded their heads.

"Young people are turning away from the church. Why? Because they hear us complain that we can't buy that new BMW, or buy that third color TV for the guest room." He stared at the audience, his face wrinkled in disgust at the vision he had painted.

"We need to be prepared to die for the Lord. What will the next generations of Christians say about us? We already are an embarrassment to heaven.

"Ah," he sighed. "God help us."

The sanctuary was so silent that his listeners could almost hear Randall Terry breathing. His head bowed, Terry looked as if he were inhaling inspiration. When he looked up, he was back on fire.

"We have to stop doing what we're doing! We are on the edge of survival. Do you want there to be a country twenty years from now? We can stop this war in one or two years. All hands on deck, folks. Some of us will go to jail. I don't want to go to jail. But I don't want my children to suffer because I'm a wimp. It is better to perish than live as slaves."

Terry said that he wanted history to show that the wave of repentance began in the late 1980s and early 1990s, that then the people turned the tide of morality and "shoved child killing back to hell." He wanted those in the congregation to tell stories to their grandchildren and their great grandchildren of how they restored the nation.

"Repentance and reformation," he said. "Transform Western civilization for the next 200 years. Maybe Eastern civilization, too."

Then, Terry asked the church full of Boston's devoted antiabortionists to splinter into groups of twos and threes to pray.

Heads bowed, hands clasped, eyes closed, the men and women slid together in their small clusters and prayed, the hum of their mumbled words rising in the sanctuary. "Please God, let the judge suspend Randy's sentence, so he won't have to go to jail," whispered one young woman with dark hair. "Please forgive our weaknesses, our fears. Make us strong. Help us fight this battle back to morality."

"I cry to you, oh Lord!" shouted Bruce Henden, his eyes clamped tightly closed. "Take away the hardness, the cruelness."

"He is Lord," Randall Terry said, and stepped down from the altar. Once again, Pat Mahoney replaced him.

"Randall Terry makes you feel uncomfortable," Mahoney said. "And I'm not sure that's negative."

Several people in the crowd squirmed. Mahoney stared down at the audience coldly.

"Randall Terry faces two years in jail," Mahoney continued. "Bill and Darroline face RICO suits. What are *you* willing to sacrifice?"

Randall Terry assumed the microphone again. His preaching over, he had summoned back his lightheartedness for comic relief. It was time for the offering.

Although Randall Terry insisted to authorities that Operation Rescue's national office in Binghamton had taken in $300,000 in 1988, most of those who studied the organization believed that Rescue's income soared into the millions. In addition to receiving backing from such luminaries as TV evangelist Jerry Falwell and Tom Monaghan, president of Domino's Pizza, Terry appealed for and got money every time he appeared on Christian television and every time he assumed the altar at a church or the podium at a lecture hall. Like the other Operation Rescue satellites around the country, the national office was not considered a nonprofit business—if it were, it would have to make public the names of its donors. Nor was it a for-profit business—for-profits have to pay taxes. Instead, the Operation Rescue chapters were designated as DBAs, or Doing Business As. This meant that the business was run solely by an individual or individuals. That way, those who claimed to run an Operation Rescue outfit could place all of their seizable assets, such as a house and car, under the name of their spouse, or parent, anyone they trusted. In case of an audit, the individuals would be examined, not the organization, and without assets, those named would suffer a minimal loss. In Boston, Operation Rescue told the Internal Revenue Service that it was operated by four people, two of whom were Bill Cotter and Darroline Firlit.

"How many of you donate monthly to Boston Operation Rescue?" Terry asked.

No one raised a hand.

"OK," he said. "How many of you eat pizza once a month?"

No one raised a hand.

"OK, how about hamburgers? Do you go to Burger King?"

"Burger King is antilife!" shouted one woman.

"OK," Terry said. "How about Domino's?"

The crowd cheered. Apparently, they knew that Domino's president supported their cause.

"I want everyone to donate their pizza money to Operation Rescue," Terry ordered. "I've noticed that Bill Cotter has gained a little weight lately, so he doesn't need the pizza. But he does need the money."

Pocketbooks clicked open, men dug into their pockets, and as the baskets passed from one to another down the pews, hands plunked down dollars and checks. The evening with Randall Terry was over.

• • •

Two days later, Sam, the former convict, told McDermott that Bill Cotter had been upset when he heard about the small crowd and lack of media at the Randall Terry rally. Only one television camera and one print reporter had been in the room, and as far as anyone knew, the story hadn't been aired or printed. McDermott was suspicious of the

"Chicago trip" Darroline and Cotter had supposedly made during Terry's visit, especially when he heard later that week that Cotter had told a reporter that the seminar was on how to hold Rescue banquets across the country simultaneously and communicate via satellite. "What??" McDermott had said, rubbing his forehead. That sounded too stupid—even for them. Something was up.

Shortly after Terry's night in town, an infiltrator had mailed McDermott an Operation Rescue newsletter announcing that the next rescue was slated for October 14. "Could be interesting," McDermott told his colleagues in the station. Maybe Rescue would try something unique to get themselves back on the map, something to pique the sergeant's interest. As usual, the Brookline police planned to outfit each of the three clinics with twenty cops and rows of barricades on the morning of the rumored rescue. If the abortion foes struck a Brookline clinic, the town's cost for clinic protection would hurdle $100,000.

That Saturday, 200 rescuers hit Gynecare and sixty-nine were arrested, hardly the overwhelming numbers Operation Rescue had hoped Randall Terry would inspire to fight childkilling. Patients made it inside the clinic without much trauma once police cleared a path. As far as McDermott could tell from his spot across the street on Boston Common, the prochoice demonstrators outnumbered their opposition two to one. The October 14 rescue earned a brief story buried inside the pages of *The Boston Globe's* Metro section.

Randall Terry's response to the rescue was not immediately known. Five days after he had warned his Boston fans of the famine and pestilence that would result from America's evil ways, Rescue's leader began serving a two-year jail sentence in Atlanta. Terry had refused to pay the $2,000 fine or stay away from Atlanta for two years, either of which would have spared him from prison. Since an anonymous donor had not come forward with money to bail him out, as the opposition had predicted, Randall Terry was digging ditches somewhere in Georgia, his wavy hair shaved from his head.

CHAPTER TEN

Too Young

Today, I am your mother
and we are waiting for your world to end.
I am sorry, perhaps if it was another time, another place,
I would bring you out of me, into the world.
you would have friends, hands, ideas. I am sorry, my baby,
I have learned more from you than most of my living has given me.
we could be making a whole life. goodbye. I am sorry.
I am ashamed to leave you.
this is your birthday
this is the end of the world.

—written by a sixteen-year-old Preterm patient

"HELLO, Preterm Health Services, may I help you?" Sue Richdale said into her telephone receiver from her desk in the clinic's phone room. The phones had rung constantly all morning, and Sue was already weary of picking up the receiver to schedule yet another abortion or gynecology appointment. Usually, the fatigue didn't hit until the middle of the afternoon after she had answered thirty or forty calls, but it seemed by eleven o'clock on this gray Monday morning in November that she had already talked to every woman in Greater Boston who sought an abortion or a chlamydia test.

But this voice on the other end of the telephone line jolted Sue to sit up straight and clasp the phone tightly to her ear, as if relaxing her grip would cause her to lose the connection. The voice, a mother's, started calmly enough, stating that her fifteen-year-old daughter was pregnant. But with each word the voice accelerated, until Sue felt that she was listening to a record playing at 78 RPM. And then the mother began to wail.

"Excuse me, ma'am," Sue interjected softly. "I can't understand you."

Sue had worked in Preterm's phone room for six months, hoping to earn enough money to pay for her last semester at Boston College, a Jesuit university a few miles from the clinic. The fact that she was raised Catholic and attended a Catholic school didn't dilute her belief in a woman's right to choose whether or not to be a mother. Sue didn't feel that she, or anyone else, was qualified to judge such an intimate decision. Although the days were long and the work repetitive as she asked each caller the same questions—"Do you have asthma? Epilepsy? Diabetes?"; rattled off the same anesthesia options—"We have a local anesthesia and intravenous sedation"; and described the same procedure—"Then the doctor will dilate your cervix . . ."—Sue felt good that she could help these women take the initial steps in solving a crisis. In the evaluation sheets—or the "green sheets" as they were called at Preterm because of their color—that patients filled out after their abortion, Sue was consistently lauded as being understanding and helpful.

But today, as the naked branches of the trees lining the sidewalk tapped in the wind against the phone room's window, Sue wondered how helpful she could be to this hysterical mother.

"It's my fault she's pregnant," the mother sobbed. Divorced, the mother felt that she hadn't spent enough time with her daughter; she was gone all day at her secretarial job, and too tired when she got home to talk to Alison. Maybe if she had arrived home earlier in the afternoon or if she had been a better listener, Alison would have told her that she was having sex, or thinking about having sex, and they could have discussed birth control. Or maybe she could have persuaded Alison to abstain.

Sue knew that asking Alison to abstain was like asking the moon not to rise at night. Once teens began having sex, they rarely returned to chastity.

"May I speak to your daughter, please?" Sue asked, explaining that the patient must make the appointment, even if she were a minor.

Sue was accustomed to parents calling for their young daughters. Often the mothers, or fathers, were angry, seething as they called their daughter to the phone. Others were sad, but supportive. It was tough to be a parent of teens, Sue knew. Her own parents had been to hell and back with her younger sister, who had become pregnant at fifteen and had decided to keep the baby. Three years later, her sister and niece still lived with her parents. Although her parents loved their grandchild, raising a baby the second time around was a struggle. Tired from rearing their own children, they didn't have much energy left to discipline, feed, and diaper their grandchild. While Sue's sister participated in the childrearing, she often let her mother do the chores. Sue's father joked about adding a new wing to the house for his second family. He might have to, Sue thought. The last time she had called home, her sister had told her that she thought she was pregnant again.

Sue was short with straight black hair that stuck straight up in front and was shaved close to her head in the back. "Punk," another phone counselor said of her hair. "Easy to take care of," Sue replied. All she needed was a little gel to make the front strands stand erect. Her face was round, her skin fair, and her voice raspy. In the phone room, Sue Richdale was a presence. She walked fast, talked fast, and said whatever came to mind. "Ciao, baby," she called one afternoon to Barbara, one of the older phone counselors, a grandmother, who had survived her own illegal abortion years ago in Jamaica. Barbara had laughed all the way to Preterm's front door.

Sue lived in an apartment with five roommates, one of whom was her longtime boyfriend. At twenty-three, she was one of Preterm's youngest employees. Scheduling appointments for abortion and gynecology patients (the sterilization clinic made its own appointments) was an entry-level job, starting at $7.50 an hour, and many of the young women who answered phones in the room just off of the administrative area either were working their way through college—Sue had one semester at Boston College left—or were recent graduates. Although the credentials of some were impressive enough to land far more lucrative jobs—Sarah had graduated Phi Beta Kappa from Brown University and Liz had just finished her thesis on Chinese women to complete her bachelor's degree from Harvard University—they chose to work at Preterm to, in their words, help women. Some had had abortions themselves and hoped to give other women the support that they had once needed and received. Others, such as Sue Richdale, were simply interested in women's health, and as Sue would say, in "working with people." Working with so many people—a phone counselor could answer up to eighty calls a day—was exhausting, and phone counselors rarely lasted more than a year before they switched jobs, often within the clinic.

On the other end of the line, Sue heard the mother gently coax Alison to the phone. After a few minutes of mumbles, Alison weakly greeted Sue. "Hi, how ya' doin?" Sue asked.

Like her mother, Alison began sobbing. "I . . . don't . . . want . . . an . . . abortion," she said, gulping for air. Sue listened carefully as Alison stumbled through her explanation, that she loved her boyfriend and wanted to have his baby.

"Uh, uh," Sue said, to make sure Alison knew she was listening.

Sue had spoken with enough teenagers to wonder if the woman/child on the other end really wanted to have the baby, or if she were merely frightened of the abortion procedure. Teenagers didn't think much beyond tomorrow, and the fear of a doctor inserting a rod into their vagina as they lay on a cold table with their legs spread apart was more terrifying than the idea of labor and delivery, which seemed too far in the future to be real. Alison, like many of the teenagers who visited Preterm's abortion clinic, had never even had a pelvic exam.

Alison gave the phone back to her mother, who still wept. At least once a day, Sue talked to a patient whose story caused her throat to tighten and tears to well, such as the woman who had tried for years to become pregnant only to find through tests that her fetus was missing most of its brain. Most times, Sue could maintain composure, but the sobbing of this mother and daughter was too much. "She's too young to have a baby," the mother moaned. "She doesn't understand the responsibility." Sue began to cry.

On another phone was Lin Sherman, who at forty-five prided herself on her ability to talk to teens, soothing them by speaking so softly that her words streamed out more like a melody than like questions. Young patients found Lin "motherly." Lin found young patients upsetting. She yearned to put her arms around the adolescent on the other end of the line and tell her that it wasn't the end of the world. Sometimes she wanted to do the same for the parent. In a crisis, Lin would often say to a distraught mother, "the first thing we lose is perspective."

"Your parents know, but they don't want you to have an abortion?" Lin said to the sixteen-year-old on her line, explaining that in the Bay State girls under eighteen needed to have both of their parents' permission or a judge's consent to have the abortion. "You have two options," Lin told the girl, "you can either go out of state for your abortion or you can go before a judge here in Massachusetts."

Sue put the mother and daughter on hold and looked around the room for support. Seven or eight phone counselors worked per eight-hour shift, each sitting at a wooden table bearing a phone, notepad, piles of admitting forms, and a plastic disk divided into months and gestation dates to help the counselors calculate how many weeks pregnant their patient was. Sue's desk formed one side of a triangle of desks, but Sarah and Jane, the two counselors at the other desks, were both on the phone, unable to offer Sue advice. Behind Sue, the three counselors at their triangle of desks were busy, too. Lin, who sat across from Sue, was hunched over her desk, immersed in her conversation with the sixteen-year-old.

"Do you have transportation?" Lin asked slowly and softly. "The Feminist Health Center of Portsmouth in New Hampshire is closest to you. Here's the phone number. Yes, this is all confidential."

Last week, Sue had fielded a similar call. A fourteen-year-old had told her that her parents had refused to sign the consent form. "You play, you pay," the girl's mother had said. "This is your problem," her father had added. "Have a baby."

That clearly wasn't the case with the duo now on Sue's phone. When Sue returned to the mother and daughter, Alison was back on the line. She said that she would make an appointment, but that she didn't promise to go through with the abortion.

"OK," Sue said. "Do you remember the first day of your last menstrual period?"

She didn't. Alison wasn't about to make this simple for Sue.

• • •

Nothing was simple about teenagers and pregnancy, especially when parents and daughters saw different solutions to the crisis—which nearly half a million girls under eighteen experienced every year in the U.S. On one side was the parent, the guardian who remained responsible for the child, whose permission was required for everything from class field trips to administering a tetanus shot. Although the daughter's body performed as a woman's, she was still a child to her parent, still a dependent, still in need of maternal, or paternal, guidance. From a parent's perspective, a teenager didn't have the life experience to make such an irreversible decision as whether or not to end a pregnancy. A teenager was too naive to realize the time and energy that babies demand, or how a baby could hinder or change forever plans for college or career. From another point of view, a teenager was too young to understand the immorality of destroying fetal life.

On the other side was the teenage girl, who alone faced a swelling belly and varicose veins and Saturday nights burping an infant. She, not her parents, would lose the freedom to dash off to the movies, or spend hours after school editing the yearbook or playing basketball or just giggling with friends. Even if her parents helped her financially, the teenage mother was ultimately responsible for feeding and housing and educating her child—for at least eighteen long years. If the teen aborted, she, not her parents, would carry the memory of ending the life inside of her. The embryo was part of her body, her life, her future. And for that reason alone, she felt that only she could make the decision.

Almost from the moment Justice Blackmun had uttered the Supreme Court's *Roe* v. *Wade* decision, stating that the reproductive rights of *all* women were protected under the constitutional right to privacy, lawmakers and laypeople alike had demanded that parents be involved in a minor's decision about whether or not to end a pregnancy. Massachusetts was the first state to act, its legislature approving a law that required every minor under eighteen to have both parents' consent before she could have an abortion. Opponents challenged the law all the way to the Supreme Court in a case called *Bellotti* (Francis X. Bellotti, who was then the state's attorney general) v. *Baird* (Bill Baird, the renowned abortion rights advocate), arguing that the restrictions violated minors' constitutional right to privacy. In 1979, the Supreme Court determined that requiring parental consent did violate a minor's constitutional right, but, in a surprising move, four justices added that the requirement could be constitutional if the state provided minors with an alternative form of authorization, such as judicial consent.

Massachusetts politicians shot back to their writing tables and revised the original law, adding the option of a judicial bypass. The new law was passed in 1980 and implemented a year later, thus requiring all unmarried girls under eighteen to get both parents' consent, or receive a judge's authorization. If minors chose not to tell their parents, they could sit before a judge, who would ask them questions to determine if they were mature enough to have an abortion. If the judge concluded that the minor was immature, that she didn't understand the gravity of her decision, the judge would decide if having the abortion was in the teenager's "best interest." Abortion rights advocates were quick to point out that if the minor was deemed too immature to have an abortion, how could she be mature enough to nurture a healthy pregnancy or care for an infant?

Since then, thirty-one states had passed laws either requiring parental consent or notification of parents by the abortion provider, but only eleven states' laws were in effect. The other legislation had been struck down in court as being unconstitutional in that it denied prompt health care and privacy to young women based solely on their age. The laws of two states, Minnesota and Ohio, had been appealed again and again, until they reached the final stage—the Supreme Court.

On Wednesday, November 29, the day after Sue Richdale's patient, Alison, had scheduled her abortion at Preterm, the high court would hear *Ohio* v. *Akron Center for Reproductive Health* and *Hodgson* v. *Minnesota*. Since the Court's other high-profile abortion case of the 1989–90 session, *Ragsdale* v. *Turnock*, which involved requiring abortion clinics to act as small hospitals, had been settled out of court earlier that month, the nation was riveted on the two cases concerning minors.

In *Ohio* v. *Akron Center for Reproductive Health*, the law under fire required that one parent be notified by the doctor who would perform the abortion. In *Hodgson* v. *Minnesota*, the challenged law demanded that the abortion provider notify both parents—regardless of whether the parents were divorced, never married, or if one parent had not been in touch with the minor for years, if ever—forty-eight hours before the procedure.

Abortion foes focused their argument on parental, not abortion, rights, claiming that since parents were ultimately responsible for the behavior of their dependent children, they should not be excluded from their daughter's decision to have an abortion. The notification and consent laws would foster family communication, they argued, and would enable parents to help their child through a traumatic time.

The laws' opponents argued that you can't legislate family relations, that teens had reasons for not telling their parents, and frequently the reason was fear of violence. Often cited was the case of Spring Adams, a thirteen-year-old girl from Idaho, whose father had shot her dead when he had learned that she was pregnant with his child. Other less brutal tales included a girl whose doctor advised her not to tell her father, who had recently suffered a stroke, or another teen who hadn't confided in her mother for worry that her mother, a recovering alcoholic, would hit the bottle again.

The only thing that these restrictive laws fostered, the opponents countered, was delayed—and therefore more risky—abortions, at best, and teenage deaths and mutilation at worst. For proof, two parents from Indiana were traveling the country, telling the tragedy of their seventeen-year-old daughter, Becky, who had been afraid to disappoint her parents with news of her pregnancy. She had considered obtaining court consent (Indiana required one parent's consent or a judicial bypass) but feared the reaction of the local judge, who was reputed to be antiabortion. So Becky Bell, a former cheerleader, had sought her own abortion means and had died less than a week later.

While no one on the Preterm staff would deny the past and potential horrors of restricting abortion to adolescents, the debate, for the most part, struck them as merely an opportunity for individuals on both sides of the issue to blast their rhetoric. The staff knew firsthand that parental consent laws didn't change the number of teens seeking abortions. In the eight years that Massachusetts' law had been in effect, the number of teenage abortions had not shifted, averaging under five thousand a year. More than two-thirds of those teens had received their abortion with at least one parent's permission (the law states that both parents' consent is requested, except if one parent has sole custody or one parent cannot be reached within a "reasonable amount of time"). The rest either traveled to states without parental consent or notification laws (each month, between ninety and ninety-five Massachusetts teenagers drove to Connecticut, New Hampshire, or Maine for abortions), or sought a judicial bypass.

Although the prospect of sitting before a judge was terrifying to minors, their journey through the state's judicial system had been eased by a group of women lawyers who had agreed to represent minors going before a judge. In conjunction with Planned Parenthood, the lawyers worked out a system in which a minor calling a clinic for an appointment would be referred to Planned Parenthood, which in turn would connect the minor with a lawyer. The lawyer would set up a court date, meet the teen at the Superior Courthouse a half hour or so before the appointment to discuss what the judge may ask, and sit with the minor in the judge's chambers as the judge asked the teen if she understood why she was there and if she knew the risks abortion entailed. After three to ten minutes of questions, depending on the judge, the judge would then issue a decision, which was usually yes.

Of the 8,000 minors who had applied for a judge's permission since 1981, only thirteen had been denied. Eleven of those cases were overturned on appeal, one girl told her parents and received her abortion with their permission, and another traveled out of state.

At Preterm, an average of 1,700 young women under age eighteen received an abortion each year. Most were either sixteen or seventeen, but thirteen- and fourteen-year-olds were not uncommon. The youngest patient anyone could remember was eleven. The adolescents arrived in their unlaced sneakers and junior-high basketball jackets, their purple nail polish chipped from fingernails chewed to the quick. The heartbreakers were the younger ones clutching stuffed koala bears and rag dolls. Lin Sherman remembered one fourteen-year-old who had arrived at Preterm wearing pajamas covered with teddy bears. Staffers always wondered "incest" when faced with a twelve-year-old patient, but rarely would the little girl divulge the dirty family secret. Occasionally older teens would admit the violation. "I don't know if this baby is my boyfriend's or my father's," sighed one seventeen-year-old.

About one-quarter of Preterm's teenage patients had gone through the courts for permission, their reasons ranging from "my parents would be crushed if they knew" to deep-seated fears of violence. "My stepfather would beat the crap out of me," said Denise, a well-developed fifteen-year-old, who with her teased red hair, skin-tight jeans, and high-heeled boots, could have easily passed for twenty-one. Her stepfather had called her a whore when he suspected she was sleeping with her boyfriend, but her mother had prevented him from kicking her out of the house. If Denise had the baby, he wouldn't think twice about evicting her, and she didn't have the money or skills to live on her own. Adoption was out of the question. "I couldn't walk down the street without wondering if every kid were mine," she had said to her Preterm counselor. Denise was nervous when she sat down in Judge Joseph Mitchell's chambers of heavy wood and leather chairs. In his black robe, he was the epitome of authority. But he was quick.

"Now, Miss," he had said, "I show you this confidential affidavit. Is this your signature?"

"Yes," she replied, thinking, Get me out of here.

"Do you know why you're here today?"

"Yes."

"Why?"

"I'm here to get court permission to have an abortion."

"Are you pregnant?"

"Yes."

"How do you know that you are pregnant?"

"I had a test."

He asked how far advanced her pregnancy was, if she had told anyone about her pregnancy, if she knew the risks involved in abortion. Satisfied with her answers, he told the lawyer, a young woman, that he thought Denise was mature, and he signed the necessary papers. At Preterm, Denise simply said to her counselor, Joan Holland, "I want it [the pregnancy] out of me." In her years at Preterm, Joan had found that by the time teens had woven their way through the court system, they had few, if any, reservations about their decision.

Teens arriving at Preterm with their parents' consent were not necessarily as certain. The presence of a mother could indicate pressure for the girl to have the abortion as easily as it could mean support for the teen's choice. Angry, protective, or teary, the parents marched their child through the picketers and up to Sonia's desk, almost as if they could will the necessary task to completion. But once the child left the admitting area for the fourth floor, the parents' involvement ended. There was nothing they could do to force their daughter onto the table to have her uterus evacuated.

And on that raw November Monday, just two days before the Supreme Court would hear representatives from both sides of the abortion issue debate the merits of parental involvement in an adolescent's abortion, Sue Richdale sat at her desk in Preterm's phone room, torn between a mother's desire to have her daughter lead a normal teenage life unencumbered by motherhood, and respect for Alison's desire to control her own destiny.

•   •   •

Hanging up the phone, Sue reached for her can of Diet Coke, the second of the morning. If it weren't for Diet Coke and M&Ms, she wouldn't make it through her shift, she often joked. On days when she needed extra energy to handle telephone demands, she could chug up to five cans of soda. This could be one of those days.

Sue had coaxed enough answers out of Alison to make an abortion appointment for tomorrow morning at eight o'clock. But she wondered if Alison would show up, and, if she did, whether she would go through with the abortion. The week before, Sue had spoken with another teenager whose mother had forced her to call Preterm. "My mother killed two babies, and now she wants me to kill mine," the teenager had said. "Tell the counselor how you feel," Sue told her. "There are alternatives." The counselor had sent the teen home to reconsider her choices. "Ambivalent," the chart read. Fireworks had probably erupted that night at the teen's home, but that was a scene over which Preterm's staff had no control. The counselors gave the teen the responsibility to make the decision and, consequently, the responsibility of handling the repercussions.

Sue stared at her ringing phone, hoping that one of the other counselors would pick up this next call. She needed a small break after Alison. Sue looked around the room. Everyone was busy. Sighing, she picked up the phone. "Preterm Health Services," she said. "Have you had a pregnancy test? . . . When was the first day of your last menstrual period? . . ."

And so the abortion rap went. The woman on the other end started out lucid enough, but just as Alison's mother had done before her, she soon became hysterical. By the time Sue got to the insurance questions, the woman was screaming.

"Are you all right?" Sue asked. She paused as the woman wailed. What she wailed, Sue wasn't sure.

"Excuse me?" Sue asked.

"I want to be booorrnnnn . . ."

Sue hung up. Another antiabortion prankster. The phone lines swelled with their calls these days. Usually they said, "Jesus loves you" and hung up. But sometimes they kept a counselor on the phone for a half-hour or more, just to tie up the line. Still others made appointments and never showed up—to congest the patient schedule.

Sue sipped her Diet Coke and wished she could take a cigarette break outside on the back steps to get some air and some distance from the morning's calls. When she had first started working at Preterm, Sue had taken many of her patients' stories home with her, such as that of the woman who feared that her former husband, who had beaten her for years, would kill her and her new boyfriend if he discovered she was pregnant. He had killed others, she said, and the restraining order she had against him did no good. He followed her everywhere, from apartment to apartment, city to city.

The longer Sue answered phones at Preterm, however, the better she became at leaving her patients' woes at work. It wasn't that the tales had become less dramatic, but rather that the more stories she heard, the more she could keep the women's plights in perspective. Her job was not to right every wrong in the world, but to help women gain control of one crisis. Still, sometimes she wallowed in the sadness of her work. The Sunday before last, while she had strolled through a department store with her boyfriend, she had picked up a book on fetal development. Numb as a statue, she had stared at the photo of a twelve-week fetus, complete with fingers and toes and ears and oversize head. "Why torture yourself?" her boyfriend had asked. But she couldn't flip the page.

The sobs of Alison and her mother tormented Sue in much the same way, echoing in her mind throughout that day and at home that night. When Sue arrived at Preterm the next morning, she raced to Sonia's desk to see if Alison had been admitted. She had. Relieved, Sue returned to her desk in the phone room.

To be sure, some teens benefited from motherhood; the responsibility increased their confidence, their sense of purpose, and for some, it kept them off drugs and the streets. But for the majority, raising a child could mean a long marriage with poverty. Sue hoped that if Alison continued the pregnancy, she would stay in school, but statistics proved that she could swing either way; half the adolescent girls who gave birth in the U.S. each year never finished high school, too burdened with child care and part-time jobs to attend chemistry classes and research history papers. Without a high-school degree, their future job options were limited, which meant that so was their earning potential. The lucky ones enjoyed some support from parents or from boyfriends, but that would not be Alison's fortune. Her mom had a difficult time earning enough to support herself and her daughter, let alone the demands of an infant grandchild. And public welfare programs—such as Women, Infants, and Children (WIC) which provided food supplements—offering medical help and food to poor women and their offspring had shriveled under recent federal and state budget cuts. Sue could only shudder at the thought of Alison's future.

Alison's future was certainly not lost on her mother. Not long after Alison, a sweet-looking girl with long brown hair and rosy cheeks, had boarded the elevator for the fourth floor, her mother had sought Sonia's ear. Perhaps because she was older, or because she appeared friendly and open, or because she sat at a desk in the family room, Sonia attracted troubled parents the way a coach attracted athletes. Whatever the reason they came to her, Sonia felt that soothing parents was her specialty, that as a parent herself she understood how they felt and could present them with a viewpoint they would hear. "What do I say to her when she comes downstairs?" they would ask. "That you love her," Sonia replied. If parents were especially upset or angry, she ushered them into the little room behind her desk that had been built at her request to offer parents and partners privacy. "What has your daughter done?" Sonia asked fuming fathers. "She hasn't robbed a bank. She made love, and her sexuality is as much a part of her as the hair on her head." To the mothers, she would say, "Don't you remember being in the back seat of a car and having two seconds to say yes or no?" Usually, the mother smiled and Sonia would launch into her narrative on how times have changed.

And they had. In Sonia's day, young women were encouraged to date a lot of different boys. That way, they would be saved from developing a relationship and the accompanying pressures to have sex. Sonia had first dated Edgar when she was fifteen, but she had continued to date others until she realized that none of them were as kind, as loving, or as fun as Edgar, whom she married at age eighteen. But today, teenagers often dated one boy, and to keep that boyfriend they often felt that they had to have sex, because everyone else was having sex. How were teens supposed to say "no" when every page they turned in a magazine, or every TV show they watched, from "Cheers" to "The Cosby Show," alluded to beds and bodies and touching?

But spewing statistics and theory wouldn't help Alison's mother. She didn't care that the average girl became sexually active at 16.4 years, and the average boy at 15.7 years. Nor did she care that most teenagers, like her daughter, didn't practice regular contraception, claiming that sliding on a rubber or slipping in a diaphragm ruined spontaneity. Girls also claimed that they didn't want to seem aggressive, as if they had planned on intimacy. Using birth control was evidence that they were having sex, something they didn't want to admit to their mothers or themselves.

Janet Cosgrove, Alison's mother, was an attractive woman in her early forties, carefully groomed except for the mascara smudges around her eyes. Sonia knew of few mascaras that would hold up through endless tears. "I am so hurt that my daughter didn't ask me about birth control," she told Sonia. "I have always told her that she can come to me about any problem."

"What's she going to say?" Sonia said gently, smiling. "Mom, can I go out to the basketball game? Mom, can I go out with my friends? Mom, can I be sexually active?"

Janet Cosgrove dabbed at her eyes and tried to smile. Sonia let her rest in privacy in the little room behind the admitting desk, just long enough to gather her composure. Sonia knew through experience that Janet Cosgrove's worst fear—that Alison wouldn't go through with the abortion—was likely to materialize. Teens were naturally rebellious, and if forced by their parents to do one thing, they would do the opposite.

Last month, a seventeen-year-old named Cindy had canceled her appointment three times before she finally entered Preterm. On the morning of the fourth appointment, Cindy's mother had called the phone room saying that Cindy would be late and that if she didn't go through with the abortion the mother would kick her out of the house. Once at Preterm, Cindy refused to fill out her medical chart, wandering back and forth to the bathroom instead. After her third trip, she returned to the family room, burst into tears, and bolted out of the clinic and into the arms of the picketers outside. Her mother stood at the doorway, watching the picketers engulf her sobbing daughter.

"What can I do?" the mother had asked Sonia. "My husband isn't Cindy's father, and he said no way. We have four other kids at home and we don't need a baby."

As much as Sonia hated to hear mothers order their daughters to have an abortion, she understood the woman's position, that she, not her daughter, would probably shoulder the 3 A.M. feedings and toilet training. With four other children at home, this mother didn't need one more responsibility. But instead of commiserating, Sonia warned the woman that adolescents forced into abortion may become pregnant again to spite the parent, or they may descend into deep depressions. "They feel that they murdered a baby," Sonia said. She recommended that the mother and daughter seek professional crisis counseling, and referred her to a qualified therapist. She also suggested that the mother do some reality testing with her daughter. "Explain that her stepfather will not allow her and the baby to live in the house," Sonia coached. "Ask her to call Medicaid for estimates on medical coverage. Have her call the telephone company, the electric company, and the gas company for prices. Then thumb through apartment rentals advertised in the newspaper."

Sonia was home sick the day the daughter returned to Preterm for her abortion.

And then there was Maureen, a plump seventeen-year-old with round eyes and long brown hair that she twisted through her fingers when she spoke. She hadn't planned to get pregnant, and she cried when the Brockton Family Planning Clinic called with positive results from her pregnancy test. She and her boyfriend had used condoms for the first couple of months that they had begun making love in Maureen's bedroom after school while her mother worked at a nearby hospital as a laboratory technician. But her boyfriend didn't like the rubbers, and promised he would withdraw before he ejaculated. For two years, Maureen didn't conceive, but then in June she had started throwing up all the time, so much that she had to quit her job waitressing at the Clam Shack. When her mother asked her if she were pregnant, she turned away. A few months earlier, when her mother had confronted her about sex, Maureen had admitted that she had had intercourse, but said that she had stopped. She didn't want her mother to think badly of her.

"You have an abortion or I'll kick you out of the house," her father had screamed when she told him of the pregnancy. Her mother, too, had nudged her toward abortion. But Maureen wasn't sure. She had dated the baby's father for almost two-and-a-half years, and although they had broken up, she didn't want to kill his child. Her friends had urged her to keep the baby; they wanted to see if it looked like her or her boyfriend. The thought made Maureen giggle. She, too, wanted to see what it would look like, if it would be as cute as the little baby down the street with the black curls. She liked the idea of strolling into Brockton High School with her cherub, the envy of all her friends. But to appease her parents, she made an appointment at Preterm, only to be sent home because of her ambivalence. "I knew this would happen," her mother said over and over again during the car ride home from Brookline to Brockton, a Boston suburb.

That night, Maureen slept at the apartment of a friend who was the mother of an eleven-month-old baby. The baby cried from midnight until six o'clock the next morning. Watching her weary friend change the baby's diaper, Maureen began to wonder if that was the life she wanted. The next day, she visited Brockton High School's day-care center, where she would place her baby from April, when it would be born, until June, when she would graduate. If she had the baby, she couldn't go to Hawaii, the trip her parents had promised her for a graduation present, and she probably couldn't go to Cape Cod Community College as she had planned. How would she earn money to feed and clothe a baby? Her parents said that if she had the baby, she was on her own. Maureen had always felt that abortion was OK only in cases of rape and incest. But after a night of listening to a baby howl, Maureen became more convinced that motherhood wasn't for her right now, that maybe abortion wasn't such a bad option.

"Is this some kind of game?" her father had asked when she said she had made another appointment at Preterm.

"No," she replied. "This is none of your business."

Alison, however, was several steps behind Maureen in her conviction. Through her colleagues upstairs, Sue Richdale learned that Alison had dragged herself through medical screening, answering the nurse in monosyllables and staring out the window at Beacon Street during the group counseling lecture on the procedure and birth control methods. In individual counseling she stated that she didn't want the abortion at all, that her Preterm appointment was her mother's idea. When Sue checked the patient log late that afternoon, she saw that Alison had been sent home because of her uncertainty.

"Bummer," Sue muttered back at her desk in the phone room. Sonia, too, was upset. Perhaps Alison would be a wonderful teenage mother. Chances, however, were that Alison and her baby would struggle for many years, and that wasn't good news for anyone.

Since Preterm held a gynecology clinic on Wednesdays, none of the abortion staff was upstairs listening for news of the Supreme Court's hearing of the Ohio and Minnesota parental-notification cases. Fran and Carolyn picked up bits and pieces of the justices' dialogue through news briefs during the afternoon. Once again, Sandra Day O'Connor held the pivotal vote, and once again she was difficult to read. Since Court protocol did not permit justices to address each other directly, Justices O'Connor and Scalia sparred through questions each asked of Minnesota's chief deputy general, John R. Tunheim. Justice O'Connor wondered if requiring both parents' consent posed an "undue burden" on young women. In turn, Scalia, the most vocal abortion opponent on the high court, questioned O'Connor's thinking. "I had assumed," Justice Scalia said, "that there is a parental interest involved as well as a filial interest." Rebutted Justice O'Connor to Tunheim: "That may be true in general, but probably you would concede there might be circumstances where it is not in the best interests of the child to tell both parents of her problem and her intention." Preterm and the nation would have to wait months before the final decision was handed down.

Carolyn shrugged off the debate. "I'm so ambivalent about this issue," she said. She felt that someone besides the doctor should participate in the minor's decision, but a judge didn't seem the proper mediator. A counselor or social worker would be better, someone who could encourage the teen to discuss her feelings, not just answer legal questions in monosyllables. The irony, of course, of the parental-consent and notification debate was the same as with the larger abortion issue: The attention was misplaced.

Instead of focusing on the question of preventing or providing abortion, Carolyn felt that both sides should concentrate on pregnancy prevention. Demoralized by what they felt as the hopelessness of their lives, some adolescents saw motherhood as offering them a sense of purpose. A baby would help them hold on to their boyfriend and give them something to love when they found no other source. Tackling poverty and despair was an overwhelming goal for society, let alone for the abortion debaters, but stronger efforts could be made to offer these young women education and contraception.

The harsh truth, though, rested in the fact that federal funds for family planning had not been reauthorized for four years, largely because of protests by antiabortion lobbyists, who were against public subsidies for birth control as well as abortion. Consequently, hundreds of thousands of poor teenagers across the country had lost reproductive health-care services and information.

Most teens did not have the pocket change to pay fifty dollars for an appointment with a private doctor plus another sixteen dollars a month for birth-control pills. Those who lived in rural areas did not always have transportation to more affordable family-planning clinics, such as Preterm, which were usually located in metropolitan areas. In countries such as Denmark, which offered comprehensive sex-education programs and affordable contraception through socialized medicine, the teenage pregnancy rate was less than half that of the United States. The nearly half a million girls under age eighteen who became pregnant every year in the U.S. represented the highest teenage pregnancy rate of all industrialized countries (almost half of those pregnancies ended in abortion). Carolyn often questioned the philosophy of a free market system when it left its population struggling to afford proper medical care.

On Thursday, the abortion clinic ran as usual with Bill Cotter standing outside for the early shift, Fred Pulsifer taking over at 10 A.M., and Alice arriving soon after. That afternoon, just before three o'clock, as Sonia gathered her purse and jacket before dashing out the door to go home, her phone rang. It was Alison.

"I talked with my mother for a long time," Alison said, her voice clear of tears. After she had left Preterm on Tuesday, she and her mother had sat down at the kitchen table in their apartment with a sheet of paper and figured out how much a baby would cost, and what motherhood would do to her life. No movies. No dates. An after-school job. Day-care costs. "May I make an appointment for tomorrow?" she asked.

Sonia called Sue, who happily checked Friday's appointments. Booked solid. But, she thought, today we had twenty-three no-shows, clearly an all-time high—Sonia had wondered if the antis were plugging up the appointment schedule again—so Sue felt safe in overbooking Friday by one.

Would Alison go through with it this time? Sonia felt that she would. Sue felt that she would. She would march past the picketers and into a Preterm counseling room, this time resolved. All she had wanted was the respect and time to make up her own mind. Sue checked the abortion appointment blackboard and jotted down Alison's name for an eleven o'clock appointment.

CHAPTER ELEVEN

The Business of Abortion

EVERY day, Carolyn Wardell seemed to grow paler, more despairing. Despite her attempts to be perky, to wear brightly colored dresses and giggle with the secretaries, she couldn't conceal the gray shadows under her eyes, which were often puffy from yet another night of restless sleep. The pressures of coping with Preterm's deficit and the inevitable staff cutbacks were apparent, and those who worked closest with Carolyn had begun to worry. "Carolyn seems so fragile," said Sarah, Preterm's bookkeeper, "as if she'll break." So distraught did Carolyn look as she sat at her desk bent over a stack of paper, that staffers would often tiptoe past even if Carolyn's door were open, which usually meant an invitation to come in.

On this blustery January day, Carolyn looked especially vexed. The crisis was doctors, or a lack of them. Doctors were always in short supply in Preterm's abortion clinic, but today Carolyn had Bill Cotter & Friends to thank. Cotter's getting slick, she thought. He may not have realized how the effects of his invasion of a doctor's office in downtown Boston this morning had resonated, but they certainly had.

The violated doctor, Sidney Levitt, performed abortions part-time at Preterm and was scheduled to work this afternoon from noon until three o'clock. But Cotter and six abortion foes lay locked together by the neck in one of Sidney's procedure rooms. Now, three hours after the invasion, the Boston police had yet to figure out a way to drill open the locks without hurting the protesters. All ten of the women scheduled to have abortions this morning at Sidney's office had decided to wait out the siege and not reschedule. Considering that the protest had left

198

Sidney with only one room in which to work instead of two, the appointments would take him well into the afternoon. Besides, even if the women had rescheduled, Sidney couldn't leave his office while seven abortion foes lay like logs behind a closed door.

Losing any doctor for an abortion shift caused a patient backup at Preterm, but losing Sidney Levitt was disastrous. He may not have had the softest bedside manner—he was gaunt and swarthy with a dark beard, thin lips that rarely smiled, and eyes as cold and blue as Rasputin's—but he was a brilliant technician. He was so fast that the medical assistants clocked him to see how swiftly he could do an abortion. Sidney Levitt could be in and out of a room in under five minutes, less than a third of the time most of Preterm's doctors took to perform the same surgery. No sooner had Sidney introduced himself to the patient and donned a pair of rubber gloves than he was gone, it seemed. The staff wondered how Sidney could be thorough, how he could remove all of the pregnancy tissue in such a short time. But Sidney Levitt's patients rarely returned to be reevacuated. He was, Carolyn recognized, simply very good at what he did.

Sidney would be sorely missed this Friday afternoon. Seventy-six patients were scheduled to have abortions. All had showed up. Already, the flow upstairs was sluggish, and by early afternoon, when most of the doctors were slated to leave and Sidney to take over, the patient bottleneck would be big enough to burst the building's walls. Carolyn didn't know what to do. Waldo Fielding had said that he couldn't come in this afternoon; he was on his way to Cape Cod. None of the other doctors whom she had called was available. Carolyn's only chance was Dr. Shiao Yu Lee, the president of Preterm's board of directors. Dr. Lee worked mostly in the sterilization clinic performing tubal ligations, but he was also adept at abortions and helped the clinic out in a pinch. Today, though, he had already canceled several of his private patients to deliver a baby. Chances looked bleak that he would be free in time to help out.

Carolyn sat at her desk piled high with staff schedules and financial statements. If Dr. Lee couldn't come in, she might have to send patients away, something she couldn't afford to do. Not by a long shot. At last glance, Preterm Health Services was $192,000 in debt.

Again and again, Carolyn had asked herself how the deficit had bloomed so out of control. And again and again, she had had to remind herself that she hadn't created the problem, but had inherited it. For the past few years, the clinic's previous administrators had blamed its increasingly shaky finances on low abortion numbers, maintaining that the clinic wasn't doing fifty-one abortions per day—the magic number that could keep Preterm solvent.

Carolyn, too, had bought that party line, but after poring over the budget books, she had discovered that Preterm's deficit had little to do with patient numbers. In fact, for the past three years, the clinic had averaged forty-seven abortion patients per day; hardly enough of a drop to account for the dramatic financial loss. Sure, last summer's numbers seemed especially grim thanks to Operation Rescue and the media attention on abortion, but summer was historically slow since most of the Boston area college students were out of town. All things considered, the number of women seeking abortions hadn't altered that much.

The truth was that Preterm's problems were much more complex. So complex, in fact, that it was easier for Carolyn's administrative predecessors to focus on patient numbers rather than delve into the real reasons behind the deficit, reasons beyond Preterm's control.

Like all health-care facilities, Preterm had fallen victim to soaring medical costs. Prices for equipment, for everything from the cannulas to the evacuation machines, had leapt. Laboratory fees had increased 50 percent in the last year alone. Every month, Preterm paid thousands and thousands of dollars for pathology reports for Pap smears, abortion tissue analysis, and gonorrhea cultures.

Salaries chewed the biggest hole in Preterm's wallet. Less than four years ago, starting nurses had earned seven dollars an hour. Then came the well-publicized nursing shortage. As demand for nurses exceeded the supply, salaries shot skyward. Now, Preterm's nurses started at $14.50 an hour, and veteran nurses collected $22, $23, or more an hour. Doctors' salaries were even more stunning. Most of the clinic's doctors earned $120 an hour for performing abortions; more if they were the doctor in charge for the shift—the doctor responsible for tending the complicated cases and answering all questions.

Preterm had always meant so much to Carolyn. She deeply believed in its mission: its commitment to provide all women, regardless of their ability to pay, with quality medical service. But Preterm's generosity, one of the clinic's greatest assets, was also one of its greatest liabilities. Caring for the "have-nots" was a major reason that Preterm teetered on the edge of disaster. In the past two years, Preterm had provided $420,000 worth of free service for women of little or no means.

An unstable economy and declining job market had taken its toll, and Preterm's phone counselors heard more and more women plead for financial assistance. Some were eligible for or were covered by Medicaid, but that meant lost income for Preterm, which was one of the three outpatient facilities in Greater Boston which accepted Medicaid for abortion services. Each year the clinic lost thousands of dollars because the state reimbursements didn't cover the costs of the service.

Many women who didn't qualify for Medicaid but who were uninsured, or whose insurance didn't cover abortion, or who didn't have the full amount for the surgery, asked to be placed on a deferred-payment plan. A little now, a little later. In the past two years, more than 1,600 women, almost double that of five years ago, had agreed to pay in increments. Of these women, Carolyn could anticipate that at least 40 percent would probably pay no more than half of the total fee. Carolyn knew of some patients who mailed the clinic ten dollars, five dollars, sometimes even two dollars a month, and planned to continue until their debt was paid. But others stopped payment after the first few installments. Writing a check to the clinic was a reminder of a painful decision that the woman had had to make, a decision she'd probably rather forget. The clinic mailed reminder notices, but it wasn't about to call out the collection agency on a former patient.

And Preterm wasn't about to raise its prices high enough to help cover costs. Despite the hard times, Carolyn remained committed to keeping abortion and health-care fees affordable for lower-middle-income patients—women whose income was too high to qualify them for public assistance and too low to enable them to afford a private doctor—who composed the bulk of Preterm's patient list. And, like it or not, providing abortions was a business. There were two other abortion providers in town with similar prices. If Preterm jacked up its fees, patients would quickly head to the other Beacon Street clinics. Carolyn didn't consider Planned Parenthood much of a threat since it offered relatively few abortion slots—ten to fifteen appointments during the week and perhaps sixteen on Saturdays. Repro, though, was stiff competition, averaging 6,000 abortions a year.

Although Repro's founder and chief physician, Dr. Howard Silverman, had recently made front-page headlines for charges of sexual misconduct with a patient in 1984, his Brookline clinic hadn't seemed to suffer. Perhaps it was advertising; every time Carolyn flicked on her radio, she seemed to hear another Repro ad. She and Fran snickered that Repro spent all of its money on promotion instead of health care. But she knew it was more than that. Repro promised to have abortion patients out of the clinic in two to three hours, and it did. Even though Preterm could argue to potential patients that it offered superior care, that women would find in-depth counseling and quality nursing at

Preterm, Carolyn was savvy enough to know that to many, perhaps most, women facing an abortion, the only requirement besides safety was getting in and out of the clinic as fast as possible.

Preterm's abortion staff was vehemently opposed to slicing counseling time, arguing that often women weren't certain of their feelings toward abortion until they were presented with the questions that the clinic's counselors were trained to ask. Carolyn agreed that Preterm wasn't in the business of steering a woman in and out of a procedure room if that wasn't what she really wanted. But what else besides counseling could be cut to speed patient flow? In November, Carolyn had instituted a standard form for counselors to sign that said that each patient had made her decision on her own, instead of requiring counselors to write a separate statement for each patient. To free more counselors for individual counseling, she had filmed a video detailing birth-control options and describing the abortion procedure. Carolyn had worried at first that patients wouldn't pay attention to a video, but then she realized that some patients didn't pay attention to the counselor in group sessions. At some point, the patient had to assume responsibility.

Those moves alone, though, hadn't remedied the slow patient flow. More doctors would help, but even if Carolyn could afford them, she wasn't sure she could get them. Across the nation, the number of doctors willing to do abortions dwindled.

"Abortionist" had always carried a tainted image, but in the past, physicians had been more willing to ignore the stigma, the ostracizing by some of their medical colleagues, and the threats by abortion foes. The bulk of those doctors were, like Waldo Fielding, veterans of emergency rooms during the era of illegal abortions. They had seen the blood and death and dismemberment caused by botched abortions. The problem was that now these doctors, like Waldo, had reached retirement age. Their replacements, younger doctors who knew only legal abortion, had not witnessed the horror of coat hangers jammed through cervixes. Raised during a time when abortion was legal, young physicians didn't understand how far a desperate woman would go to end a crisis pregnancy. They knew only the havoc that performing abortions could play with their professional and personal lives.

A 1985 study conducted by the American College of Obstetricians and Gynecologists found that 84 percent of its 4,000 members polled felt that abortion should remain legal and available, but only a third of those doctors actually performed abortions. Of those who did, most performed very few. Some felt that the paradox between delivering babies one hour and destroying fetuses the next was too great to be justified. Others felt that abortionists were treated as pariahs by the medical community and that they would be rejected by their peers and possibly by their patients—women seeking obstetrical and gynecological services—if they performed abortions on the side.

Many others feared harassment by antiabortion activists. Doctors across the country had walked out of their homes and private offices to find a picket line of protesters shouting "murderer" and holding posters of blackened fetuses purportedly killed through saline injections—not a welcome sight to either the doctors' patients or family. Anonymous callers had threatened to kill or kidnap doctors, their spouses, or their children. And then there were the ever-present possibilities of arson attacks and bombings. Or, as Sidney Levitt knew, of invasions.

In rural areas where small-town pressure not to do abortions was especially intense, doctors often succumbed to the public scrutiny and disdain of their work. The Alan Guttmacher Institute found that between 1985 and 1988 the number of abortion providers in non-metropolitan areas had plunged by 19 percent. For years North Dakota had had only one abortionist, and when he retired, the one clinic that offered abortions was dependent on doctors flying in from other states, which meant that the patients and clinic were held hostage to weather conditions and flight schedules.

Massachusetts wasn't North Dakota, yet abortion providers were far from smug. Even though the Bay State's plethora of medical schools spawned hordes of residents, hordes of residents did not ask to learn abortion skills. Of those who did, not all utilized them. Finding doctors to fill the abortion-clinic schedule was a constant challenge for Carolyn, with or without Operation Rescue invasions. She was well aware that as committed as her doctors were to helping women solve a problem, they, too, constantly evaluated the pros and cons of working at Preterm.

For Kate Horowitz, performing abortions paid well and allowed her to work part-time, which meant that she could still practice medicine but could also spend most of her week with her toddler son. Moreover, unlike family practice, when the day was through, so were her responsibilities. Emergency phone calls no longer woke her up at 4 A.M. since Preterm employed two doctors to be on call at all times to handle crisis. Kate, who never volunteered for the job, was grateful that when she came home she could be a mom, not a doctor anticipating a call from a frantic patient.

The drawback was that Kate lived in fear of driving home to a cluster of picketers parading up and down her street, which would terrify her son and annoy the neighbors. Kate was selective of whom she told about her work. She hadn't yet divulged her occupation to her neighbors. Having them discover antiabortion pamphlets under car windshields and in mailboxes was not the way Kate wanted them to find out. Her address was unlisted, as was Dr. Lee's, but that hadn't protected his neighborhood from being blanketed once with photos of bloody fetuses.

Beyond that, the work itself was routine, repetitive. Each abortion took between twelve and twenty minutes, which meant that time with the patient was minimal. Because the doctor saw the patient only once, no bond was formed. There was no history to the relationship, nor would there be a future. In fact, an abortion took so little time that it was easy to forget that there was a mind and a heart inside the body on which the doctor worked. Kate made it a point to talk to the patient both before and after the procedure, not only to assuage the patient's fears, but also to remind herself that the woman was a human being with feelings, not just a body. Many doctors, though, rarely uttered more than an introduction.

And then there was the inherent gruesomeness of the procedure itself, the sadness of sorting through parts of what had just been alive. The antiabortion movement was quick to send to podiums former abortionists who claimed that they had finally seen the light and denounced the morality of ending fetal life. One such doctor, Bernard Nathanson, became a leader in the antiabortion movement and produced the documentary, *Silent Scream*, which depicted a fetus recoiling in utero from the suction. Abortion rights advocates countered that if Nathanson considered the act of abortion murder, how could he calmly film such an atrocity? Kate Horowitz didn't deny the horror of sifting through fetal parts and admitted that she constantly had to remind herself that what she did was what she had been asked to do by the patient. When she felt her perspective was especially clouded, Kate thought of a card she had received from a patient, a woman whom she didn't even remember.

On the outside, the card was inscribed: "Taking time to thank you for taking time to care." On the inside, the woman had written:

This has been one of the hardest times of my life. I am sure there will be many more but I can only hope that someone like you will be there to care. You make a huge difference in this world and I want you to know it is greatly appreciated.

That was the proof Kate needed to reinforce that she was doing something important.

Carolyn Wardell counted on that sense of commitment to balance the negatives of performing abortions. But all the commitment in the world didn't seem to help Carolyn find a doctor today.

Staring at the mess on her desk, Carolyn felt out of touch with her clinic and so caught up in money and staffing problems that she had to remind herself that patients sat not 100 feet from her office door. She felt so isolated from her staff and its work that she sometimes yearned for the days when her major worry had been how to protect the clinic from Operation Rescue. At least then she had felt as if she and her staff worked together, not as if she were struggling alone to make ends meet. Driving home from her New Year's holiday in Pennsylvania with her family, Carolyn had actually hoped that Rescue would plan an attack in January. That way, she could once again do what she did best: organize and direct. A rescue was tangible. Unlike the budget mess, it had a clear beginning, middle, and end.

Thus Carolyn was delighted when, on her first day back after the New Year's break, Fran showed her the Operation Rescue newsletter announcing a January 13 rescue. She was even delighted when she received a frantic phone call from the clinic just before seven o'clock yesterday morning warning her that twenty picketers were circling in front of Preterm singing hymns and carrying signs. Carolyn had rushed Lorena to school, explaining that she had to get to work because people who didn't like Preterm wouldn't let patients in.

By the time Carolyn arrived at the clinic, six cops stood guard over seven protesters who had charged the front door, which was locked. Another ten or so demonstrators sang on the sidewalk. McDermott had ordered that no one be allowed inside the building unless they were clinic staff, so Carolyn asked the counselors to don escort pinnys and steer patients to Dunkin' Donuts, or to another safe and warm place, for half an hour. Eventually, the door blockers stood up and joined the others on the sidewalk. There were no arrests.

It turned out that Preterm had been only a decoy. The real surprise attack was on Planned Parenthood, where forty-seven protesters had attempted to invade at the same time that the seven had tried to rush into Preterm. Since Planned Parenthood's first-floor door was still locked when they arrived, the demonstrators had lain down in the entryway, occupying every inch, body to body, head to feet, feet to head. By nine o'clock the hallway was clear, and seventy-one demonstrators—those on the inside plus some on the outside—had been arrested.

Bill Cotter had told a reporter that Operation Rescue's activity would intensify in the New Year. Maybe he meant it. If he were smart, and Carolyn knew he was cunning, he would try new tactics. The blockades had lost steam. The last one on December 9 at Repro had shown new aggression between the prochoice and antichoice forces, but patients had walked into the clinic without much trouble. A fresh approach was needed to stop clinic operation. The fact that seven protesters lay locked together in Sidney Levitt's office at this moment confirmed Carolyn's worst fear: The fresh approach was invasion.

Invasions were scary. You didn't know what damage the abortion foes could do if they got inside a clinic. Two months before, in November, a twenty-seven-year-old man had gone on a violent rampage at the Planned Parenthood in Worcester, smashing windows and furniture, tossing bricks at clinic staff and police, and knocking over file cabinets which, in turn, spilled thousands of pages of medical records and destroyed a computer terminal. Staff and patients hid behind locked doors and under desks until the police corralled him. The man, who listed his address as the Public Inebriate Program, had been arrested twice in 1986 for attacking the Worcester Planned Parenthood. On his first visit, he had destroyed two evacuation machines with a snow shovel. The next day he had returned with a baseball bat. He was found not guilty because of mental illness and later committed himself to a mental institution. Police said that the man initially had identified himself as Jesus Christ.

Bill Cotter wasn't mentally ill, but Carolyn wasn't so sure about some of his followers. They were sheep, willing to be led, apparently ready to do anything for their cause and their leader. Cotter may no longer lure to clinic steps the hundreds of last spring, but those who composed his inner circle might be capable of anything.

Last summer, Carolyn had researched renovating Preterm's fourth floor to make the medical area more secure, but the estimates started at $30,000. Considering that Preterm was so broke that it had stopped offering ice packs to patients, a major construction project was out of the question. Carolyn liked the idea of a buzzer system downstairs allowing Sonia to admit only patients and their escorts, but that, too, was expensive. Preterm couldn't lock the building's front door; that wouldn't be fair to the other tenants or their clients. So for now, Carolyn resorted to placing a staffer on the fourth floor to make sure that the women entering the medical area were patients. One fake patient the clinic could handle. But a fake patient followed by a band of lock-laden zealots would be overwhelming.

The phone rang, interrupting Carolyn's reverie. It was Dr. Lee. He would, after all, be able to do some procedures at Preterm late in the afternoon, between four and four-thirty. That was late, which meant that some patients would have an eight- or nine-hour day. But it couldn't be helped. They could either wait or reschedule. Carolyn knew that if she were a patient who had already invested a day at Preterm, she could wait another hour instead of returning again tomorrow. Carolyn called upstairs with the good news.

One dilemma solved. Now on to the next. What would Cotter try? she wondered. Would he slip somebody inside? McDermott thought that Rescue would soon hit Preterm. The warriors had struck Repro on December 9, Planned Parenthood on Thursday, and Gynecare every other time since last October. It was Preterm's turn. Charged with a mixture of dread and excitement, Carolyn stood up and walked into Fran's office to make sure that the church had been reserved for patients tomorrow, just in case they couldn't get inside the clinic.

•   •   •

The escorts' faces looked grim underneath their ski hats and fur hoods, taut with anticipation. Arriving at Preterm shortly before 6 A.M., they resembled puffy snowmen in their down parkas and thick wool scarves wound around their necks and over their mouths. It was a brutally cold morning, even for January in New England, and Carolyn envied the care with which the escorts had dressed. She was freezing. She had thought her long wool coat too cumbersome for trotting back and forth between Preterm's back and front entrances, and had chosen instead to wear her winter jacket. This kept her torso warm but not her legs, which were clad merely in sweatpants. Sarah, her bookkeeper, had loaned her a sweater to wear over her sweatshirt, and she had borrowed a pair of mittens to wear on top of her knit gloves, but she refused to slip a hat over her earmuffs. Conceding to vanity, she didn't want a hat to flatten her hair.

And so Carolyn shivered as she stood on the sidewalk in front of Preterm in the early morning darkness, worried that if she dipped inside to warm up in the building's foyer, she'd miss Operation Rescue's arrival. A police lieutenant had told her that from what he had heard from McDermott, who was parked at St. Ignatius Church where the abortion foes had congregated earlier this morning, Bill Cotter's gang were headed for Preterm. "Oh goody," Carolyn had said, clapping her mittened hands.

She was ready for some excitement, for the challenge of outmaneuvering the opposition. Up since 4 A.M., Carolyn was fortified with a bowl of Lorena's Honey Crisp cereal and the largest cup of coffee Dunkin' Donuts offered: a sixteen-ounce tumbler called "The Big One." The church was reserved, the phone room was staffed to handle calls from frantic patients, and the metal barricades stood firmly in place in front of Preterm's front steps. Twenty Brookline cops, dressed in their blue leather coats and hats with earflaps, stood in the middle of the metal corral, clapping their hands and stamping their feet to keep circulation moving. Carolyn's primary worry was that a prochoicer, an antichoicer, or a clinic escort would push too far and a brawl would ensue.

Despite all of Carolyn's attempts to cut Saturday morning chaos in front of Preterm by cutting appointment hours, tension between the prochoice demonstrators and the antis had increased. The cast of characters on both sides had stabilized, which meant that Saturday after Saturday, the same prochoicers faced the same antichoicers. With familiarity came knowledge of the others' tactics as well as aggression. As soon as the escorts spotted Marie Henden, or Speed Bump as they called her, trotting toward a patient, they bolted after her. Likewise, when the prochoicers approached a patient, Marie Henden wasn't far behind. It was difficult to say who elbowed whom, but the Saturday police detail were forever separating demonstrators crying "assault."

Worse, the animosity had spread beyond the clinic's sidewalk. Two escorts had reported that they had received prank phone calls late at night. Another, Alexis Williams, said that her parents had been awakened at three o'clock several mornings in a row in their Connecticut home by a threatening male caller. On the first night, he asked the Williams if they knew where their daughter was. On the second, he asked whether they knew if their daughter was all right. Then he asked whether they knew that their daughter killed babies, and that they should tell her to stop. The fourth time he called, he said that their daughter was in danger, that her life was threatened. Alexis's mother was hysterical. So, too, was Alexis. But after discussing the call with her fellow escorts, she calmed down. A picketer had traced her car's Connecticut license plates back to her parents, she suspected, and she wasn't about to let a picketer intimidate her. After several Saturdays passed and nothing happened, Alexis's fear was replaced by a sense of righteousness: The escorts were right and the antis were terrorists.

Not long after, several escorts, Alexis among them, discovered that their names had been placed on a sexline. Their phone would ring and the man at the other end of the line would ask them to share their erotic fantasies. To retaliate, the escorts placed Marie Henden's name on the sexline. Only when Marie reported the violation to the police did the pranks stop, but not before water and sugar had been poured into the gas tank of the Hendens' car during the night.

As Carolyn looked at the unsmiling faces of both the escorts and the NOW demonstrators who had gathered protectively in front of the barricades, she wondered if today would be the day that punches would replace pranks. The police, eying the prochoicers suspiciously, seemed to share her thoughts. At the December 9 rescue, the pro-choicers had formed a human chain in front of Repro, a move which they claimed had kept the clinic safe from invasion. The police, though, had claimed that the prochoicers had hindered their ability to maintain control. Both Carolyn and the police knew that the more visible the prochoicers were, the more aggressive the abortion foes became.

There was little reason for them not to be aggressive. To Carolyn's great frustration, the charges against those arrested for blockading clinics had been dropped. Everyone, including the abortion foes, knew that the prisons were overcrowded already without adding clinic block-aders to the cells. After requiring the arrested protesters to attend a number of pretrial hearings, the courts would announce that the cases had been tossed. Except for missing a few days of work to attend the preliminary trials, the Soldiers of God walked away unpunished. All of that might change if the Supreme Judicial Court upheld the injunction against blockading abortion clinics, but the panel of judges had yet to rule on the court order which threatened a longer jail sentence and higher fines.

It was 6:35 A.M., and Carolyn had been standing outside in the slush for half an hour. God, she was cold. Where were they? Their meeting spot, St. Ignatius Church, was fewer than three miles away. How long could it take them to organize? Was Cotter plotting to send in a fake patient? Carolyn's heart froze. A blockade she could handle, but a fake patient accompanied by a kamikaze troupe with locks around their necks could really back up patient flow, not to mention destroy expen-sive equipment and furniture.

Carolyn turned toward Cleveland Circle and spotted the flashing lights of a police car moving very slowly down Beacon Street. The lights had an eerie quality as splashes of blue punctuated the early morning darkness. Even eerier was the caravan of headlights behind the cruiser, a caravan that seemed to stretch from Brookline to Newton—a caravan that heralded the arrival of Operation Rescue. Would the crusaders stop at Preterm as McDermott had predicted? Or would they continue on to Repro, or Planned Parenthood, or Gynecare? Carolyn held her hand over her mouth, waiting for the morning's fate.

Inching along, the cruiser pulled a U-turn in front of Preterm. The cars, one by one, parked across the street.

"Bill Cotter's supposed to be in jail!" Carolyn cried when she saw Rescue's leader emerge from a car. Six hours after he and his six cohorts had locked themselves together in Sidney Levitt's procedure room yesterday, they had volunteered the keys. Watching the protesters rush to the bathrooms, the Boston police figured that their bladders had given up long before their determination. Carolyn had suspected that the seven invaders would play martyr and spend the weekend in the Charles Street jail in downtown Boston. But Cotter must have felt that today's rescue was too important to miss.

Carolyn glanced at the human fortress of prochoicers linked around the perimeter of the barricade, prepared for battle. The rest of the opposition—Carolyn estimated about 100 people—stood in a cluster behind Bill Cotter across Beacon Street. Weird, Carolyn thought. In April, they had marched down the sidewalk toward Preterm quickly, defiantly, with purpose. What were they waiting for? An invitation?

Then, with Cotter in the lead, the flock crossed Beacon Street and headed toward Preterm, stopping at the curb a block away. In unison, they began to sing, "How I Love Thee." On cue, they gingerly stepped off the curb and toward Preterm.

But instead of dropping in front of the barriers and attempting to crawl toward the clinic entrance as they had done at every other rescue, the abortion foes congregated on both sides of the barricades and stood, waiting for instructions.

"Why aren't they blockading?" Carolyn wondered. When the pro-lifers began to sing, the prochoicers defending the barricades began to chant, "Prolife, who you kiddin'? You're prowar and antiwomen."

It was almost seven o'clock and the morning sky had brightened enough for Carolyn to see with whom she was dealing. Close to 300 people had gathered in front of her clinic. Most of them were abortion rights advocates, but enough of the opposition was present to spark some violence. Beside her was a group of elderly men, one of whom pointed to the prochoicers and said, "Those are the prodeath people. They get paid for being here." In front of her was a woman wearing a bathrobe over her ski parka and curlers in her hair and holding a sign that said "EVERY MONTH IS A WASTED CHANCE." A tampon splashed with red paint dangled from the cardboard.

Lovely, Carolyn thought. Almost as tasteless as another sign she spotted: "MASTURBATE, DON'T PROCREATE," which was adorned with a drawing of a hand holding a penis.

The antis rarely responded with more than a headshake to visual taunts, and today was no exception. In fact, today they were particularly passive. Forty-five minutes after they arrived, Bill Cotter's people still hadn't attempted to block the door. They simply stood or knelt beside the barricades, singing and praying. The only active abortion foes were the sidewalk counselors, and Carolyn guessed that they, too, would calm down if the clinic escorts and prochoicers backed off.

Before a patient had even opened her car door, two or three escorts were at her side, followed by a set of Cotter's sidewalk counselors. The escorts surrounded the patient as the sidewalk counselors shouted "Please don't kill your baby" and tried to duck under the escorts' arms to get to the young woman. Each time this scene played, Carolyn held her breath, wondering if a sidewalk counselor would belt an escort, or vice versa. At one point, a blond woman planted her feet on the sidewalk and spread her arms to stop the train of escorts leading a patient. A tall man, a psychiatrist who carted a "STAND UP FOR CHOICE" sign during demonstrations, grabbed the blond woman's coat. The circle of escorts led their patient to Preterm's entrance.

"Assault!!" the woman yelled.

"I saw the whole thing," a policeman told her. "You were blocking."

"No, I wasn't, officer," she said, shaking her head vehemently for emphasis. "No, I wasn't."

The police officer walked away. So far, the police had made only three arrests. The first was a prochoice demonstrator who was charged with assault and battery for raising his arm to a man from Cotter's group who had allegedly pushed him. The second and third were a couple of well-known Saturday picketers who had sauntered toward Preterm's entrance pretending that they were a patient and her escort. "Hey, I recognize you," a policeman said. "You're under arrest." But at 7:25 A.M., almost an hour after Operation Rescue had arrived, not one of Cotter's people had attempted to blockade the entrance. Would they?

"In time," Cotter told a reporter.

A Budget Rent-A-Truck parked across Beacon Street reminded Carolyn all too clearly of last July, when Bill and Darroline had opened the back of a truck to release a mob of antis. But this truck just stood there, engine idling, not moving, not even looking as if it were about to move. The escorts stared at the truck as if it might drive into the crowd. Carolyn tried to calm them, to tell them that their job was to make themselves available to patients, not protect the clinic, but they didn't hear her.

"I hope there aren't any victims today!" Alice, the picketer whom the staff called Earmuffs and the police called Frog Mouth, shouted to Carolyn.

"There are never any victims," Carolyn retorted.

"Just ask them five years from now, dear."

Alice frequently talked to Carolyn. When she saw Carolyn with Lorena, she sweetly said, "Ooohh, how nice. You have a daughter."

Word reached Carolyn that a NOW demonstrator had overheard two of Cotter's people say, "They got in," and shake hands. Did that mean that a fake patient had gotten inside her clinic?

Within a heartbeat, Carolyn found Sonia and instructed her to require all patients to produce a fresh urine sample, proof of pregnancy, before they were allowed to go upstairs. That meant a lot of congestion in the family room, which meant Sonia would be frantic. But Carolyn couldn't afford to let a fake patient wander through her clinic.

Sonia, indeed, was mortified. For the past three months she had endured the Saturday crowds in her family room as the clinic struggled to accommodate fifty-plus appointments by 10 A.M. Two weeks ago, one patient's partner, standing six deep in front of Sonia's desk, had hollered, "Do we take a number?" just as if he were waiting to buy sliced turkey at a deli counter. On these Saturdays, Sonia felt as if she were working in a factory, and that embarrassed her. The least she could do, she decided, was to explain to the patients why they had to produce a fresh urine sample and wait an extra half hour downstairs.

"Are you aware that seven antiabortion protesters locked themselves together in a doctor's office yesterday afternoon?" Sonia said, standing in front of her desk. Some heads nodded, most faces stared at her blankly. Sonia then launched into the story of the attack at Sidney Levitt's. When she finished, she explained that to make sure that the day went without interruption from invaders, Preterm had to double-check every patient.

More heads nodded in understanding. Sonia felt better.

Outside, Carolyn watched Cotter carefully. He was acting strange, almost nonchalant, not the Billy she remembered bouncing from one side of the sidewalk to the other, shouting to his people to drop down and crawl their way toward the door. He simply stood back, watching

with an almost bemused expression. It was hard to tell what his expression was, since two hats covered his forehead and a scarf wound around his neck and over his chin.

At 7:45 A.M., an hour after he and his people had arrived, Cotter walked in front of the group, straightened his shoulders, and waved his hands. On cue, a block of his followers, more than 100 by Carolyn's estimation, turned away from Preterm and marched to their cars. One by one, just as they had arrived, the cars pulled from their parking spaces and headed east on Beacon Street, toward Boston. They were bound for Gynecare, Cotter had told a reporter.

In pursuit, the prochoice forces packed up their signs and hopped into their vans and station wagons. By eight o'clock, barely a handful of demonstrators stood in front of Preterm. It was as if the clinic had given a party and all the guests had left at once. For the first time all morning, Carolyn walked inside. All of a sudden she was cold again. The protesters could still return—Captain Hayes had ordered ten cops to wait at Preterm for another three hours, until they were sure that the Budget Rent-A-Truck still parked across the street didn't harbor any surprise visitors.

It didn't. At 10:15 A.M., the truck pulled away from the curb and returned to the rental agency. At 10:30 A.M. another truck, this one with a silver hood over the flatbed, parked in front of Preterm. It looked like a food truck. But considering the odd events of the morning, you couldn't be sure. Carolyn and the policemen huddled in the clinic's foyer watched a man hop out of the driver's seat and open the latch to the back of the truck. Would twenty-five antis jump out? The driver didn't look familiar.

Pop. The back was open. Instead of facing a row of protesters, the crew inside Preterm stared at bran muffins and coffee urns and ham sandwiches wrapped in cellophane.

"I wonder if he has hot dogs," a cop said as he and his colleagues dashed out of the building to greet the food truck.

Carolyn was delighted. At every rescue, she had wished that a food truck would appear. The great equalizer. Speed Bump passing the cream for coffee to a NOW demonstrator. Bill Cotter handing Carolyn a straw. A temporary truce as members of both sides snacked. But the two antis left didn't venture near the truck, which was flanked by cops chewing hot dogs.

"Breakfast," one cop mumbled between bites.

Carolyn merrily sipped her coffee, cheered by this symbol of normalcy amid the insanity. Inside the family room had cleared, and the upstairs flow had smoothed out. Fifty-two patients were safely in the clinic. So much, she thought, for blockades.

•   •   •

January slipped by with its usual erratic temperatures of subzero one day and balmy the next, but Carolyn's mood hadn't veered much above depressed for weeks. The temporary lift she had felt after the fizzled rescue of January 13 had quickly faded. Carolyn was tired. Tired of struggling to keep Preterm afloat. Tired of feeling her staff's venom.

Intellectually, she knew that as manager, she would be the staff's scapegoat. Who else would they blame for laying off two nurses? Who else was responsible for cutting the CMAs' work week from five days to four? Who else had decided to charge patients for Pap smears, which had always been offered for free? To many of her staff, Preterm was not a business but a family that nurtured all within its embrace. Unpaid bills and budget deficits didn't seem relevant compared to the trauma of a woman deciding to end a pregnancy. To the staff, patient comfort was priority. Staff comfort ran a close second. Carolyn had heard rumors that the nurses were furious that she had ended Preterm's tradition of providing staff with free coffee and all the crackers they could munch.

Carolyn was not immune to her own decisions. She had cried during the staff meeting when she announced that she had to release two nurses and cut CMA hours. But she was also proud of some of the strategies she had developed to increase patient flow and cut costs without further hurting staff. To soften the loss of two nurses, she had added a new position called medical assessor. Instead of using four nurses to screen abortion patients for their medical history, Preterm would use two nurses and two medical assessors: former CMAs who would be trained to work with patients who had uncomplicated medi-cal histories. Two nurses would handle the more difficult patients. That still meant that the CMAs would be short by two, but at least no one would be fired.

Nonetheless, the staff remained cold to her. Carolyn understood that staffers feared for their jobs. But couldn't they see that she was working as hard as she could to make sure that Preterm wouldn't go under? When she suggested to Marian Wolfsun, the director of counseling, that she hold an all-clinic meeting to discuss Preterm's changes, Marian shook her head. "The staff doesn't really trust you now," Marian said. Carolyn ran into the office of Sarah, the bookkeeper, and burst into tears.

Was there a solution? On this Thursday afternoon at the end of January, when the street and sky and buildings all shared the same desolate shade of gray, it didn't seem so. As Carolyn bent over her desk to tackle the latest fiscal numbers, a flash of orange caught her attention. It couldn't be. It was. Down Beacon Street and up Englewood toward Preterm's back entrance zoomed an orange-and-white ambulance.

What now? Carolyn cradled her head in her hands and closed her eyes.

At Preterm, complications requiring hospital care were so few in number that it was easy to forget that they existed. Out of the nearly 10,000 abortions performed each year, the clinic averaged 140 complications, the vast majority of which were treated at the clinic. These complications included infection (which usually meant that the patient had not kept her vagina clear of outside materials, very often a penis), retained tissue (which meant that the evacuation process had not removed all of the pregnancy and the patient needed to be reevacuated), continuing pregnancy (the woman may have been pregnant with twins, and the evacuation only removed one pregnancy), or perforation. The most serious of all complications, perforation of the uterus, was also the most infrequent. In one year, Preterm was responsible for only ten "perfs" as they were called. That was ten too many from Carolyn's perspective, but only the ignorant would expect all medical procedures to be flawless.

Carolyn picked up the phone and dialed the fourth floor. Mary, who directed the medical center, was too busy to talk. So were the nurses. Someone would call Carolyn back later.

Carolyn assumed that a patient had been perfed. In most cases, the puncture wound healed immediately, shrinking to the size of a pencil tip as the uterus contracted. After resting in the recovery room for a few hours under close observation, the patient was allowed to go home if her bleeding had diminished. A Preterm nurse would call the next day to check the patient's condition. If heavy bleeding continued, the patient was taken to the hospital. Often, the uterus required stitching, which meant that the patient spent a few more hours in the hospital and was ordered to avoid exerting herself for several weeks. Rarely did a perforation result in sterility.

Anyone who worked in health care recognized that any invasive surgery, be it forging a root canal or removing an appendix, carried a risk. Although abortion carried less than most, any slip was magnified because the surgery was controversial. Consequently, the ambulance company had agreed not to flash its lights or flick on its siren when it approached or left the clinic.

Contrary to the picketers' claim, Preterm was not buried in lawsuits by former patients. Since its inception, the clinic had fielded a variety of litigation, most of which was either dismissed or settled out of court, some of which was still pending. While Carolyn wasn't comfortable knowing that a patient had sued her clinic for what the patient considered to be wrongdoing, she wasn't surprised. She was directing a medical facility in an era when patient lawsuits against doctors were so common that malpractice insurance rates had more than doubled, and in some cases tripled, in the past seven years. It was not unusual for an obstetrician-gynecologist to pay more than $60,000 in insurance in 1990. Considering the ratio of lawsuits to the number of patients Preterm saw every year, or even the number of letters women wrote thanking the clinic for its care, Carolyn preferred to dwell on the latter. Still, the sight of the ambulance was unsettling. What had gone wrong?

Sitting at her desk, Carolyn found it hard to believe that just a year ago, she had been thrilled to accept this job, a job she thought would allow her to develop Preterm into the clinic she knew it could be. She had entertained such glorious plans. As director, she would add a sexually transmitted disease clinic for women and men. She would recruit national experts and sponsor seminars, perhaps on hormonal treatments for postmenopausal women, for her medical staff and other members of Boston's medical community. She would educate the lay public and offer educational programs on abortion and family planning. But between Operation Rescue and the budget, she hadn't had time to finish revising the counselors' manual, let alone launch anything new.

The phone rang. It was the fourth floor calling with details of today's "comp". Carolyn listened intently, her eyes focused on her shoes. A fifteen-year-old patient who had had a Caesarean section four months ago had been perfed. Hysterical from the moment the doctor had entered the room, the young girl had worked herself into such a state that her vaginal muscles had tensed too tightly for the doctor to insert his finger for the pelvic exam. A second doctor had been able to open the canal enough to perform the pelvic exam and dilate the cervix, but when he had evacuated, nothing came out. Fearing that the cannula had punctured the uterus and was suctioning air instead of a pregnancy, the doctor had suggested calling an ambulance. Howling, the teenager had been taken to Beth Israel Hospital, accompanied by her mother and a Preterm nurse.

Carolyn hung up, feeling as if the blues would never leave, that spring would never come. Could something go right? Whenever she felt hopeful that some decision or new idea would improve Preterm's condition, the hope was quickly dashed. Like this morning's meeting, for instance. Jeffrey Allen, chairman of Brookline's Board of Selectmen, had gathered representatives from the three clinics, the Brookline police, and the prochoice community around the conference table in the selectmen's office. As soon as Carolyn entered the room and saw five prochoicers sitting on one side of the table, the providers on the other, and the police and Jeffrey Allen at either end, she knew the battle lines were too thick to cross. Only Bill McDermott seemed objective: He sat away from the table, his arms and legs crossed as he watched the show.

Jeffrey Allen had opened calmly enough, describing how Rescue's tactics had changed from blockades to invasions and suggesting that each clinic tighten its security. Adding more police detail was not an option, since the Brookline cops considered clinic duty the worst job in town. Most of the police even preferred calming the drunken brawls during the night shift at the International House of Pancakes, because at least there they got fed. Captain Hayes had forbade the force to accept anything from the clinics, even coffee. The providers nodded. And then the room exploded.

The prochoice people were getting in the way at rescues, Jeff said. After every rescue, police morale dips. Their authority was questioned, and their work was made more difficult by women surrounding the barricade attempting to ward off protesters—the job the police were paid to do. The five prochoicers countered that without the prochoice presence, Operation Rescue would invade the clinic. They, the prochoice community, kept the clinics open.

Jeff Allen yelled. Captain Hayes yelled. Even Alice, Planned Parenthood's clinic director, entered the fracas. One Saturday, Alice said, she had thought that Operation Rescue had struck, judging from the number of people surrounding Planned Parenthood's doorway. But on closer inspection she saw that the crowd was composed of abortion rights advocates. If *she* were intimidated by the sight, she said, what must the patients feel?

The prochoicers, looking unfamiliar in business dress instead of their Saturday jeans and sneakers, claimed that if the police did their job and arrested the abortion foes, prochoice efforts wouldn't be necessary. McDermott argued that the prochoice protesters were pawns in the antiabortionists' game plan, that Bill Cotter realized he didn't have the numbers and was delighted to share clinic turf with the prochoice army. The abortion foes recognized that patients couldn't tell who supported their right to an abortion and who didn't, and that the crowd could intimidate women into turning away. Rescue's goals had changed, McDermott said. The antiabortionists no longer wanted to change the law on Saturday morning; they wanted to "save one baby's life."

"They may not have saved shit," he said, "but if they can go back to their people and say one baby's life was saved, they feel like they've done their job."

Carolyn added that Preterm had its own escorts, that it didn't need NOW demonstrators to guide the patients inside. But the prochoicers held their ground, never yelling, but instead using the counseling techniques Carolyn knew so well. "We just want to talk calmly," one woman said. "Now please listen. We have something important to say."

But no one listened to any perspective but their own. McDermott warned that the prochoicers would be arrested if they entered the police zone, just like the antis. Carolyn returned to Preterm, struck by the similarity between the prochoice and antichoice forces. Both sides were myopic, and for a reason. Protecting a clinic was one way the prochoicers felt that *they* could exercise control. Attacking a clinic was one way the antichoicers felt that *they* could exercise control. Neither side could see anything but its own agenda. Compromise was not an option and, therefore, neither was peace.

All Carolyn could control was her own clinic escorts. She made a note to call a meeting to emphasize the escorts' limited responsibility. If they were calm and approached a patient one at a time instead of in groups of four and five, the antis might be calmer. The picketers never grabbed patients before the escorts became more aggressive.

Meanwhile, she had plenty of other crises to consider. The longer she sat at her desk, the more she realized that Operation Rescue wouldn't bring Preterm to its knees, but that the inherent problems of running an abortion clinic might. Maybe she no longer had to worry about 500 rescuers descending on Preterm, but Bill Cotter and a small but dedicated band would still risk their all to do what they felt they had to do to stop abortion. An invasion was likely. What more could she do to make the clinic secure, given her limited budget?

Then there was all the other stuff. The doctor shortage. The deficit. An angry staff. Would Preterm be around a year from now? Two years? Would *she?* There were easier ways to make a living. She sometimes thought of moving to Pennsylvania to be closer to her sisters and to live in an area less congested and expensive than Brookline—an area where maybe she could afford to buy a house and offer Lorena a backyard with a swing.

The phone rang. It was the fourth floor. Beth Israel had called. The teenager had not been perforated. In fact, she wasn't even pregnant. The Preterm staff wasn't to blame; the teenager had shown all the signs of pregnancy, from an enlarged uterus to testing positive on not just one, but two pregnancy tests. Still, a mistake was a mistake, and the young girl had suffered.

Carolyn glanced at her desk, once clean and organized, now a collage of demands. Only one piece of paper cheered her: the one that reported that Preterm's first batch of fund-raising letters, mailed only last week, had elicited $550 already. In Preterm's seventeen years, the clinic had not launched any formal fund-raisers and had applied for only one small grant. Now that Rescue had calmed down, Carolyn hoped that Fran could devote more time to seeking grants and donations.

Carolyn had taken other steps, also. Although abortion numbers would remain constant (unless the French abortion pill, RU 486, was approved in the U.S., which meant that many women would no longer need the invasive evacuation), medical costs would probably continue to soar. This meant that the abortion clinic, which used to support the rest of the clinic, would lose more and more money. Carolyn had suggested to Preterm's board of directors that the sterilization clinic be expanded, as should breast screening. Preterm had barely advertised its mammogram program, yet its market was unlimited: With the baby boom generation hitting the over thirty-five mark, more and more women would need the service.

Carolyn looked at her clock. Almost 5 P.M. She slipped off her shoes, stuffed them in the lower drawer of her file cabinet, and replaced them with her sneakers. It was time to pick up Lorena at day care. Maybe they would go to the mall in Watertown tonight and shop, maybe have dinner at one of the cafés.

There were, she reminded herself, other things in life besides Preterm Health Services.

CHAPTER TWELVE

Elusive
Victory

F RAN burst into Carolyn's office, her hands flying, a cloud of hair covering one side of her face. Carolyn was accustomed to Fran's spurts of excitement, to the eyes that opened wide as the words tumbled out. But there was something about the demeanor of Preterm's spokeswoman this morning that demanded extra attention.

"We got the injunction," Fran said breathlessly.

Carolyn twirled around in her chair, away from her desk, and toward the doorway, where Fran stood. The injunction? The court order forbidding Operation Rescue to blockade access to all abortion clinics in Massachusetts? The order that had bounced from court to court and judge to judge for nine long months, ever since last May? Without uttering a response, Carolyn stared at Fran, waiting for the rest of the story, which Fran was only too happy to share.

Leslie Loveless from Planned Parenthood had just called, Fran said. Details were blurry, but the gist of the news was that the state's Supreme Judicial Court had voted four to one to uphold Judge Catherine White's order from last July, the one that White, a Middlesex Superior Court judge, had issued two days after the abortion foes had attacked Gynecare and Preterm only to have the order negated on appeal three weeks later.

Carolyn jumped up and clapped her hands.

"That's *some* good news," Fran said, grinning, as she left Carolyn's office to spread the word throughout the clinic.

Carolyn settled back in her chair and turned to face her desk, the top of which suffocated under a blanket of papers so thick that she could barely see Lorena's photo through the pile. This was, as Fran said, some good news. There was no denying that the SJC's vote sent a clear message to Bill Cotter and his friends: The highest state court considered Operation Rescue's blockades a violation of the patients' constitutional right to an abortion and not, as had been stated last summer when the order was struck down, an exercise in freedom of speech. No longer would those arrested for trespassing or blocking entrance to the clinics be arraigned and tried in district court, which often had resulted in dropped charges. From now on, the judicial system would play hardball. After a rescue, the abortion foes would be marched straight to superior court, where their punishment would be determined by the judge. And if the superior court judges were as liberal as they were reputed to be, anyone who prevented a woman from seeking an abortion could end up on a prison road crew.

Carolyn was not naive enough to think that this morning's ruling would cause Operation Rescue to shrivel up and die within the week, but there was little likelihood that the abortion foes would appeal the ruling to the next judicial level: the U.S. Supreme Court. One deterrent was that there was no guarantee that the high court would agree to hear the case. Another was that the appeal required money, big money, for legal fees. If Operation Rescue:Boston were as broke as Cotter pleaded in every newsletter and at every rally, it couldn't afford to challenge the ruling. Up until now, much of Rescue's legal work had been done pro bono; but how much longer could those lawyers remain altruistic? Not only were they not paid for their Rescue work, but they forfeited other paying cases to help the antiabortionists. Even lawyers couldn't afford to work for nothing forever; they had families to feed and mortgages to pay. Besides, the outcome was questionable. Other Operation Rescue satellites had challenged injunctions and lost. In New York, a federal appeals court had fined Operation Rescue $25,000 for each violation of the order prohibiting blockades.

The weakness in the injunction upheld this morning by the SJC was that it included no specific penalties. Planned Parenthood's original plea, which was enjoined by the clinics and several prochoice organizations, had suggested fines and jail sentences, but Judge White had declined to include them in her court order last summer. That meant that the punishment would be determined by the individual judge who heard the cases. Without clear penalties, Operation Rescue could be tempted to test the injunction's teeth.

On the other hand, the state attorney general, Jim Shannon, had asked the SJC if he could intervene and add more specifics. His office had called Carolyn and the other providers requesting details about the demonstrations and asking what would be considered a logical "safe access zone," an area in which only clinic staff and patients could enter. If protesters entered the zone, they could be subject to a fine of $5,000 or two-and-a-half years in a house of correction or both. If anyone was injured, the accused could be fined $10,000 or face imprisonment for up to ten years, or both. Now *that* injunction had teeth, but whether the SJC would uphold it was another question.

So for now, the issue was whether this injunction was strong enough to keep the abortion foes home in the mornings sipping coffee instead of plastered on Preterm's doorstep. Carolyn was unsure. Would someone who locked himself by the neck to the undercarriage of a police bus in the name of saving babies take a judge's order seriously? Would someone who kept fetal remains in jars in her home drop her crusade? Carolyn was still stunned by the thought of Darroline stealing POCs, or having someone else steal them, from an abortion clinic for a fetal funeral she had yet to hold. If Darroline could justify stealing those scraps of tissue as following God's will, wouldn't she be able to justify defying the Massachusetts judicial system? These people claimed that God would protect them, but did they believe that He would protect them from a $2,000 fine?

Still, Carolyn couldn't help but feel a little hopeful. Saturdays had been quiet lately. Since the January blitz of attacks, Operation Rescue had ignored Brookline, choosing Planned Parenthood in Worcester for its February siege. But even that had been a bust. Operation Rescue's strategy was as familiar now to the clinics as it was to the rescuers, and it didn't take much effort by police and clinic staff to open a pathway through the pack of bodies and sweep the blockaders into the police bus.

Even the abortion foes who dedicated themselves to prayer rather than physical intervention had faded in number. Perhaps the reason was the slush and snow of winter. Perhaps they were simply tired of spending their weekend mornings kneeling on cement sidewalks, taunted by prochoice demonstrators. Or perhaps the fun had gone out of Saturdays since Preterm's escorts had changed methods.

Carolyn had called a meeting of the fifteen volunteers several weeks earlier to ask them to stop charging at the patients the minute the women stepped out of their cars. The escorts' intensity aggravated the antichoicers, making them more aggressive, she explained. She asked that the escorts ignore the prochoice demonstrators who told them that

they weren't doing their job if they let a sidewalk counselor walk with a patient uninterrupted for a block and a half. "Your role is limited," Carolyn told the volunteers. "You can't make the picketers disappear or shut out the ugly things they say. They lie, they're obnoxious, but you have to remember your job." Their job, she said, was to offer help to patients if they wanted help, to make themselves accessible to patients, but not to force themselves on the women. The escorts should stand apart from the crowd, maybe near the end of the block, anyplace where they were easily visible. One at a time, they should approach the women to offer help, but not in groups.

The tactic had worked. The escorts had calmed down and so had the picketers, whose presence seemed to evaporate more every Saturday. Since the middle of February, Preterm's patients had walked past only a handful of prolife picketers, and, to Carolyn's extra delight, only a handful of prochoice demonstrators.

Not long after the January meeting with the town, the providers, and the prochoice representatives, the number of prochoice demonstrators in front of the clinics on Saturdays had begun to drop. From twenty-five or thirty regulars, now only two or three women congregated on the sidewalk with their "STAND UP FOR CHOICE" signs. Fran had wondered if enthusiasm had faded because the prochoicers had heard about a letter that Preterm had planned to pass out thanking them for their support but detailing Preterm's concerns about the demonstrations. The letter emphasized that blocking the sidewalks was against the law in Brookline and, more important, that the clinic feared the potential for violence. The antis were looking for ways to take the prochoicers to court, and the tension caused by rushing to patients created an environment ripe for shoving, elbowing, possibly a punch or two. The letter explained that Preterm had its own escorts, and whether the other demonstrators agreed with the clinic's methods or not, Preterm was legally responsible for the safety of the patients and staff.

On the first Saturday that the letter was slated for distribution among the demonstrators, only two prochoicers had showed up. Ellen Convisser, president of Boston NOW, claimed that her demonstrators hadn't given up their Saturday vigil because of pressure from the town and clinics, but rather because they no longer saw a need for such a strong prochoice presence since the number of antiabortion protesters had tapered off. Instead, NOW sent out "orbiters," people who patrolled Beacon Street in their cars scouting the clinics for possible trouble. They could orbit all they wanted as far as Carolyn was concerned, as long as the sidewalk in front of Preterm remained peaceful.

Maybe, Carolyn hoped, this was the beginning of happier times at her clinic—in all arenas. Although the figures still glared red in the budget books, relief seemed imminent. Every day brought more checks in response to Preterm's first fund-raising letter, checks that already added up to $6,971, $2,000 more than anyone had expected. Although donations alone wouldn't reverse the clinic's fortune, Waldo's salary might. The man who had helped form Preterm, who had lent his name and title to bring respect and legitimacy to the fledgling clinic, was retiring. This meant a savings of over $100,000 a year for Preterm. Some of that money, of course, would pay new doctors, but not all. Between Waldo's salary, fund-raising, and Carolyn's budget cuts, maybe Preterm's deficit would disappear—along with Operation Rescue.

Maybe.

•   •   •

Bill McDermott couldn't have asked for a better birthday present. Well, the dissolution of Operation Rescue would have been better, but the Supreme Judicial Court upholding the injunction was close enough. On Friday, February 23, the day after the SJC announced its verdict, the police sergeant had turned forty-two. He didn't like to make a big deal out of his birthday, or at least that was what he claimed, so he spent the evening of February 23 driving around Brookline and Newton looking for his Operation Rescue sources. He was eager to find out their reaction to the injunction and whether the court order had jarred them enough to stay home on Saturday mornings—which meant that McDermott could do the same.

At a Newton coffee shop frequented by his "muffins," the sergeant had found the guy he called "the wino" for his scarlet nose and pink face and Sam, the ex-convict who had found religion while serving his prison sentence for armed robbery. Sipping coffee with the two, McDermott listened carefully as Sam claimed he had had it with Rescue. He was tired of Bill Cotter's weak leadership, tired of always hitting Boston when Brookline, "the abortion capital of the world," was the real enemy. And Sam didn't like being excluded from plans. Since he wasn't part of Bill Cotter's inner circle, Sam hadn't been told about the invasion of Sidney Levitt's office. Feeling snubbed, Sam had refused to rescue the next day. He told McDermott that he might not participate in any more protests. His parole officer wouldn't be crazy about him violating a court order, which could be a criminal offense.

"The wino" was an older man who was active in McDermott's

family's church. Devoutly Catholic, "the wino" believed that abortion was murder because the church said it was murder. Whenever McDermott challenged him, citing examples of poor women, sick women with AIDS, twelve-year-olds raped by their fathers, or any other example that might justify terminating a pregnancy, "the wino" countered that killing babies was against God's Law. "The wino" rarely blockaded, preferring to videotape the demonstrations. McDermott sort of liked the guy, sensing that he was a good man who sincerely believed that he was doing God's will. McDermott also liked him for the information he had given the sergeant throughout the year about meetings and the mood among the minions. Sitting at the coffee shop on the day after the injunction was upheld, "the wino" said that he hadn't heard of any activity for the weekend, and that even if he had, he'd think twice about kneeling down in front of an abortion clinic door. He didn't need thousands of dollars in fines.

"They're scared shitless by the injunction," McDermott told himself, chuckling, the next morning, as he cruised up and down Beacon Street. It was Saturday and the sidewalks in front of Repro, Planned Parenthood, and Preterm were clear, save for two or three women in down parkas holding "KEEP ABORTION LEGAL" signs, and a few sidewalk counselors gripping pamphlets. It was as if a giant hand had suddenly swatted most of the players off the stage, leaving only a few as symbols of more lively days.

They should be scared shitless, he thought, if the court system had the backbone to implement tough penalties for violating the court order. The next time those muffins were found guilty, they were going to go to jail, and it wouldn't be the garage of the Brookline police station. We're talking real jail. Camp, as the cops called it. Just the thought of spending a night or two with convicted rapists and murderers would be enough to deter the bulk of Cotter's crusaders.

And that could mean the final blow to Cotter's movement. This was the second major setback to his people in three weeks. At the end of January, the day after Randall Terry had been released from his work camp in Fulton County, Georgia, when an anonymous donor had paid his bail, Terry had held a press conference to announce the dissolution of Rescue's headquarters in Binghamton, New York. Terry couldn't afford to pay the $70,000 that the outfit owed in debts or the $50,000 fine imposed by a New York state court. He added that Operation Rescue affiliates across the country would continue activity without the benefit of the central office. Would Randall Terry hold a close-out sale on Kryptonite locks? McDermott wondered.

Bill Cotter said that Operation Rescue:Boston would continue with "business as usual." He told reporters that Terry's closing the central office didn't change anything; Operation Rescue:Boston didn't receive money from Binghamton—only guidance. "Just because the Bible publisher goes out of business doesn't mean you stop living the Bible's teachings," he had said.

Even if Cotter didn't feel the blow of the Binghamton's office closing, McDermott suspected that most of the other rescuers did, at least psychologically. The symbolism of losing the national headquarters was stunning. What would grass-roots groups do without a central office? Cotter didn't have Terry's charisma, nor his connections with sources of money. If Terry couldn't keep his organization together, how could Cotter?

Between the demise of Operation Rescue national and the court injunction, McDermott was ready to bet that he and Brookline had seen the last of the 500-person rescue. Small invasions were the wave of the future. Although the crowds would stay home, McDermott knew that the small core of "nut nuts," as he dubbed the hardcores, would never give up the fight. After the January 12 attack at Sidney Levitt's, McDermott had written in his police report that it was "time for toys and trinkets," that the abortion foes were ready to haul out every device they could muster, from triple locks to cement blocks, to make trouble for the clinics and police. A small group of people inside could do a lot more damage in a lot less time than hundreds outside, McDermott figured. Preterm's elevator was a perfect target. McDermott envisioned a group of six chained and locked inside that elevator while another six stormed upstairs to overturn a few evacuation machines and superglue some cannulas together. If they were hurt in the process, they were hurt. What better laurel for an abortion foe than to say, "Charlie lost his ear saving a baby. He did it for the Glory of God."

If the injunction frightened Darroline Firlit, she hadn't let on to the press. Her people weren't scared, she said. On the contrary, she maintained that she had received phone calls of support from her people, all of whom claimed that they would continue to rescue. Facing stiffer penalties "is a small price to pay for the life of a baby," she was quoted as saying in *The Boston Globe*. To *The Boston Herald* she said, "We have an obligation before God to continue to rescue. In this case, we are obeying a higher law."

She would rescue until she was dead, she added. Even the broken disk, or broken jaw, or whatever ailment Darroline claimed she had received from the police "tossing bodies" on her during the January 11 attack on Planned Parenthood, hadn't prevented her from blockading Planned Parenthood in Worcester a month later. Her crusaders claimed that they were inspired by Darroline's dedication as they watched Darroline hobble into Operation Rescue headquarters to continue her work to save babies. "At least I haven't been torn limb from limb like those babies in the abortuaries," she told them.

And why should she stop? McDermott thought. She was a tough kid from New Bedford with little education. Through Rescue she now had an office, reporters calling for quotes, her face on the evening news, and a few followers who worshiped her. Without the abortion fight, she'd have nothing. McDermott could see Darroline locking herself to evacuation machines until one of the criminal charges against her landed her in prison.

Cotter's dedication, McDermott thought, was more suspect. Billy C. had been more forthright than Darroline with the press, admitting that he wasn't sure how deeply the injunction would affect his rescuers, but that he would continue to "do what was right." McDermott wondered if that were so. The sergeant sensed that Rescue's leader would like nothing more than to win the applause of abortion foes across the country for the sacrifices he made to save babies. But McDermott wondered if Cotter would challenge the system to the point where he would be tossed in prison for a few years. But then, Cotter could always surprise him. Ego was a powerful force.

Was it ego that had caused those two to continue leading the battle when they had faced charges of organized crime in the RICO suit, Brookline's litigation against Operation Rescue under the federal racketeering law? Or had they been confident that the suit would die somewhere in the legal channels? If they had been motivated by the latter, they were right. The last McDermott had heard about it, the case lay in a stack of papers in a box on the windowsill of detective-turned-towncounsel George Driscoll's office. It was difficult for the town counsel to make the RICO suit a priority when it was evident that neither Darroline, Cotter, nor any of the other leaders named in the suit, had the money or the assets to pay $75,000 in retribution for the town's costs in combating early rescues. Nevertheless, Jeffrey Allen, chairman of the Brookline Board of Selectmen, insisted that the RICO suit had done its job; that it had scared off potential rescuers and was largely responsible for the group's dwindling numbers. On December 9, after two prayer rallies designed to recruit more blockaders and prayer supporters, fewer than 200 abortion foes had braved the bitter wind to save babies. On January 13, Cotter hadn't even been able to get that many.

If that were the end of the big rescues, McDermott was thrilled. He had to admit, though, that Cotter & Company had provided plenty of laughs. The sergeant had almost been kicked out of Brookline District Court on the afternoon of January 11, when seventy-one of his "muffins" were arraigned for that morning's attack on Planned Parenthood. The small courtroom was standing room only as those arrested and their supporters filled the pews, spilling out into the aisles. The Hispanic teenager arrested for shoplifting didn't understand enough English to know why his arraignment was stalled. As soon as all of the arrested had filed in, the crowd stood up and sang "God Bless America." Without taking a breath, they launched into "We Shall Overcome," followed by "Glory, Glory, Hallelujah." McDermott, who had positioned himself by the door in case he needed to quickly exit, covered his mouth with his hand to hide his grin. But as they launched into "Jesus loves the little babies . . ." he was laughing so hard his shoulders shook.

"Order in the court! Order in the court!" shouted the court clerk, a short fellow with red hair who earlier had confided in McDermott that he was suffering from an ugly hangover. Turning to a giggling reporter, the court clerk snapped, "You have to stop or you'll have to leave." McDermott howled under his breath. "And you, too, McDermott," he hissed.

It was not yet nine o'clock on this Saturday morning, and the clinic sidewalks were still empty. McDermott headed his car toward the Busy Bee, a coffee shop across from Planned Parenthood. There he might find some of his sources seeking company or comfort from the cold. There he might hear some chatter providing clues about the future of Operation Rescue.

·

•　　•　　•

Nearly eight months had passed since the Supreme Court had issued the *Webster* decision. Contrary to predictions, abortion's availability had changed very little. Hundreds of abortion bills lay waiting in legislative committees across the country, but in the late winter of 1990, no state had yet codified a woman's right to an abortion in case the Supreme Court ever overturned *Roe* v. *Wade*, nor had any state successfully made the procedure illegal or even substantially diminished a woman's access to abortion. Even in Missouri, which had implemented the controversial restrictions stated in the *Webster* case, the number of abortions hadn't altered much. The statute's preamble, which stated that human life began at conception, had not caused IUDs and certain birth-control pills (contraceptions that worked as abortifacients by disturbing the fertilized egg) to be taken off the market, nor had it challenged all abortion, as had been feared. The preamble was a statement, not a law, and it could not be used as a law. The ban on abortions performed in public hospitals by public employees had, however, created a hardship for women in the central and western parts of the state where there were no outpatient clinics, only hospitals, which forced those seeking abortions to travel out of state or to a St. Louis clinic. For many, this meant unnecessarily prolonging the pregnancy, which in turn could mean a riskier abortion.

The only state that had made a definitive move on the abortion issue since the *Webster* decision was South Carolina. Its state legislature had passed a law requiring minors to notify their parents before having an abortion, or acquire a judge's consent. This new legislation, though, was actually more liberal than the one it replaced, which hadn't offered the judicial bypass.

As much as the prochoice forces would have liked to believe that they had won the battle, however, the political activists knew that danger loomed perilously near. Among the proposed abortion legislation that lay scattered in state houses from coast to coast and beyond were restrictive laws that the antiabortionists hoped would be challenged all the way to the Supreme Court. The prochoice forces recognized that any one of those laws could be the vehicle that the Supreme Court used to reexamine *Roe* v. *Wade*.

In Louisiana, the state legislature was predicted to pass a bill that would outlaw abortion even in cases of rape and incest. Backers of the bill said that rape should be included because in order to obtain an abortion, women might lie and say that they had been raped when they hadn't. Doctors providing abortions would receive up to a ten-year prison sentence under the new law, although women obtaining abortions wouldn't be prosecuted. Whether or not Louisiana's governor, Buddy Roemer, who had said he was against "abortion on demand," would veto the bill was anyone's guess.

Antiabortionists were hopeful that Idaho's governor would accept the state legislature's proposal that all abortion be outlawed. Unlike Louisiana's bill, the Idaho legislation made exception for rape and incest, but only if the rape survivor reported the violation within seven days, and only if the incest victim were under eighteen.

The two biggest threats rested in the hands of politicians in Pennsylvania and in the U.S. territory of Guam, an island lying 3,000 miles west of Hawaii. Pennsylvania's House and Senate and governor had approved legislation that banned all abortions after the twenty-fourth week of pregnancy, barred "sex selection" abortions, restricted use of fetal tissue in research, and required husbands to be notified of their wife's intent to have an abortion and women to wait twenty-four hours between visiting the clinic and having the procedure. Abortion rights advocates immediately challenged the law, arguing that spousal notification and a twenty-four-hour wait violated a woman's constitutional right to an abortion. The controversial legislation lay in legal limbo as it waited to be heard by a federal court on appeal.

Labeled "Pearl Harbor for women" by a lawyer from the American Civil Liberties Union, Guam's law was even more lethal to abortion access. The territory's legislature had voted unanimously to outlaw virtually all abortions, even in cases of rape, incest, and fetal abnormality, allowing the procedure only if the mother's life were threatened, and then only if the surgery were approved by two independent physicians whose judgment would then be reviewed by the Guam Medical Licensure Board. Performing or assisting in an abortion would be a felony, and soliciting an abortion a misdemeanor.

It was expected that Guam's governor, Joseph Ada, would sign the legislation into law, and that the law would be immediately challenged. Abortion rights activists hoped that a judge would place an injunction forbidding the law to go into effect while the legislation chugged through the channels of the court system. The antiabortionists claimed that they would fight for the law all the way to the Supreme Court, which the ACLU's Reproductive Freedom Project predicted could be as soon as the fall of 1991 if the lower courts pushed the appeal through quickly.

There was little doubt in either the prochoice or antiabortion camp that the high court would hear one of these controversial cases. When handing down the *Webster* decision in July 1989, several justices had made it clear that they sought a case that would allow them to reexamine whether or not the right to abortion was included in the constitutional right to privacy.

The prochoice contingent was especially nervous about the Supreme Court composition when and if the cases were heard. Three of *Roe's* staunchest supporters—Justices Thurgood Marshall, Harry Blackmun, and William Brennan, Jr.—were octogenarians and, most likely, not far from retirement. The Bush administration had made no secret of the fact that it would seek a conservative replacement for any Supreme Court justice who retired from the bench, and abortion rights advocates inferred that to mean a judge who shared the administration's wish to overturn *Roe*. Losing even one of the three liberal justices could mean the end of legal abortion.

Or maybe not. There was no assurance that the U.S. Senate would approve a new justice who held strong antiabortion views. President Ronald Reagan's nomination of Robert Bork, an outspoken conservative and abortion foe, had sparked an angry battle among senators, which ended with the nomination's defeat. Perhaps George Bush had learned a lesson and would nominate a judge of moderate persuasion. But even in the highly unlikely case that Bush selected a liberal, the abortion rights supporters had learned that they could never rest. As long as there were abortion foes, the right to abortion would be challenged.

The only thing that might render the abortion battle in front of abortion clinics obsolete would be the distribution of RU 486, the French abortion pill, which could be taken in the privacy of a doctor's office or a woman's home. Already available in France and ready for dissemination in Europe, RU 486 had proven nearly 100 percent effective when used in conjunction with prostaglandin in the first seven weeks of pregnancy. The pill prevented the uterus from receiving the hormone progesterone. This caused the uterus to shed the fertilized egg. Since it was nonsurgical, RU 486 was safer than the evacuation procedure or a D&C, and it didn't require a hospital or medical setting—only a doctor's supervision. Freestanding clinics would remain to provide abortions for later-term pregnancies, but patient flow would be cut dramatically. Without a multitude of patients to approach, the antiabortionists would, the abortion rights activists hoped, vanish from the clinic sidewalks.

• • •

By 10 A.M. on Saturday, March 3, 1990, one day shy of the anniversary of Preterm's first Operation Rescue attack, the activity in front of 1842 Beacon Street had reached its peak. Four NOW demonstrators stood huddled by the front entrance next to two sidewalk counselors. Another sidewalk counselor covered the back entrance. The police detail yawned as he leaned against the wall in the foyer, surrounded by a handful of escorts who sat on the floor, their legs stretched in front of them. The morning was mild, the temperature almost hitting the forty-degree mark, and the escorts debated who would leave early.

The day before, Carolyn and Fran had stood at the watercooler near the secretary's desk reminiscing about what they had been doing last year at this time as they had prepared for the March 4 rescue. It seemed a little odd, but very comforting, that they weren't worrying about pinnys and escorts and police barricades for this weekend. Operation Rescue hadn't announced any plans for a blockade or a prayer vigil, and the regular picketers had all but disappeared the past few weeks. Whatever the reason—the injunction, fatigue, the end-of-winter doldrums—Fran and Carolyn weren't about to question the peace. They knew all too well that the calm could shatter in a minute.

Outside of Preterm on this Saturday the calm was interrupted only by the sidewalk counselors' pleas to patients.

"We have financial help and housing," Marie Henden called to a woman walking toward the clinic entrance. The woman ignored her. "Postpone your appointment, and come out to talk to us. You don't have to go through with the abortion."

"Don't bother me," the woman snapped. "I'm not in the mood."

Marie stared after her, then slowly turned toward Beacon Street, as if to spot more patients on their way in. Marie had been standing in front of Preterm on Saturday mornings for almost a year when Operation Rescue came to town. At first she had been dubious of the organization's philosophy of purposely breaking the law. But once she saw how a blockade forced the patients to stand outside longer, which gave Marie and her colleagues more time to talk to them, she became a believer. She had spent too many mornings being ignored not to see the possibilities in having more than thirty seconds to make her pitch.

Marie believed that her job was to present information, alternatives to abortion, to act as a liaison between God and these women. She prayed that hearts of the women entering the clinic would be open to God's word. Earlier this morning, a patient hadn't listened but the boyfriend of the friend who accompanied her had. He said that he would call the patient's boyfriend.

She approached another patient, who also ignored her. The woman's partner turned to Marie and said, "Too bad your mother didn't visit a place like this."

"That is a real live baby!" yelled Barbara Bell, a large black woman whose voice could be heard four blocks away. "Abortion is killing a baby! You'll never be the same!"

The woman, a thin blond, turned toward Barbara when she reached the top of the stairs. Her hand on the front door latch, she hissed, "Are you going to pay for this baby?"

"Yes!" Barbara bellowed.

The cop walked down the stairs and over to Barbara to tell her to quiet down. "I'm sorry, officer," she said. "I can't help it. No one is telling these women the truth. I have to answer to a higher power."

He shrugged and retreated to the warmth of the foyer.

At 11:40 A.M., twenty minutes before the last patient was scheduled, one of the escorts, Laura Jones, sat down on the outside steps and munched on a cruller. The only escort left on duty, Laura was petite with black hair and a gentle smile. She had once worked as a counselor at Preterm, before she became a social worker. Horrified by Operation Rescue's tactics, Laura had volunteered to escort patients on Saturdays. She was glad for today's quiet, and the quiet of the past few Saturdays, but Laura had observed the antis long enough to doubt that the reprieve would last for long. They were as determined to thwart the patients' access to abortion as Laura was to provide it.

Hugging her knees as she sat, Laura watched old Bill Clarke point to a little boy walking by on the sidewalk. "There's one who got away!" Bill cried gleefully. Turning his attention to Laura, Bill Clarke launched into his comparison of the Holocaust and abortion. Laura rolled her eyes.

"I've been doing this for almost a year," she said, shaking her head. "Will I be doing this forever?"

Sources

A<small>LTHOUGH</small> this book is based on the information I gathered during the year I spent at Preterm Health Services observing staffers perform their jobs and talking to patients, picketers, and police, I also consulted a variety of references. Forming the backbone of my research were daily stories from *The Boston Globe, The Boston Herald*, and *The New York Times*, and weekly stories from *The Brookline Citizen* and *The Brookline Tab*. In addition, I consulted *The Wall Street Journal, The Philadelphia Inquirer, The St. Paul Dispatch, Sojourner, The Cape Cod Times, The Boston Phoenix, The Binghamton Press and Sun-Bulletin, The Burlington Free Press, The Hartford Courant, The Seattle Times, The Washington Post, The Miami Herald, The Los Angeles Times, The Herald* of Everett, Washington, and *The Newburyport Daily News*. Articles in *U.S. News & World Report, Time, Newsweek, The Atlantic Monthly, Mother Jones* ("Where Did Randy Go Wrong?" by Susan Faludi), and *The New York Times Magazine* added depth to my research.

The Alan Guttmacher Institute's studies and booklets such as *Abortion and Women's Health* and *Abortion Services in the United States* were invaluable for statistics and background information as were publications by the National Abortion Federation (*The Truth About Abortion*), the National Abortion Rights Action League (*Who Decides; A Reproductive Rights Issues Manual* and *Who Decides? A State by State Review of Abortion Rights in America*), and the Planned Parenthood League of Massachusetts (*Questions and Answers about Abortion: a Handbook for the Citizens of Massachusetts*). The 80 Percent Majority Campaign newsletter provided insight into the antiabortion movement. The American Civil Liberties Union/Reproductive Freedom Project's *Reproductive Rights*

Liberties Union/Reproductive Freedom Project's *Reproductive Rights Update* offered details of political events that often went unrecorded in the daily press.

The highlights of my book list were:

Bender, David L., and Leone, Bruno, eds. *Abortion: Opposing Viewpoints.* St. Paul, Minnesota: Greenhaven Press, Inc., 1986.

Benderly, Beryl Lieff. *Thinking About Abortion.* Garden City, New York: Doubleday & Co., 1984.

Boston Women's Health Book Collective. *The New Our Bodies, Ourselves.* New York: Simon and Schuster, 1984.

Dash, Leon. *When Children Want Children: The Urban Crisis of Teenage Childbearing.* New York: William Morrow, 1989.

Faux, Marian. *Crusaders: Voices from the Abortion Front.* New York: Birch Lane Press, 1990.

————. *Roe v. Wade: The Untold Story of the Landmark Supreme Court Decision that Made Abortion Legal.* New York: Macmillan Publishing Co., 1988.

Franke, Linda Bird. *The Ambivalence of Abortion.* New York: Random House, 1978.

Gilligan, Carol. *In a Different Voice.* Cambridge, Massachusetts: Harvard University Press, 1982.

Ginsberg, Faye D. *Contested Lives: The Abortion Debate in an American Community.* Berkeley and Los Angeles, California: University of California Press, 1989.

Howe, Louis Kapp. *Moments on Maple Avenue: The Reality of Abortion.* New York: Macmillan Publishing Co., 1984.

Irving, John. *The Cider House Rules.* New York: William Morrow, 1985.

Luker, Kristen. *Abortion and the Politics of Motherhood.* Berkeley and Los Angeles, California: University of California Press, 1984.

Merton, Andrew. *Enemies of Choice: The Right to Life Movement and Its Threat to Abortion.* Boston, Massachusetts: Beacon Press, 1981.

Nolen, M.D., William A. *The Baby in the Bottle.* New York: Coward, McCann, & Geoghegan, Inc., 1978.

Scheidler, Joseph M. *Closed: 99 Ways to Stop Abortion.* San Francisco, California: Ignatius Press, 1985.

Tribe, Laurence H. *Abortion: The Clash of the Absolutes.* New York: W. W. Norton & Co., 1990.

Worldwatch Paper 97: The Global Politics of Abortion. Washington, DC: Worldwatch Institute, 1990.

Index

Index